Not Strangers in These Parts

Urban Aboriginal Peoples

Edited by

David Newhouse & Evelyn Peters

CP22-71/2003
ISBN 0-662-67604-1

Table of Contents

Preface

Edited by Professors David Newhouse, Trent University, and Evelyn Peters, University of Saskatchewan, this volume is a collection of papers devoted to analyzing the realities of urban Aboriginal peoples in Canada. It is the first volume in a series of thematic publications of proceedings from the Aboriginal Policy Research Conference.

Held in November 2002, the conference was co-hosted by Indian and Northern Affairs Canada (INAC) and the University of Western Ontario (UWO), with the participation of over a dozen federal departments and agencies as well as four national Aboriginal organizations. The conference was the largest of its kind ever held, with over 640 Aboriginal community leaders, academics, and policy-makers coming together to examine and discuss state of the art research on Aboriginal conditions in Canada.

During the conference, representatives of the Policy Research Initiative (PRI), the Federal Interlocutor for Métis and Non-Status Indians Division, INAC, and UWO agreed to produce a series of thematic publications. As with this volume, subsequent publications will be based primarily on presentations from the conference, but will also include related studies not available at that time.

With an increasingly important number of Aboriginal people living, studying, and working in urban areas, there is a particular need for multidisciplinary research into the many issues facing Aboriginal people in urban settings. The papers contained in this volume are both timely and relevant, not just to interested researchers and policy-makers, but to all Aboriginal people for whom the urban experience forms an integral part of either their own lives or the lives of family and friends.

On behalf of the PRI, I am extending my thanks to our colleagues at the Federal Interlocutor for Métis and Non-Status Indians Division, INAC and UWO, to our editors, and to the many authors who have contributed to this collection. I would also echo Professors Newhouse and Peters in acknowledging the many Aboriginal people, indeed all people, who are working within urban centres to ensure that more Aboriginal people are able to lead healthy, rewarding lives in those communities. We are confident this book will provide a broad range of insights into the complex issues that face Aboriginal peoples in Canadian cities.

Jean-Pierre Voyer
Executive Director, Policy Research Initiative

For more information on the conference or for updates on forthcoming publications, readers can visit the conference web site at
<http://www.ssc.uwo.ca/sociology/aprc-crmpa/>. Accessed June 16, 2003.

Acknowledgements

The editors want to acknowledge the many Aboriginal people who are living in urban centres and working hard to create places of dignity and respect for Aboriginal individuals, communities, and nations within them. We hope our small contribution may assist in their efforts.

We owe special thanks to many whose contributions made this text possible. First to the authors who agreed to write and share their research with us. Writing is no small feat. As the project managers responsible for this book, Roger Roberge and Johanne Valcourt of the Policy Research Initiative shepherded us through the laborious process of editing, revisions, production, and design. A very special thanks to Danny Jette who took on the difficult task of co-ordinating the various authors and working with us to keep us on track and on time.

We owe similar debts of gratitude to Alfred LeBlanc, Eric Breton, and Jeff Frank, whose vision and dedication in the early stages of this project were instrumental to the realization of this collection. Special thanks also go to Jean-Pierre Voyer, Executive Director of the PRI, for backing this project and seeing it through.

Susan Anzolin, Mary Lou Kenney, and Allan Macdonald of the Office of the Interlocutor for Métis and Non-Status Indians were enthusiastic and essential contributors to this project, bringing to the table authors, ideas, and necessary support.

Dan Beavon of Indian and Northern Affairs Canada, along with Jerry White and Paul Maxim of the University of Western Ontario, welcomed the association of this project with the Aboriginal Policy Research Conference in November 2002. Many of the authors featured here were presenters at the conference, speaking on issues of tremendous importance to Aboriginal peoples in Canada. We are pleased that this collection will serve as the first of a series of publications from the Aboriginal Policy Research Conference, and we are grateful for the opportunity to contribute to the legacy of that historic conference.

Introduction

David R. Newhouse
Department of Native Studies
Trent University

Evelyn J. Peters
Department of Geography
University of Saskatchewan

"You have to live in the world you find yourself in."
Fred Wheatley, Ojibway Elder in response to Trent student
question about tradition and modernity, circa 1985.

Aboriginal people live in cities. This simple declarative statement hides a complex reality. Life in small towns and large cities is part of Aboriginal reality as is life on reserves and in northern and Métis communities. Relationships with urban landlords, searching for employment in urban economies, making spaces for Aboriginal cultures and languages in city places, interacting with neighbours from different cultures and building urban Aboriginal programs and institutions is as much a part of Aboriginal realities as are land claims, conflicts over logging, hunting and treaty rights, and rural economic development. City life is now an integral component of Aboriginal peoples' lives in Canada. This fact generates new mental images, research frameworks, and policy challenges.

In 1951 the Census of Canada showed that 6.7 percent of the Aboriginal population lived in cities.[1] By 2001, that proportion had increased to 49 percent. Now 245,000 Aboriginal people, or 25 percent of the total Aboriginal population reporting Aboriginal identity, live in 10 of the nations largest cities: Winnipeg, Edmonton, Vancouver, Calgary, Toronto, Saskatoon, Regina, Ottawa-Hull, Montréal, and Victoria.[2] Aboriginal people are now a part of the urban landscape and will remain so, most likely in increasing numbers, over the decades to come. Understanding this complex reality in sufficient detail and depth is a major research challenge. Using this understanding to guide policy-makers is the policy challenge.

Many Canadian cities emerged in places used by Aboriginal people as gathering spots or settlement areas. Understanding contemporary processes of Aboriginal urbanization means we also need to acknowledge the story of Aboriginal peoples' removal from emerging urban centres, a facet that is not a familiar part of Canadian urban history. While there are no histories that examine urban Aboriginal peoples and cities, there are numerous examples to suggest the general absence of Aboriginal people in cities before the mid-1900s resulted at least in part from policies that actively displaced them from urban areas.

These policies included the selection of reserve lands far from urban centres and practices that confined First Nations peoples to these areas, the dispossession of Métis people from their lands and their settlement on urban fringes, and the expropriation of reserves and communities overtaken by expanding urban boundaries. The idea of an urban Aboriginal person became incompatible with the images of Aboriginal peoples that had developed over the last century. Consequently, Aboriginal people who chose to live in cities were seen as an anomaly or as people who had turned their backs on their culture.

This history reminds us that urban Aboriginal people do not arrive in cities like other migrants, national or international. Clearly, Aboriginal people moving to cities face some of the same challenges of other migrants – challenges associated with integrating into urban economies, interacting with diverse people from many origins, and finding appropriate housing and education. Like other migrants, many Aboriginal people also retain close ties to their communities of origin. Unlike these other migrants, though, many Aboriginal people are traveling within their traditional territories. Many have expectations that their Aboriginal rights and identities will make a difference to the ways that they structure and live their lives in urban areas. The clarification of Aboriginal rights in urban areas, particularly those dealing with self-government, represents a major contemporary challenge for governments, both Aboriginal and non-Aboriginal.

Assumptions about the nature of the urban Aboriginal experience have historically shaped policy responses. Around the start of the 20th century, most writers saw the presence of Aboriginal people in cities as detrimental to the moral and physical conditions of both Aboriginal peoples and urban areas, providing one rationale for removing Aboriginal people from city areas. For decades, public discourses have defined Aboriginal and urban cultures as incompatible. Migration to the city was interpreted as a decision to leave rural communities and cultures, and to assimilate into mainstream society. The federal government's emphasis on provincial responsibilities for Aboriginal peoples and programs off reserves supported this interpretation as did the responses of many Aboriginal peoples themselves. Fledgling attempts by some First Nations governments to maintain connections with their urban members dissolved in this context.

While much of the challenge of early urbanization was framed as one of cultural adaptation, by the 1980s the emphasis shifted to poverty, and the challenges facing urban Aboriginal people were framed as unemployment, inadequate housing, and low levels of income and education. Federal and provincial government programs attempted to address the economic and educational needs of Aboriginal people in urban areas. With the exception of some Métis organizations on the prairies, provincial and national Aboriginal representative bodies ignored urban Aboriginal communities, except that their offices tended to be located in urban centres and they served as employers for local urban Aboriginal populations. Instead, it was urban Aboriginal organizations, many with roots in the earlier period of migration, that provided spaces for the celebration of Aboriginal cultures and developed culturally appropriate ways of delivering services.

The federal government defined its responsibility quite narrowly and focused primarily on Indians residing on Indian reserves. Provinces and municipalities tended to see all Aboriginal peoples including those residing in cities and towns as a federal responsibility. Despite this narrow focus, there have been several federal initiatives which have been directed at urban Aboriginal peoples. The major policy responses from the federal government were through the Migrating Native Peoples Program in the 1970s which changed into the Aboriginal Friendship Centre Program since the 1980s. One of the major achievements of the friendship centres in the early 1980s was to convince the federal government of the legitimacy of the urban Aboriginal population and its institutions. CMHC provided support in the 1980s for urban Aboriginal housing primarily through an off-reserve housing program, since discontinued. Employment and Immigration Canada, now Human Resources Development Canada, provided support for training and education of Aboriginal individuals residing in urban areas and seeking employment. Many First Nation communities provided support for members to attend urban colleges and universities.

These efforts focused, to a large extent, upon individual adjustment to the urban environment. The issues were addressed through the lens of individual social problems, taking a labour economic approach to the issues. The problems that Aboriginal peoples were experiencing were problems of "lack": lack of education, lack of training, lack of job experience, lack of industrial cultural experience. The solutions then were to fill the individual deficiencies.

The report of the Royal Commission on Aboriginal Peoples (RCAP) represents accurately the contemporary discourse on the urban Aboriginal experience: tension between loss and opportunity. On the one hand, the city represented loss – loss of culture and community for Aboriginal migrants, yet there was an emergent urban Aboriginal culture, a creative blend of Aboriginal traditional cultures and urban popular culture. On the other hand, it represented opportunity – a chance for better education and employment but it drew many of the best and brightest away from reserve and rural communities, draining intellectual capital needed for building healthy rural communities and nations. The RCAP report brought to the forefront the desire of many Aboriginal peoples to live good lives within cities, to maintain and develop a distinctive Aboriginal culture which is more than a heritage and to exercise significant governance over their daily lives, both as individuals and as communities.

In this context, the Commission made an important contribution in its emphasis on the importance of Aboriginal cultures to the well-being of urban Aboriginal peoples and to the social futures of cities. The urban Aboriginal situation however is awkwardly and incompletely linked to other Commission recommendations and analyses, though, and it is clear that urban Aboriginal people were not seen as central to the discussion of Aboriginal futures.

The contemporary situation calls for ways to describe and respond to the urban Aboriginal experience. We must move away from Donald Fixico's description in *American Indians and the Urban Experience*[3] of urban Indians as "an unseen, little understood Indian identity." He echoes the findings of the RCAP report when he says "Indian people have struggled to learn a new culture of mainstream urbanization, but rather than being absorbed into the process, they have survived to form a new identity of their own." RCAP reported that (urban) "Aboriginal people stressed the fundamental importance of retaining and enhancing their cultural identity while living in urban centres...maintaining that identity is an essential and self-validating pursuit for Aboriginal peoples in cities...Contemporary urban Aboriginal people, in particular, are more positive about their Aboriginal identity than at any time in the past."

There is a growing recognition of the contribution of Aboriginal people to the social and economic future of urban areas in Canada. There is evidence that strong and diverse Aboriginal identities exist in cities as well as in rural reserves and communities. Some Aboriginal people experience marginalization in urban areas, others experience success. Many Aboriginal people maintain strong connections with their rural communities of origin, but many do not. There is an emphasis on self-determination and self-government in cities, as well as in communities defined by reserve or Métis settlement boundaries. There are strong, semi-autonomous urban Aboriginal organizations representing urban Aboriginal communities, as well as an increasing interest in urban residents by national and provincial Aboriginal political bodies. There are attempts to co-ordinate government (federal, provincial, municipal, Aboriginal, for example through the Urban Aboriginal Strategy) responses to the situation of Aboriginal people in Canada.

What is important is that we begin to see urban Aboriginal peoples both as individuals and as communities, with interests, aspirations, needs, goals, and objectives that they wish to pursue within the urban landscape rather than as objects of public policy or victims of colonization or displacement.

These papers represent some issues that face public policy-makers as they begin to work toward programs and policies that will address the aspirations and needs of Aboriginal people and communities in urban areas.

Levesque's paper introduces this volume by emphasizing the way that urban areas have become central to Aboriginal economies and cultures. Urban areas are important nodes in mobility patterns, they support the growth of an Aboriginal civil service, and they represent important gathering places. At the same time, Levesque illustrates an important feature of Aboriginal urbanization: while urbanization is part of the contemporary transformation of Aboriginal cultures and economies in Canada, activities and development in cities are not disconnected from Aboriginal communities in rural areas. The boundaries between rural and urban are not murky and hazy.

Several papers explore the demographic processes associated with urbanization. Guimond addresses definitions of Aboriginality in census statistics and their implications for explaining the growth of urban Aboriginal populations. He makes two main points: there are many different ways of defining these categories with census definitions, and Aboriginal responses to census questions about Aboriginal identity have changed over time. Guimond shows that a significant part of the growth of urban Aboriginal populations from the 1980s to the present appears to derive from changing patterns of Aboriginal self-reporting. Norris and Clatworthy demonstrate that migration is not the major factor affecting urban Aboriginal population growth, and that there is substantial migration of Aboriginal people to rural reserves and Aboriginal communities. Norris and Clatworthy explore some of the cultural and demographic factors associated with different migration and mobility patterns. Both point to a complex identity community.

Maxim, Keane, and White focus on Aboriginal settlement patterns within the city, exploring the degree to which North American Indians live in inner cities, and whether they are concentrated or dispersed relative to other groups. They argue that there is no single pattern that describes residential locations in urban areas. Individuals who identified only a single North American origin were more concentrated than visible minorities, but individuals who identified North American Indian and other ethnic origins were less concentrated than visible minorities. The diversity of residential patterns and the lack of a geographic centre for community create dilemmas for many of the standard public policy approaches to programming.

Aboriginal peoples in urban areas are diverse. This diversity is explored in the papers by Norris and Jantzen, Siggner, Jaccoud, and Brassard, and Wotherspoon. Norris and Jantzen emphasize Aboriginal languages in urban areas – an area that has received virtually no attention. They found that while there is less Aboriginal language use and transmission in urban than in non-urban areas, Aboriginal languages still have a significant presence in cities. Cities vary both in levels of Aboriginal language use and transmission, and in the number of Aboriginal languages present in urban Aboriginal populations. Siggner's paper complements Guimond's analysis by comparing the differences in socio-economic characteristics for Aboriginal populations defined by origin and by identity. Siggner found that the Aboriginal identity population tends to have higher poverty and unemployment levels than the population that reports Aboriginal origins but does not identify as Aboriginal. He cautions analysts to pay attention to the definitions they employ in their analyses. Jaccoud and Brassard contribute to our understanding of the diversity of urban Aboriginal populations by describing the situation of a small group of marginalized Aboriginal women in Montréal. They found that moving to an urban area did not, by itself, worsen or improve these women's opportunities. Jaccoud and Brassard's work reminds us that there is not one single urban Aboriginal experience. Using various indicators, Wotherspoon identifies a small, but distinct segment of the urban Aboriginal population that occupies middle class socio-economic positions. He explores some of the barriers to movement into the middle class as well as conditions that facilitate this movement. Wotherspoon's findings are important as they give some indication of the future of public policy interventions: stable, economically well off urban Aboriginal peoples.

Some of the papers focus on government programs and services for Aboriginal peoples in urban areas. In his paper on the Aboriginal policy and program environment in major western cities, Hanselmann bridges the topics of urban Aboriginal organizations and government responses. He recommends that both federal and provincial governments need to be involved in urban Aboriginal policy and program development, and that governments should encourage the development and participation of representative urban Aboriginal organizations. Three papers address specific policy sectors in urban areas. La Prairie and Stenning focus on Aboriginal people in the criminal justice system. They argue that, while the Aboriginal population appears to be over-represented on the basis of population numbers, this over-representation disappears when age, income, and education are taken into account. In other words, Aboriginal people are represented in the criminal justice system at rates similar to those of other populations with the same socio-economic characteristics. This analysis raises questions about the role of culturally appropriate programming in the criminal justice system, suggesting that perhaps interventions that help economic adjustment may be more meaningful. In response to the La Prairie and Stenning paper, Trevathan documents the success of Aboriginal-specific programming for Aboriginal offenders. Her analysis suggests that, although the factors leading to Aboriginal over-representation in the criminal justice system may relate to socio-economic rather than cultural characteristics, culturally based programs represent part of the solution. Richards and Vining explore the correlates of Aboriginal student success off reserves. They recommend facilitating Aboriginal participation in the school system through strategies such as the introduction of a distinct Aboriginal school system or the development of schools with specialized mandates to honour Aboriginal traditions.

Finally, the focus turns to community organizations and governance issues. These papers emphasize the development and role of urban Aboriginal organizations. Loxley and Wien emphasize Aboriginal initiatives in urban economic development. They describe three kinds of strategies – initiatives by urban reserves, attempts by rural First Nations and Métis groups to develop opportunities in urban areas, and economic development efforts by urban Aboriginal populations without a land base. They note that there have been few government interventions that support the latter. With the increasing size of an urban Aboriginal population without a land base, this appears to be an important area for policy and program development. Newhouse addresses the issues of urban Aboriginal organizations more generally. He documents the changing nature of urban Aboriginal institutions and argues that they play an important role in defining urban Aboriginal communities and mediating urban Aboriginal community life. This important role is often ignored by policy-makers. Todd builds on Newhouse's analysis by documenting some of the issues associated with the development of urban Aboriginal self-government. He describes the evolution of projects and programs under Aboriginal control in the city of Vancouver, and identifies some of the challenges facing urban Aboriginal organizations in developing effective Aboriginal governance. Finally, LaGrand explores some of the directions that Aboriginal organizations in U.S. cities have taken. His paper provides a unique comparative perspective.

The picture that emerges from the research, albeit tentative and incomplete, is that of urban communities, geographically distributed, culturally and linguistically diverse in which many members retain strong links to rural and reserve communities. These communities have developed an infrastructure of institutions and organizations over the last two decades in particular, are desirous of maintaining a distinct Aboriginal cultural identity willing and desirous of participating as Aboriginal peoples in the social and economic life in cities and urban areas, and working hard to ensure their members can do so. We read the literature as one of determination and strength in the face of adversity and challenge. Urban Aboriginal peoples have not sat back and waited for solutions.

The incredible range of Aboriginal organizations, their many community services and garnering of community effort demonstrate to us an institutional capacity to effectively deal with many of the challenges facing them. We have not documented or explored all the challenges in any great depth: racism and discrimination, lack of integration of Aboriginal institutions into municipal planning structures and processes, difficulties of language and culture development in small communities, sorting through the contestations of governments and organizations for jurisdictions, relationships with other ethnic and cultural groups in cities and the many social problems. These can include poor and inadequate housing, low and under-employment and low participation rates at all levels of education. Communities which are dealing with such overwhelming problems require high levels of sustained assistance.

We argue that public policy approaches to urban Aboriginal peoples must recognize the institutional infrastructure that has emerged over the last two decades and build key roles for them throughout the policy development, implementation and review processes. Defining the issues ought to be done jointly with Aboriginal, municipal, provincial, and federal institutions. Improved policies and programs, based on jointly commissioned research, ought to be the outcomes of these joint efforts. There is a strong desire by Aboriginal peoples to use traditional knowledge in this effort. This ought to be a central part of the work to be done. The experience of the last 125 years of Indian public policy ought to point out the folly of doing things for Indians instead of helping Indians do things for themselves.

Notes

1   Peters, E.J. (2002) "Our City Indians: Negotiating the Meaning of First Nations Urbanization in Canada, 1945-1975," *Historical Geography*, 30: 76. The count in 1951 did not include Métis.

2   <www.12.statcan.ca/english/census01/products/analytic/companion/abor/canada.cfm>. Accessed March 2003.

3   Lobo, Susan and Kurt Peters, (eds.) (2001) *American Indians and the Urban Experience*, Altamira Press.

Urban Aboriginal Populations: An Update Using the 2001 Census Results

Andrew J. Siggner
Housing, Family, & Social Statistics Division
Statistics Canada

Introduction

This publication was originally scheduled to be released in late 2002, prior to the dissemination of the 2001 Census data on Aboriginal peoples in January 2003. However, due to a delay in the release of the former, the Census results have become available. While not all Census data have been released as of the time of writing, it was felt worthwhile to add some of the more recent demographic data on the urban Aboriginal population. Therefore, by way of introduction to the subsequent articles, many of which drawprimarily on earlier Census data, selected 2001 Census results on Aboriginal peoples are presented below.

Population Size and Distribution

The 2001 Census asks a series of questions to count Aboriginal peoples:

▸ a question on the ethnic/cultural origins of a person's ancestors;

▸ a more direct question on whether or not a person self-identifies with an Aboriginal group (namely, North American Indian, Métis, or Inuit);

▸ whether or not a person is a Registered (or Treaty) Indian according to the *Indian Act*; and

▸ if a person is a member of an Indian Band or First Nation.[1]

Depending on the application, counts using any of these concepts may be appropriate for defining the Aboriginal population. Thus, as analysts and other data users will see in the subsequent articles, defining the Aboriginal population statistically for their purposes can be an important decision that can, and does, affect the outcomes of their research.

The 2001 Census of Canada reported 1,319,850 persons as having at least one Aboriginal ancestor (North American Indian, Métis, or Inuit), up 20 percent from 1,101, 960 in 1996 (see Chart 1). On the more direct question of asking about Aboriginal self-identity, the 2001 Census reported 976,305 with an Aboriginal identity (namely, North American Indian, Métis, or Inuit), up 22 percent from 1996.[2] Using a separate concept in the Census from the ethnic origin and identity concepts, 558,175 reported they had registered Indian status according the *Indian Act*.[3] It should be pointed out, however, that the Registered Indian count overlaps with a portion of the Aboriginal identity count and, thus, is not mutually exclusive.

Chart 1: Ratio of those Reporting Aboriginal Identity per 100 of those with Aboriginal Origins in Selected CMAs, 2001 Census

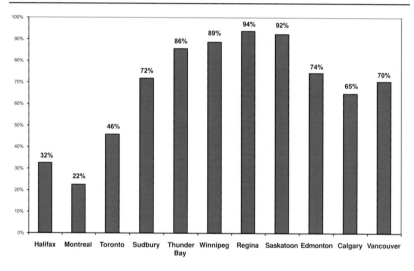

Using these different definitions, the Census can tell us the size of the population living in urban areas across Canada. In Canada, 495,095 of the total Aboriginal identity population resided in urban areas, representing 49 percent of total. However, if the broader Aboriginal origin definition were used, the number of people reporting at least one Aboriginal origin and living in urban areas was 758,455 or 56 percent of the total Aboriginal origin population.[4] As will be seen in subsequent articles, the socio-economic characteristics of the Aboriginal origin-based population living in urban areas varies when compared to those with Aboriginal identity.

In Chart 2, a selection of urban areas across Canada shows the size and ratio of those reporting an Aboriginal identity to those reporting Aboriginal origins. Two general observations can be made. There is a much higher correspondence in the size of the identity and origin-based Aboriginal populations from Manitoba and points west, compared to those cities in the eastern part of Canada. But, as one moves north, even in Ontario, the ratio of Aboriginal identity to origin increases. It is in the more southern and eastern cities where a much larger number of people report some Aboriginal ancestry, but do not identify themselves as Aboriginal on the more direct Aboriginal identity question in the Census (see Chart 2). For the remainder of this 2001 update, the focus will be on the Aboriginal identity population.[5] Readers can go to the Statistics Canada Web site, <www.statcan.ca> for further information on the Aboriginal origin-based population.

Chart 2: Ratio of those Reporting an Aboriginal Identity per 100 of those Reporting an Aboriginal Origin, for Selected CMAs, 2001

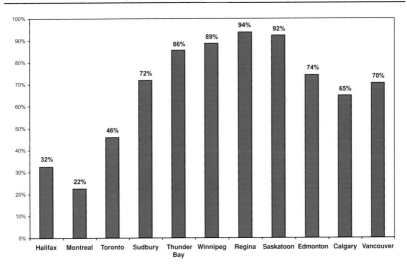

Using the Aboriginal identity concept, both large and small urban areas gained in the shares of the total Aboriginal population between 1996 and 2001 (see Chart 3). In 2001, the percentage living in urban census metropolitan areas (CMAs) grew from 26.3 to 27.8 percent in five years, reaching about 280,000 Aboriginal people. The smaller urban areas (i.e., those with less than 100,000 population) had about 214,000 or 21.3 percent of all Aboriginal people. Those on Indian reserves and in rural non-reserve areas both saw slight losses in their respective shares between 1996 and 2001. The reader should remember that even though there were losses in percentage shares in these latter locations, the absolute populations still grew over the five years, but just not as fast as in the urban areas. For example, both reserve and rural non-reserve Aboriginal populations grew by about 14 percent over the 1996-2001 period, while both small and large urban areas saw their Aboriginal populations grow by 23 and 26 percent, respectively.

Chart 3: Aboriginal Identity by Area of Residence, Canada, 1996 and 2001

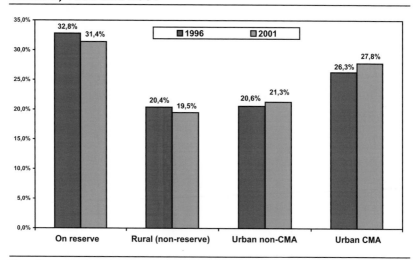

Note: Data are adjusted for incompletely enumerated Indian reserves in both years.

A variety of factors may be contributing to the more rapid growth of the urban Aboriginal population over the 1996-2001 period. Some of this growth in urban areas will be due to natural increase (i.e., births minus deaths) among the resident Aboriginal population. Another factor is the net migration into urban areas among the Aboriginal population. While this factor added to the urban CMA growth, there actually was a net loss of migrants in smaller urban areas. Therefore, other factors are contributing to the overall growth in both urban non-CMAs and CMAs. These factors likely include the potential for improved coverage in 2001 in these areas compared to 1996, but also may include the impact of "ethnic mobility." This factor is more fully discussed in the subsequent articles by both Siggner and Guimond.

Ethnic mobility occurs when someone changes how they report their ethnic origin or identity from one census to the next. Over the last several censuses, there appears to be a large number of people changing their affiliation both in terms of their ethnic origins and their Aboriginal identity. On the origin question, people appear to be shifting from reporting a non-Aboriginal origin in one census to reporting an Aboriginal origin in the response to the ethnic origin question in a later census. This same phenomenon appears to be occurring in the Aboriginal identity population, as well. As will be demonstrated in later articles, the ethnic mobility factor is affecting the rapid growth of urban Aboriginal populations. The exact amount of its contribution is not known. However, the phenomenon and its impact should not be ignored by policy-makers and planners, when examining the socio-economic conditions of Aboriginal peoples.

Finally, while it was the North American Indian population, which was the fastest growing 10 years ago (i.e., between 1986 and 1991), by 2001, it was the Métis who had the largest percentage growth (43 percent) over the 1996-2001 period. The Métis also tend to be more urban-based (68 percent) than their North American Indian counterparts (41 percent).

Notes

1   The 2001 Census data on Bands/First Nations will be released later in 2003.

2   The Aboriginal identity count includes persons who do not necessarily have any Aboriginal ancestry, but who did report self-identifying with an Aboriginal group, or who may have Registered Indian status or band membership without having Aboriginal ancestry.

3   Registered Indian status is a legal concept with eligibility criteria defined in the *Indian Act*. While the vast majority of Registered Indians reports that they are North American Indian on the Aboriginal identity question of the Census, some non-Aboriginal, Métis, and Inuit people can have and do report legal Indian status on their census form. These are included in the 558,175 reported above.

4   Both the Aboriginal origin and identity counts have been adjusted for the incompletely enumerated reserves in 2001, to obtain a more realistic percentage in urban areas. An estimate of 30,000 was added to the total Aboriginal populations in the denominator in both cases. Also, the urban Aboriginal population excludes any reserves within urban boundaries.

5   Readers can go to the Statistics Canada Web site <www.statcan.ca>, and for further information on the Aboriginal origin-based population click on the Census box, find the Previous releases box and click that, then the January 21, 2003 release. This should take readers to the 2001 Census/Ethno-Cultural & Aboriginal Home Page. Scroll down to the bottom of the page and click on Thematic Tables. Once the list of table appears, review for the tables containing Aboriginal origin data. These can be viewed and printed, or downloaded.

Definitions of Aboriginal Peoples

Aboriginal Population

There are many ways of defining the Aboriginal population, which can result in different estimates of its size. There is no single or "correct" definition of the Aboriginal population, and the choice of a definition depends on the purpose for which it is to be used. Different definitions/counts are used depending on the focus and requirements of the user.

The Census provides data that are based on the definitions of ethnic origin (ancestry), Aboriginal Identity, Registered Indian, and Band membership.

Aboriginal Ancestry/Origin refers to those persons who reported at least one Aboriginal origin (North American Indian, Métis, or Inuit) on the ethnic origin question in the Census. The question asks about the ethnic or cultural group(s) to which the respondent's ancestors belong.

Aboriginal Identity refers to those persons who reported identifying with at least one Aboriginal group (i.e., North American Indian, Métis, or Inuit). Also included are individuals who did not report an Aboriginal identity, but did report themselves as a Registered or Treaty Indian, and/or Band or First Nation membership.

The terms, North American Indian, Métis, and Inuit are the terms used in the Aboriginal identity question on the Census form. These terms allow the individual respondent to report the specific Aboriginal group with which they self-identify. There are no official definitions provided in the Census for these terms. They do derive from the terms used in the Constitution in relation to Aboriginal peoples.

The term, North American Indian is used for those persons who self-identify as such, and generally refers to persons who consider themselves as part of the First Nations in Canada, whether or not they have legal Indian status according to the *Indian Act* of Canada. Métis generally refers to people who are of mixed Aboriginal and non-Aboriginal ancestries and who self-identify as Métis. The Inuit are Aboriginal people who originally lived north of the tree line in Canada, and who self-identify as such.

Registered, Status or Treaty Indian refers to those who reported they were registered under the *Indian Act* of Canada. Treaty Indians are persons who are registered under the *Indian Act* of Canada and can prove descent from a Band that signed a treaty. The term "treaty Indian" is more widely used in the Prairie provinces.

Member of an Indian Band or First Nation refers to those persons who reported being a member of an Indian band or a First Nation of Canada.

The counts from the **2001 Census** using the different definitions:

Aboriginal Origin 1,319,890
(single and multiple responses)

Aboriginal Identity 976,305

▸ North American Indian 608,850

▸ Métis 292,310

▸ Inuit 45,070

▸ Multiple Aboriginal identity groups
  or Registered Indians/Band Members
  without Aboriginal identity 30,080

Registered Indian 558,175

First Nation/Band Membership 554,860

The Presence of Aboriginal Peoples in Quebec's Cities: Multiple Movements, Diverse Issues

Carole Lévesque
Institut national de la recherche scientifique
Université du Québec

Introduction

The presence of Aboriginal peoples in several Quebec cities is becoming more and more visible and diverse.[1] Although this phenomenon is more recent in Quebec than in the western provinces where it dates back to the 1950s, it has greatly intensified since the early 1980s, mostly in Montréal but also in Québec City, Val d'Or, Chibougamau, Sept-Îles, La Tuque, and Gatineau (Gill et al., 1995; Laplante, 1991; Montpetit, 1989; RCAAQ, 1997; Roy, 1993). No longer is this presence simply a matter of individuals; it is also a matter of communities, institutions, networks, and projects. Indeed, while for many Aboriginal people the city is still a destination or a stopover in their educational and/or career path, and a refuge or place of exile for many others, it is also becoming a relay point between Aboriginal communities on the one hand, and different First Nations on the other. As this occurs, new ties are being forged between cities and Aboriginal communities[2] that are as yet little discussed. More and more often, bridges are being formed between these two living environments that have long been seen and portrayed in studies as being opposed to, if not incompatible with, one another (Peters, 1996a,b). These new types of ties unquestionably stem from the position that Indian groups and the Inuit occupy in the political arena at the national and provincial level. These ties result from Aboriginal peoples' demonstrations of their affirmation of identity, which are characterizing their progress toward self-government and their quest for legal, social, and cultural recognition.

Already, the debate surrounding self-government has markedly turned in recent years toward political issues associated with the question of the rights of Aboriginal people living in urban areas. The Royal Commission on Aboriginal Peoples, as we know, paid a great deal of attention during its mandate to the living conditions of this population (RCAP, 1996). We should also remember that in 1999, Corbière recognized the right to vote of all band members, those living in the community and those outside, thus extending the pool of voters beyond the territorial boundaries attributed to bands, and pronouncing itself at the same time on the social and cultural bond represented by the Indian band, a bond that transcends geography and territory.

Many movements are therefore driving the contemporary phenomenon of the Aboriginal presence in the city. New forms of organization, production, and communication are emerging, and their impact is already visible, as we will see in the next few pages. These new realities reflect the modernity that characterizes contemporary Aboriginal societies, to paraphrase Newhouse (2000). This modernity must be understood, and its scope measured and assessed. Within the context of such a perspective, this article looks at three aspects of this new relationship that Quebec's Aboriginal peoples now have with the city. The first involves the current forms of movement between Aboriginal communities and the city. The second examines the Aboriginal process of institutionalization now occurring in the Montréal area and in other Quebec cities. The third more directly concerns the city's new role as an Aboriginal public space. My comments are inspired by documentary information on Quebec's First Nations, and by the empirical data collected from a group of Aboriginal women living in Montréal and a second group of Aboriginal women from the North Shore and the Abitibi region (Lévesque et al., 2001; Lévesque and Trudeau, 2001).[3]

New Forms of Mobility

The Aboriginal presence in the city has long been seen as the opposite of community life and, therefore, understood as the result of a break with the community of origin. In the past, particularly in the cases of generations of women forced to leave their communities because of their marriages to non-Aboriginal men, the departures were synonymous with a break, and were often permanent. Today, due to a family or community context that is particularly difficult and restrictive, many people may cut their ties with the community temporarily or for long periods of time. All of these situations, which effectively lead to a break, correspond to realities experienced by many individuals and, as we know, more particularly by women and children (Gill et al., 1995). However, this no longer explains all the movements of Aboriginal people to the city or from the city, which are now also often part of a dynamic of continuity with, or extension of, community life.

The data gathered in Montréal between 1997 and 1999 support this observation. Indeed, one of the particularities of the sample of women interviewed in Montréal was the large number of moves to various locations in the years before they came to reside in the city. In fact, three out of four informants mentioned at least three moves to various cities, towns, or villages. Many listed more than six; and these moves were spread out over several months or years. This phenomenon cannot be explained by either age or family situation: both younger and older women might present similar profiles, and no greater mobility was seen among single women, single parents, or women living within a couple, whether or not they had children. However, the women's origin appears to be a significant variable since women who came from the remotest communities, in a rural or isolated area, listed the greatest number of moves. In addition, for the majority of informants, this was not their first stay in Montréal. Many women had lived there at least once before, and some on several occasions.

But the Montréal informants did not hold a monopoly on mobility. In fact, it was found that the sample of informants from the regions also presented singular characteristics in this regard. Surprisingly, more than half the women interviewed who were then living in their community of origin were found to have also stayed in other places for various periods of time, and more than a third of the sample had already made at least three significant moves in their past. While some of these women had resided in cities and towns near their community, others had also lived in Montréal or Québec City for several years and did not rule out the possibility of going back there.

One can readily infer from these results that the women interviewed in Montréal and in the regions were characterized by a great deal of mobility. Nonetheless, underlying this evident mobility or *hypermobility*, to use the term cited by Frideres and Gadacz (2001), one finds a newly emerging relation to space and time. The women themselves stated that their presence in the city was neither transitory nor unusual. It was part of their way of life and their identity. Numerous other observations recorded in the past few years have corroborated these findings to the effect that mobility is today a key part of one's personal and professional life for many segments of the population, whether they live in the communities or in the cities.[4]

In some ways, at least within Quebec, cities and Aboriginal communities have grown closer. The regular activities of Aboriginal organizations, and the participation in study committees, task forces, meetings, conferences, and training sessions bring Aboriginal people to the city for periods often longer than we would likely expect. For a number of individuals, mobility is no longer associated with a setback but rather with a personal or professional advantage. This presence in the city now requires new analytical perspectives, as does life in the communities. It even appears quite clear that, when it is a question of mobility, these two places of residence, whether stayed in for short or long periods of time, can no longer be studied separately.

Moreover, it appears that mobility has become a significant feature not only of movements between the city and the community of origin, but also of the circulation of individuals between various Aboriginal communities. The empirical data available to us also show that many of the women interviewed in both Montréal and the regions had stayed a certain amount of time in an Aboriginal community other than their community of origin. These movements, especially in the context of professional activities, seem to represent, for the time being, a new form of intercommunity rapprochement. It is not unusual for Aboriginal people to go to work for a First Nation other than theirs for several years. An apparently growing number of cases can be seen in sectors such as public security, economic development, the environment, and health. Many of the women interviewed also felt that a stay in another Aboriginal community was an experience they would like to have.

We can undoubtedly hypothesize that the ways in which cities and Aboriginal communities have grown closer in the past decade have fostered the emergence of this new intercommunity mobility. Indeed, the two types of mobility (urban and intercommunity) now seem to go together. As the relationship with the city is changing (the city is becoming closer and more accessible), the relationship with the community of origin is also changing, as it is now in interaction with other Aboriginal communities. In this respect, the situation in Quebec differs somewhat from the situation seen in western Canada where a significant proportion of Aboriginal people living in urban areas were born in the cities, have lived there for several generations, and no longer necessarily maintain ties with rural communities (Frideres and Gadacz, 2001; Newhouse, 2000). Ninety percent of Quebec's urban Aboriginal population is still from the communities, so close ties exist with the communities of origin and ancestral hunting grounds. There is nothing to indicate that these ties are weakening. On the contrary, the new forms of the Aboriginal presence in the city are now strengthening relations that until the early 1990s had shown signs of eroding.

An Aboriginal Civil Service

A second aspect likely to influence discussion on the new ties with the city more directly concerns the job market in the Montréal area. Our survey also brought out some very interesting information in this regard. In fact, it was found that 23 of the 26 women in our Montréal sample held a job in an Aboriginal organization at the time of the interview. Although this situation may be due to the way in which the sample was formed, it may also indicate that an important change is taking place. A growing population, expanding needs in the area of health, education, and social services, and an ever-increasing demand for employment have led, in the past few years, to the creation of institutional and community structures whose principal characteristic, in addition to offering a more appropriate array of services that reach a larger clientele, is to become an outlet for the Aboriginal workforce in Montréal.

Some studies, and especially the research work undertaken in the context of the Royal Commission on Aboriginal Peoples, have clearly identified the obstacles facing Aboriginal people in terms of employment when they find themselves in urban areas (RCAP, 1996; MSRQ, 1995). Lower education levels and a lack of relevant work experience limit access to the job market or relegate individuals to precarious employment. But more importantly, it would appear that continual comparisons with non-Aboriginal people and difficulties in adapting to the non-Aboriginal work environment are what affect people the most. Many of the women interviewed in Montréal who had already held jobs in both Aboriginal and non-Aboriginal settings pointed to major differences between the two environments. In the non-Aboriginal environment, the work climate was deemed to be stressful, rigid, individualistic, and competitive, whereas the Aboriginal environment was deemed to be more flexible and open, and marked by greater collaboration. In addition to these perceptions, the women also noted the very great advantage of finding oneself among other Aboriginal people and, therefore, as some stated, less disoriented and more self-confident.

For the moment, it is evident that the organizations concerned operate mainly in the service sector. Employment and training programs, paralegal services, programs aimed at countering violence, and housing assistance, to name but a few, have for the most part been administered and managed since the 1990s by Aboriginal organizations, such as the First Nations Local Commissions, Native Friendship Centres, or Quebec Native Women.[5] New programs or specific agreements between governments – federal or provincial depending on the area of responsibility – and Aboriginal authorities sometimes also lead to the setting up of temporary structures. Although the number of jobs created in this Aboriginal civil service is ultimately limited in relation to the demand, the mere fact of their existence is already helping to change the sphere of work, which now offers opportunities and prospects where there had been very few before. At the same time, this is helping to change the nature of relations between Aboriginal people.

Service points are more numerous and thus more accessible, and this is facilitating exchanges between Aboriginal people of various backgrounds. Innus interact with Atikamekw, Crees with Algonquins, etc. Networks are being created whose effectiveness is seen when it is time to hire more staff or fill vacant positions. But these networks are also working in other circumstances, distributing information, encouraging mutual help, providing support, ending isolation and, at times, performing a mediatory role between Aboriginal and non-Aboriginal people. In addition, these networks do not only operate in the city. Their impact extends to the communities, given, as was underscored previously, the great mobility of the population as well as the new attitudes toward moving to the city or leaving the city. Ties forged between people from different communities or backgrounds are often maintained beyond the place of residence.

Moreover, a number of political organizations at the regional and provincial levels have offices in the city or nearby. In Wendake, a community adjoining Québec City, we find the secretariat of The Assembly of First Nations of Quebec and Labrador and its numerous administrative divisions; and the Naskapi Development Corporation also has an office in Québec City. Quebec Native Women is established in Montréal, as is the Cree Regional Authority and the Makivik Corporation.[6] The employees of these organizations are mostly Aboriginal and their work mandates generally last for several years. There is every reason to believe that there will be an increase in the number of these organizations and their staff in the coming years, given their growing involvement in the major social issues raised by the progress of Aboriginal self-government. In addition to these potential employers, there are now also Aboriginal non-profit organizations, community groups and, in some cases, private businesses. This situation is not specific to Montréal or Québec City. It can be seen in several other cities in the province, such as Sept-Îles, Val d'Or, and La Tuque.

The City as a Gathering Place

The third aspect associated with a re-examination of the various forms of the presence of Aboriginal people in the city leads us to now envisage the city as a new public space for Aboriginal people in Quebec primarily, but also for Aboriginal people from elsewhere.[7] While many Aboriginal organizations are offering more and more services to people established in urban areas, we must take into account the fact that it is from the city that many of them also offer support, services, and expertise to the communities they represent. We thus see a constant circulation between the communities and the cities, be it large centres such as Montréal and Québec City, or localities on the North Shore or in the Abitibi, Lanaudière, Mauricie, or Saguenay regions. Indeed, the city often becomes the needed relay point between remote and isolated communities. In addition, in the case of provincial agencies such as The Assembly of First Nations of Quebec and Labrador and Quebec Native Women, the city is now the link between First Nations who would otherwise have little contact among themselves.

While the city is becoming closer to Aboriginal communities, several communities are also working to facilitate the stay of their members in the city by creating welcoming infrastructures. This is particularly the case with the residential facilities for people needing care or medical follow-up. People can stay as long as necessary, along with members of their families if need be. These facilities, run by local authorities, are community initiatives, and most First Nations have such a service in Montréal, Québec City or in cities near their communities. Projects for student residences in several locations are also being studied; Aboriginal students' associations have already been set up in the past few years in Quebec universities. In short, the number of meeting places and meeting points is continuing to grow, and each in its own way is helping to shape a new Aboriginal urban reality. The informants interviewed in Montréal and in the regions often mentioned these new landmarks, these new spaces that help to lessen the isolation and disorientation often experienced by newcomers to the city.

Needless to say, the new urban landscape involves not only individuals but also communities and institutions. The Aboriginal presence in the city is no longer the sole concern of the domestic or family sphere, as was long the case. A new appropriation of the city is occurring on the part of organizations, communities, and political bodies, which are increasingly helping to enliven the urban landscape for the benefit of Aboriginal people.

The sports tournaments that are gaining in popularity each year are a good illustration of this. These hockey, broomball, or even baseball tournaments bring together teams from several First Nations and generally take place in cities located near the Aboriginal communities that initiate them. Thus, the Cree of Eeyou Istchee hold their hockey tournament in Val d'Or. The Atikamekw of the Lanaudière and Mauricie regions go to La Tuque for hockey as well, but also more and more for other sports activities.[8]

These tournaments have become highly valued annual gatherings in which people from the communities and Aboriginal residents of the cities participate. The decision to hold these events in the cities is mainly tied to material considerations. Indeed, few Aboriginal communities have the infrastructures necessary to welcome the thousands of people these tournaments attract over several days. The economic benefits for hotels and from retail sales are therefore very important to the host cities. However, benefits of a different order must also be taken into consideration since these gatherings help to strengthen ties between First Nations on the one hand, and between younger and older people on the other. First Nations from other provinces are also often invited to such tournaments. Moreover, while the teams involved in the tournaments mostly comprise Aboriginal people, the general public is also welcome, thus helping to bring Aboriginal and non-Aboriginal people closer together.

The increasing number of activities such as exhibitions, music concerts, and plays must also be considered when looking at contemporary cultural manifestations in the heart of the city. For example, in Montréal, Terres en vues/Land InSights, a non-profit organization founded in 1990, is devoted to the promotion of Aboriginal culture in all its forms. This organization, which also employs Aboriginal staff and is headed by a board of directors that includes members of several First Nations, is behind the Aboriginal Presence, a multidisciplinary festival organized annually in June since 1991. In addition to offering a varied program of films – documentaries, fiction works, archive films, experimental films and videos – and welcoming Aboriginal productions from Quebec, other provinces, the United States, and elsewhere, the festival is the meeting place for artists in visual arts, dance, music, and theatre, including craftspeople, painters, storytellers, and singers. The activities take place over 10 days and culminate on June 21, National Aboriginal Day. During this festival, several concert halls in the greater Montréal area welcome a growing audience of Aboriginal and non-Aboriginal people.[9] In addition to its function as a facilitator, *Terres en vues/Land InSights* plays a direct part in bringing different First Nations and cultures closer together.

So not only are Aboriginal peoples now coming to the city in a different way, but this renewed presence, expressed and actualized in new ways, also represents a fresh contribution to the urban fabric of a number of major centres in Quebec and Canada. Around the mid-1990s, clear tendencies in this direction could already be observed, which have since been confirmed.

> In contrast to views of aboriginal culture as either incompatible with or irrelevant in an urban environment, aboriginal people have argued that supporting and enhancing aboriginal culture is a prerequisite for coping in an urban environment. These perspectives recognize that aboriginal cultures and the Euro-Canadian cultures that dominate Canadian cities are distinct in many ways, but they insist that aboriginal cultures can adapt to and flourish in urban areas, and that supporting aboriginal cultures will enrich cities as well as make them better places for aboriginal people (Peters, 1996a: 319-320).

Conclusion

The contemporary presence of Indian and Inuit people in Quebec's cities, three particular aspects of which have been highlighted in this article, clearly demonstrates the multiple realities that must be better documented and from which much can be learned. Profound transformations are under way on the social, political, economic and cultural levels; and new alliances are forming that are the modern-day manifestations of Aboriginal peoples' affirmation of identity and of the forms their civic participation and involvement are taking. But there is still too little discussion of all this.

In an article published in 2000, David Newhouse calls on researchers interested in, among other things, the issue of Aboriginal people living in urban areas to change their working framework and to re-examine the concepts underlying their thinking and analytical approaches. For example, the concept of urbanization, which has long been discussed from the sole perspective of acculturation or cultural dispossession, clearly needs to be updated in light of all the changes that have marked the path taken by Aboriginal people over the past three decades. In western Canada, the urban Aboriginal population, now several generations old, has become so large that its demographic growth no longer depends on migratory flows from rural communities. A full-fledged urban Aboriginal population with a distinct lifestyle has emerged, which no longer has ties to the rural communities. Similarly, the concept of assimilation is no longer appropriate in discussing the ways in which the dominant culture and Aboriginal cultures are meeting in cities. In this meeting of cultures, we are seeing new modes of expression that are more closely associated with a strengthening of Aboriginal cultural identity than with its fragmentation and disintegration.

As we have emphasized, Quebec's urban Aboriginal population presents characteristics that distinguish it from urban Aboriginal populations elsewhere in the country, if only in terms of its composition and relatively recent history. However, the concept of urbanization, still widely used in Quebec, does not seem to be any more appropriate in discussing the contemporary realties that can be observed here. Moreover, the very notion of urbanization in the special context of Aboriginal issues still too often conveys an evolutionary view of development, where the only path is that of the majority, in this case, that of the west. The contemporary forms of the Aboriginal presence in Quebec cities reflect a new kind of modernity. It is a modernity that is not that of the Québécois, nor is it probably that of Aboriginal people in western Canadian cities, but it is nonetheless anchored in the present. It is a modernity that is, in many ways, the sum of the history, heritage, and contemporary imperatives of life in society, which may be constraining in some circumstances, but which also offer the potential for renewal in other circumstances.

Notes

1   The Aboriginal population in Quebec (estimated at approximately 80,000 people) is made up of members of 10 First Nations and the Inuit of northern Quebec. In addition to the Aboriginal people of many origins who can be found in urban areas (roughly 25 percent of the total population), there are 55 distinct communities, most of which are located in rural or isolated areas. The Cree form nine communities established in the James Bay region, which they call Eeyou Istchee. The Algonquins also have nine communities, which are mainly located in the Abitibi-Témiscamingue region. Nine Innu communities are located on the North Shore and in the Saguenay region. The Naskapis live in Kawawachikamach, located 15 kilometres from the former northern mining town of Schefferville. The three Atikamekw communities are situated in the Lanaudière and Upper Mauricie regions. The Micmacs, who form three communities, are found in the Gaspé Peninsula. The Malécites have protected lands at Cacouna near Rivière-du-Loup. The two Abenaki communities are located near the city of Sorel, 50 kilometres north of Montréal. The community of the Huron-Wendats is situated in Wendake, near Québec City. The three Mohawk communities are established in the southern region of the province, near the cities of Montréal, Oka, and Cornwall, Ontario. And finally, the Inuit are found in 15 villages scattered along the northern shores of the province.

2   Throughout this text, the term "community" will be used as synonymous with Indian reserve. In Quebec, it is common usage to use this preferred term to designate Aboriginal communities.

3   These data were gathered in the context of a study conducted between 1997 and 1999 under Status of Women Canada's Policy Research program. This study provided an initial assessment of the use and effectiveness of employability programs for Aboriginal women in Quebec. It was characterized by an ethnographic method that led to 60 interviews being conducted with informants from the Montréal area (26 informants) as well as from cities and communities located in the regions (34 informants). Data related to employment and the job market were therefore continually placed in their social and cultural context. This study also led to another 20 interviews being conducted with Aboriginal and non-Aboriginal resource persons working in governmental, para-governmental, and Aboriginal organizations.

4   We are referring here to movements between the city and the community and not to movements of people from different Aboriginal communities who visit their ancestral hunting grounds.

5   It should be noted that following pressure from Aboriginal organizations in the 1980s and especially in the 1990s, a majority of programs are today entirely run by Aboriginal agencies. Several specific agreements to that effect have been signed in recent years. For example, a regional bilateral agreement was signed in 1996 between the Government of Canada and the Assembly of First Nations of Quebec and Labrador regarding employment and workforce training.

6   Many other organizations in the areas of business, health, education, communications, and culture also have offices in Wendake, Québec City or Montréal, notably the Association des gens d'affaires des Premiers Peuples, the Société de communication Atikamekw-Montagnais, the Cree School Board, Avatak Cultural Institute, The Native Trail, etc.

7   Many Aboriginal people from other Canadian provinces and from the United States, Mexico, and South America can also be found in Montréal, attracted by both the bilingualism of the city and the services offered to Indian and Inuit clienteles.

8   Little information is available on these activities since they have not been the focus of specific studies as yet. Only the regional newspapers discuss them regularly. Several items on this subject can be found for example in *L'Écho de La Tuque*, *La Tribune*, *Le Nouvelliste* or *The Nation* (a monthly newspaper distributed in the James Bay Cree communities). Another useful source is the press review produced by *The Covenant Chain* (a Quebec business), which gathers all the items published in Canadian newspapers on Aboriginal issues on a weekly basis.

9   In 2001, Terres en vues/Land InSights co-ordinated the tricentennial celebration of the Great Peace of Montréal, another important activity aimed at stressing the role played by Aboriginal people in the history of Montréal. The Great Peace was signed in 1701 by some 30 First Nations and the representatives of New France to mark the end of the Iroquois wars that had lasted for nearly a century.

References

Frideres, J.S. and R.R. Gadacz (2001) *Aboriginal Peoples in Canada. Contemporary Conflicts*, Scarborough: Prentice Hall Allyn and Bacon Canada.

Gill, L. et al. (1995) *La réserve et la ville : Les amérindiennes en milieu urbain au Québec*, Ottawa: Status of Women Canada.

Laplante, M. (1991) "Les Autochtones de Val d'Or. Étude sur les Autochtones vivant en milieu urbain," Val d'Or: Centre d'Amitié Autochtone de Val d'Or.

Lévesque, C. and N. Trudeau (2001) "Femmes autochtones et développement économique ou la rencontre des modernités," in *La tension tradition-modernité. Construits socioculturels de femmes autochtones, francophones et migrantes*, A. Martinez and M. Ollivier, (eds.), Ottawa: University of Ottawa Press, pp. 15-27.

Lévesque, C., N. Trudeau et al. (2001) *Aboriginal Women and Jobs: Challenges and Issues for Employability Programs in Quebec*. Ottawa: Status of Women Canada.

Montpetit, C. (1989) "Trajectoires de vie de migrants autochtones en milieu urbain," Master's thesis (Anthropology), Université de Montréal.

Newhouse, D. (2000) "The Development of Modern Aboriginal Societies," in *Expressions in Canadian Native Studies*, R.F. Laliberte, P. Sette, J.B. Waldram et al., (eds.), Saskatoon: University Extension Press, pp. 395-409.

Peters, E. (1996a) "Aboriginal People in Urban Areas," in *Visions of the Heart. Canadian Aboriginal Issues*, D. A. Long and O. P. Dickason, (eds.), Toronto: Harcourt Brace & Company, pp. 305-333.

—— (1996b) "'Urban' and 'Aboriginal': An Impossible Contradiction," in *City Lives and City Forms: Critical Research and Canadian Urbanism*, J. Caufield and L. Peake, (eds.), Toronto: University of Toronto Press, pp. 47-62.

Quebec, MSRQ (Ministère de la Sécurité du Revenu du Québec) (1995) *Profil des personnes autochtones aptes au travail, à l'aide de derniers recours*, Direction générale des politiques et des programmes, Direction de la recherche, de l'évaluation et de la statistique.

RCAAQ (Regroupement des centres d'amitié autochtones du Québec) (1997) *L'emploi et la formation chez les autochtones qui vivent en milieu urbain. Les mythes et la réalité*, RCAAQ.

RCAP (Royal Commission on Aboriginal Peoples) 1996 *Rapport de la Commission Royale sur les Peuples Autochtones. Volume 4 : Perspectives et Réalités*, Ottawa: Canada Communication Group.

Roy, F. (1993) "De la réserve à la ville : urbanisation montagnaise dans la région de Québec," Master's thesis (Anthropology), Université Laval.

Fuzzy Definitions and Population Explosion: Changing Identities of Aboriginal Groups in Canada

Eric Guimond
Research and Analysis Directorate
Indian and Northern Affairs Canada

In their collective eagerness to research and document Aboriginal social issues, demographers and other population specialists, both Aboriginal and non-Aboriginal, have most often overlooked two fundamental questions. Why is it so difficult to define Aboriginal populations in Canada? What is the explanation behind the recent population explosion? The answer to these questions is critical because of their implications for the enumeration of Aboriginal populations (definition to use), the monitoring of their socio-economic characteristics (interpretation of recent trends), and the development of policy and programs to improve the quality of life of Aboriginal populations. The purpose of this article is to discuss and provide an answer to these two fundamental questions strictly from a demographic perspective.

The first section presents existing concepts and definitions of Aboriginal populations in the Canadian statistics to illustrate the fuzziness of "Aboriginal boundaries." The second section of this article focuses on the recent demographic explosion of Aboriginal populations, and shows that the classic factors influencing growth (i.e., fertility, mortality, and migration) cannot account for all the observed growth. Finally, we introduce the phenomenon of *ethnic mobility* to explain the existence of fuzzy boundaries and the recent demographic explosion of Aboriginal populations. Ethnic mobility is the phenomenon by which individuals and families experience changes in their ethnic affiliation.[1]

Fuzzy Definitions

Who is Aboriginal in Canada? Many definitions of the concept of Aboriginality have been proposed over the years, and more so since the early 1980s with the increased awareness of Aboriginal issues in Canadian society. Unfortunately, no single definition has prevailed to date. The Census of Canada, which is still the only source of demographic and socio-economic data that covers all Aboriginal groups for all of Canada, collects information on four concepts – ethnic origin, Aboriginal self-identity, Indian legal status and First Nation membership – designed to estimate the size and characteristics of the Aboriginal populations of Canada, in their totality or in part. Lets take a look at the first three concepts, which are more widely used for definitional purposes.

Ethnic origin has been the most frequently used ethnocultural characteristic in Canada to determine Aboriginal affiliation. Since 1871, all the Canadian censuses have enumerated Aboriginal populations by means of a question on ethnic origin. The concept of origin refers to the ethnic or cultural group to which one's ancestors belonged. In theory, this concept could identify the descendants of the populations who were living in America when the Europeans arrived in the 16th and 17th centuries (Robitaille and Choinière, 1987). In reality however, since very few persons have a comprehensive knowledge of their ethnocultural genealogy, only a fraction of the actual descendants of precolonial Aboriginal peoples self-declare an Aboriginal origin on a census form. In addition to genealogy, census data on ethnic origin can also vary according to the preoccupations of mainstream society[2] and the nature of the socio-political relationships it maintains (or not) with Aboriginal populations.[3] The 1996 Census of Canada reports 1.1 million persons self-declaring at least one Aboriginal origin.

Self-identification is now used more often to define affiliation with an Aboriginal group. Ethnic identity is a subjective indicator of a person's affiliation with an ethnic group. Given the ineffectiveness of objective affiliation indicators (such as ethnic origin and mother tongue) with respect to acculturation and intermarriage, ethnic identity undoubtedly constitutes one of the best available indicators of ethnicity. The concept of *Aboriginal self-reporting*[4] was first introduced in 1986[5] to improve the enumeration of Aboriginal populations (Statistics Canada, 1989). According to the 1996 Census of Canada, nearly 780,000 persons self-identified with an Aboriginal group.[6]

In Canada, as in many other countries with an Aboriginal population, there are legal definitions of Aboriginality (Lee, 1990). The *Indian Act* is the main piece of Canadian legislation which explicitly defines a specific subset of the Aboriginal populations: Registered Indians. The post-Confederation version of the *Indian Act* dates back to 1876 (Savard and Proulx, 1982). According to the Census of Canada, the population self-declaring Indian registration as defined by the *Indian Act* of Canada stood at 488,000 persons in 1996. Unlike for the other Aboriginal groups (non-status Indians, Métis, and Inuit), there is a second valuable source of data available for the Registered Indian population: the Indian Register.[7] This additional source estimates the population of Registered Indians in Canada at 593,050 persons as of December 31, 1995 (INAC, 2002), 105,000 more than the 1996 Census conducted five months later. Even though most of the difference between these two data sources has been accounted for by specialists (Nault et al., 1992; Nault and George, 1992; Perreault et al., 1985; Siggner and Brûlotte, 1975; Romaniuk, 1974), for the majority of individuals interested in Aboriginal issues, the existence of two significantly different estimates of the Registered Indian population further complicates the issue of definitions.[8]

Figure 1. Three Dimensions of the Concept of Aboriginality

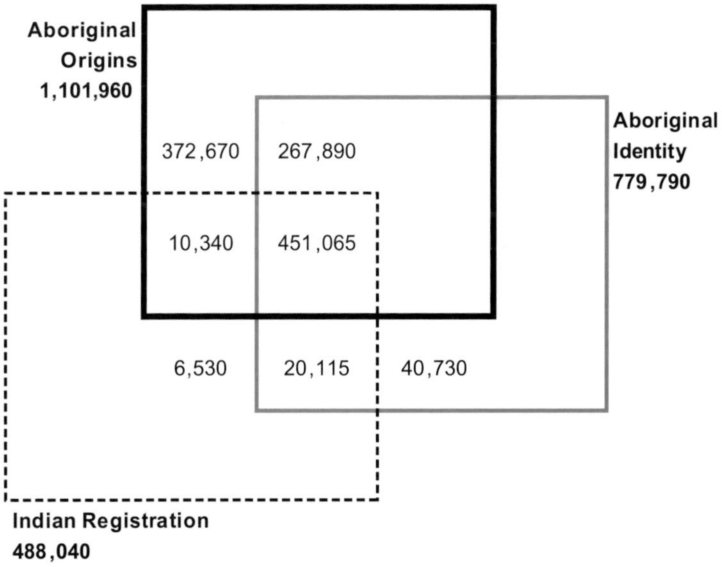

```
Aboriginal
  Origins
1,101,960

         372,670    267,890              Aboriginal
                                         Identity
                                         779,790

         10,340     451,065

          6,530     20,115     40,730

Indian Registration
488,040
```

Source: Statistics Canada, 1996 Census of Canada, custom tabulations.

Intuitively, one could think that there is some sort of "hierarchical structure" to these three concepts of Aboriginality: the Registered Indian population could be a subset of the Aboriginal identity population, which could be a subset of the broader Aboriginal origin population. Regardless of how convenient this view of the world might be, data reveal a far more complex reality (Figure 1). The populations defined by these three concepts partially overlap each other. When brought together, the concepts of Aboriginal origin, Aboriginal identity, and Indian registration define seven subsets of varying sizes. The two largest subsets are made of individuals who report an Aboriginal origin, an Aboriginal identity, and Indian registration (451,100) and of individuals who report only an Aboriginal origin (372,700). The two other "unidimensional" subsets, Aboriginal identity only and Indian legal status only, stand at 40,700 and 6,500 individuals respectively.

Already complex for most people, this illustration of the fuzziness of "Aboriginal boundaries" still oversimplifies reality. To further illustrate fuzziness, we have in Table 1 the 1996 Census population by Aboriginal origin and Aboriginal identity. In this table, there are 15 different origin responses, covering both single (e.g., Indian) and multiple (e.g., Indian and non-Aboriginal) responses. For Aboriginal identity, the question in the Census question allowed eight possibilities: North American Indian, Métis, Inuit, non- Aboriginal and four multiples (e.g., Indian and Métis). According to this "bidimensional" representation of Aboriginality, there would be 119 different ways of being Aboriginal in Canada, 17 times more than in our previous illustration of the fuzziness of "Aboriginal boundaries." If we try to further improve this representation by adding other dimensions such as Indian registration (with or without) and First Nation/band membership (with or without), then the definition becomes analytically unmanageable with 479 "types" of Aboriginal persons.

With this brief analysis of concepts and definitions, one can clearly conclude that there is no simple, single answer to the question of *who is Aboriginal in Canada*. Obviously, each definition yields a different population count and a different level of complexity. It is not perfectly clear where "Aboriginal boundaries" stand presently. However, there was a time, before the first contact between Aboriginal populations and European settlers, when group boundaries were clearly defined. Why is it more difficult to define and enumerate Aboriginal populations today? The answer lies within the concept of ethnic mobility.

Table 1: Population by Aboriginal Origin and Aboriginal Identity, 1996 Census of Canada

Ethnic Origin	Total	Aboriginal Identity					Non aboriginal identity
		Total	North American Indian	Métis	Inuit	Multiple Aboriginal Identities[1]	
Total	28 528 120	779 790	529 035	204 120	40 225	6 415	27 748 330
Aboriginal / Total	1 101 960	718 950	494 830	178 525	39 705	5 880	383 010
Aboriginal / Total single responses	477 635	450 850	360 925	56 395	32 515	1 020	26 780
North American Indian	394 550	371 685	358 120	13 005	95	460	22 865
Métis	49 805	46 515	2 675	43 295	45	510	3 285
Inuit	33 280	32 650	130	95	32 375	50	625
Aboriginal / Total multiples responses	624 330	268 100	133 915	122 130	7 195	4 860	356 225
NA Indian and non aboriginal	438 475	161 150	121 410	38 005	95	1 645	277 330
Métis and non aboriginal	137 550	69 455	2 925	65 735	25	775	68 100
Inuit and non aboriginal	12 695	6 975	145	580	6 200	45	5 720
Aboriginal multiples / Total	35 605	30 520	9 440	17 815	870	2 390	5 080
NA Indian and Métis	10 795	10 525	4 820	4 905	0	790	270
NA Indian and Inuit	910	865	390	10	310	150	45
Métis and Inuit	290	265	0	55	130	80	30
NA Indian, Métis and Inuit	100	100	20	25	20	30	0
NA Indian, Métis and non aboriginal	20 930	16 965	3 985	12 020	0	955	3 970
NA Indian, Inuit and non aboriginal	1 305	805	180	155	290	170	500
Métis, Inuit and non aboriginal	1 110	875	15	595	105	160	240
NA Indian, Métis, Inuit and non aboriginal	145	125	35	40	15	40	25
Non aboriginal / Total	27 426 165	60 840	34 200	25 590	510	530	27 365 325

Note: 1. Includes North American Indian and Métis, North American Indian and Inuit, Métis and Inuit, North American Indian, Métis and Inuit
Source: Statistics Canada, 1996 Census of Canada, custom tabulations.

Population Explosion

On taking a closer look at the data, one can discern another interesting feature: regardless of the concept used in order to define Aboriginality, the Aboriginal populations experienced phenomenal growth during the 1980s and 1990s. Between 1986 and 1996, the populations of Aboriginal origin, of Aboriginal identity and of Registered Indians recorded relative 10-year increases of 55 to 60 percent.[9] By comparison, the non-Aboriginal population increased by only 14 percent during the same period.

Looking specifically at the different Aboriginal identity populations, we observe differences in growth patterns (Figure 2) (Guimond, 1999). At the national level, the North American Indian population, which accounts for nearly two thirds of the whole, went from a population explosion between 1986 and 1991 (7.1 percent per year) to a remarkably slow growth (0.9 percent) during the following period, lower than the Canadian growth (1.1 percent). Already increasing at a vigorous pace from 1986 to 1991 (5.1 percent), the Métis population grew even faster from 1991 to 1996 (6.7 percent). Modest by comparison, the annual growth rates of the Inuit population for the 1986-91 (3.4 percent) and 1991-1996 (2.3 percent) periods are still two to three times higher than those of the Canadian population.

The overall exceptional growth of Aboriginal identity populations during the period 1986-91 occurred off Indian reserves, especially in urban areas (Figure 3): 6.6 and 9.4 percent per year respectively in rural and urban areas. On Indian reserves, the growth was more modest (1.7 percent). For the period 1991-96, the marked slowdown in the growth at the national level resulted from a steep decline in the growth of populations in rural (0.8 percent) and urban areas (2.3 percent). On Indian reserves (3.8 percent), the growth accelerated and even surpassed that of off-reserve populations.

Fertility is very often mentioned as the principal component of the exceptional demographic growth of Aboriginal populations. It is true that Aboriginal women have more children than other Canadian women, but natural growth (excess of births over deaths) cannot account for all of the extraordinary growth observed during the 1980s and 1990s. A natural growth of 5.5 percent[10] per year implies a fertility of 10 children per woman. The fertility of Indian, Métis, and Inuit women varies between two and four children per woman (Norris et al., 1995). A population maintaining a growth rate of 5.5 percent per year doubles every 13 years. After a hundred years, that population would be more than 200 times larger than at the outset.

Figure 2. Total Growth Rates* of Aboriginal Identity Populations, Canada, 1986-91 and 1991-96

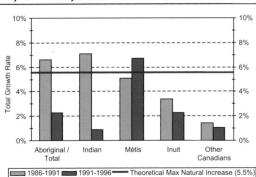

Note: * Adjusted for partially enumerated Aboriginal communities and for the inclusion of non-permanent residents since 1991.

Sources: Statistics Canada, 1986 and 1996 censuses of Canada, custom tabulations. Statistics Canada, 1991 Aboriginal People Survey, custom tabulations.

In practical terms, the contribution of international migration to population growth may be considered nil. In the 1991 Aboriginal People Survey, 2,200 persons of Aboriginal identity indicated that they were living outside Canada five years earlier (Clatworthy, 1994), which represent less than two percent of the total growth observed during the 1986-91 period. For the 1991-96 period, the number of international in-migrants totalled 2,500 Aboriginal persons.[11]

Figure 3. Total Growth Rates* of Aboriginal Identity Populations by Place of Residence, Canada, 1986-91 and 1991-96

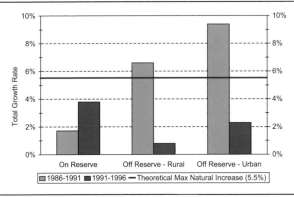

Note: *Adjusted for partially enumerated Aboriginal communities and for the inclusion of non-permanent residents since 1991.

Sources: Statistics Canada, 1986 and 1996 censuses of Canada, custom tabulations. Statistics Canada, 1991 Aboriginal People Survey, custom tabulations.

The contribution of migration to population growth remains marginal even at the sub-national level. Clatworthy (1994) and Norris et al. (2000) have shown that, contrary to popular myth, Indian reserves overall experienced net gains during the 1986-91 (+9,540) and 1991-96 (+13,585) periods. In addition, urban areas have exhibited an overall net loss for these two periods (-2,865; -10,835), indicating that individuals leaving the cities outnumber those moving to them. In large metropolitan areas, migration (+5,540) accounts for less than eight percent of the observed growth of the Aboriginal identity populations between 1986 and 1991 (+75,295).[12] Thus, the spectacular growth of urban Aboriginal populations cannot be explained by migration from Indian reserves.

The third element of the "demographic growth equation" is the quality of data. Every census, some individuals are missed while others are counted more than once. The difference between these two enumeration problems is called net undercoverage. If the percentage of net undercoverage varies, then measured growth rates are biased.[13] If undercoverage is constant, then we have a "true" measure of relative growth. According to the information on the population residing on fully enumerated Indian reserves, there was no major change in the quality of the enumeration between 1991 (12.6 percent)[14] and 1996 (13.4 percent).[15] Therefore, the observed population growth is not attributable to the quality of data.

Clearly, there is more than just births, deaths, and migration underlying the observed increases of Aboriginal populations. What is the cause of this extraordinary growth? Again, the answer lies within the concept of ethnic mobility.

Ethnic Mobility

The phenomenon by which individuals and families experience changes in their ethnic affiliation is known as *ethnic mobility*. Ethnic mobility has long been a component of the demographic growth of Canada's Aboriginal populations. This phenomenon has also been witnessed in the Aboriginal populations of the United States (1960-90) (Passel, 1996; Eschbach, 1993) and Australia (1981-96) (Ross, 1996). For convenience, individuals who experienced ethnic mobility are referred to as *ethnic drifters*.

There exist two types of ethnic mobility. The first type, intergenerational ethnic mobility, which relates to families, can occur when a child's ethnic affiliation is first stated. Parents and children do not necessarily have the same affiliation, especially when parents do not belong to the same ethnic group. This type of ethnic mobility, by creating "new types of Aboriginal persons," contributes largely to the increasing fuzziness of ethnic boundaries documented earlier (Figure 1; Table 1). The Métis, the second largest Aboriginal group, are the product of this particular type of ethnic mobility. Particular historical/commercial/cultural circumstances relating to colonization led to the emergence of this third Aboriginal cultural entity made up of descendants of North American Indians and European fur traders. From the 1996 Canadian Census data, Robitaille and Guimond (2001) estimated that, in husband/wife families with mixed ethnocultural background (e.g., Métis and non-Aboriginal), one out of two children of Métis descent were not identified by their parents as Métis. For the North American Indian and Inuit, the proportion of ethnic drifters among children in mixed families falls to 41 percent and 30 percent respectively (Figure 4).

Figure 4. Proportion of Non-Aboriginal Children* in Mixed Husband/Wife Families (Aboriginal and Non-Aboriginal), by Aboriginal Identity, Canada, 1996

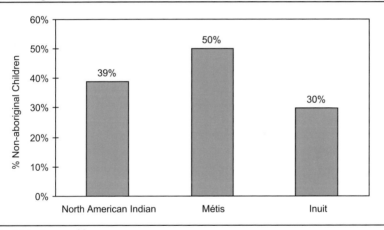

Note: * 0 to 4 years old.
Source: Statistics Canada, 1996 Census of Canada, custom tabulations.

The second type, intragenerational ethnic mobility, results from a change in individuals' ethnic affiliation over time. This type of ethnic mobility is responsible for the exceptional growth of Aboriginal populations from 1986 to 1996. For the entire decade, the proportion of total growth that can be attributed to intragenerational ethnic mobility reaches 41 percent for the North American Indians and 56 percent for the Métis (Figure 5).[16] In other words, for the two largest Aboriginal identity populations, close to half of the growth witnessed between 1986 and 1996 is due to ethnic mobility. In urban areas, the contribution of ethnic mobility to the population growth could be as high as 60 percent!

Figure 5. Proportion of the Total Growth of Aboriginal Identity Populations Possibly Attributable to Intragenerational Ethnic Mobility, Canada, 1986-96

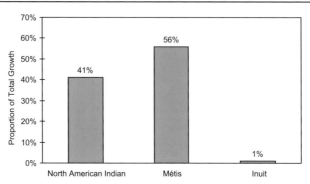

While there is no definitive answer to explain the observed intragenerational ethnic mobility of Aboriginal populations, three types of factors may be cited (Guimond, forthcoming 1). First, we have predisposing demographic factors. In major urban centres of Canada, we see people from different ethnocultural backgrounds meet, marry, and have children. These children, with their mixed ethnocultural background, have the possibility of choosing at their own convenience their ethnic affiliation. In short, mixed ancestries can lead to intragenerational ethnic mobility.

Social factors can also be cited as an explanation of ethnic mobility among Aboriginal populations. Socio-political events and their media coverage, spontaneous (e.g., Oka crisis in the summer of 1990) or organized (e.g., Royal Commission on Aboriginal Peoples, 1991-96), have all served to heighten the awareness of the public and, most importantly, to restore the image and pride of Aboriginal peoples. The increased public attention and the improved general self-perception of Aboriginal peoples could have influenced individuals to self-report as Aboriginal.

Finally, policy and legal decisions (or lack of) can foster ethnic mobility. The 1985 amendments to the *Indian Act* (Bill C-31) had a tremendous demographic impact on the size and growth of the Registered Indian population. At the end of 2000 (December 31), a total of 114,512 individuals had (re)acquired registration under the provisions of Bill C-31 (INAC, 2002). Except for Bill C-31, policy and legal factors (e.g., employment equity, land claim settlements) and their relation to Aboriginal identity have not yet been closely studied by social demographers. One area of research which will certainly require attention is the demographic implications of the policy and legal landscape regarding the Métis.

Concluding Thoughts

Aboriginal affiliation is not necessarily permanent, nor is it automatically transferred to the next generation. This mobility of individuals across ethnic boundaries is the main reason why there is such a wide range of definitions and population counts of Aboriginal peoples. Ethnic mobility is also the principal component to the recent demographic explosion of North American Indian and Métis populations. Failure to consider ethnic mobility in the analysis of Aboriginal populations would preclude proper understanding of the fuzziness of definitions, multiplication of estimates, and recent population growth. The very existence of the Métis, born from the contact between Indians and European colonizers, more than justifies a four-component analysis of Aboriginal population change in Canada that focuses on fertility, mortality, migration, and ethnic mobility.

Ethnic mobility also impacts (Guimond, forthcoming 2) the evolution of socio-economic characteristics (e.g., education) and other demographic phenomena (e.g., fertility, migration). To fully appreciate statistics on educational attainment, one has to consider the possibility that ethnic drifters might be partly responsible for the observed improvements. For example, within the cohort of persons 35 years of age and over in 1986, the number of university graduates of Aboriginal identity rose from 2,045 to 4,025[17] between 1986 and 1996, representing a phenomenal leap of 97 percent. By comparison, the number of non-Aboriginal university graduates increased by only one percent.

Looking to the future, it is clear that such high "ethnic mobility driven" population growth will not last forever, otherwise all Canadians would declare an Aboriginal affiliation by year 2048. However, if the US American Indian experience is an indication of things to come (Passel, 1996; Eschbach, 1993) – sustained ethnic mobility from 1960 to 1990 – we can expect ethnic mobility to contribute significantly to the growth of urban Aboriginal populations in Canada well into the new millennium. The multicultural make-up of Canadian cities will definitely be a fertile ground for future ethnic mobility and increasingly fuzzy ethnic boundaries. In all likelihood, more and more city dwellers from different ethnocultural backgrounds, including Aboriginal peoples, will marry and raise children in a multicultural family setting. Where the "mixed" children hang their "ethnic hat" when they become adults will have a significant impact on the ethnic make-up of our cities.

Notes

1　Also referred to as "ethnic switching" or "passing." See Guimond (1999, forthcoming 1); Robitaille and Choinière (1987).

2　As reflected by the evolution of the wording used to depict Aboriginal populations. See Goldmann (1993) and Guimond (forthcoming 1).

3　As reflected by the absence of the Métis in most of pre-1981 censuses.

4　This is the official wording of the concept of Aboriginal identity used for the 1996 Census of Canada. See Statistics Canada (1999: 5).

5　The 1986 Census data on Aboriginal identity have never been the subject of an official release, partly because of reporting errors detected within the non-Aboriginal population (Crégheur, 1988). The data on the Aboriginal identity of populations of Aboriginal origin is considered reliable (Guimond, 1999).

6　The 1996 Census published count of the "Aboriginal identity" population is 799,000. This figure includes individuals who did not report identifying with an Aboriginal group, but who reported being a Registered Indian as defined by the *Indian Act* and/or who were members of an Indian Band or First Nation (Statistics Canada, 1999).

7　In 1951, the Government of Canada established the Indian Register and assigned responsibility for its maintenance to the department now known as Indian and Northern Affairs Canada. Only persons recognized as Indians pursuant to the *Indian Act* may be registered.

8　The general belief is that the "real number" lies somewhere in between the Indian Register and Census counts. For the Indian Register, the two most important deficiencies are late-reporting and under-reporting of births and deaths. The quality of Census data is mostly affected by undercoverage and non-participation by Indian communities.

9　Adjusted rates for partially enumerated Aboriginal communities, for the inclusion of non-permanent residents since 1991 and for variations to the collection methodology of the concept of Indian status. See Guimond (forthcoming 1).

10　The theoretical maximum rate of natural increase (5.5 percent per year) is obtained from the highest crude birth rate (60 per 1,000 persons) observable in exceptional conditions from which is subtracted the lowest crude death rate (5 per 1,000 persons) (Tapinos, 1985; Pressat, 1979). Such a combination of a high birth rate and a low death rate has probably never been observed. Today, the highest national rates of natural increase in the world are approximately 3.5 percent per year.

11　Statistics Canada, 1996 Census of Canada, custom tabulation.

12　Statistics Canada, 1991 Aboriginal People Survey and 1996 Census of Canada, custom tabulations. Adjustments were made for the partially enumerated Aboriginal communities.

13　In order for differential undercoverage to explain half of the 7.1 percent/year increase of Indians between 1986 and 1991, the quality of enumeration would have to have improved by more than 15 percent between 1986 and 1991. Such variations in undercoverage are practically impossible.

14　Author's calculations. See Norris et al. (1995).

15 Author's calculations. Statistics Canada, 1996 reverse record check survey, unpublished table.

16 Estimates of net intragenerational ethnic mobility are obtained by the method of estimation by residual. See Guimond (1999, forthcoming 1).

17 Statistics Canada, 1986 and 1996 censuses of Canada, custom tabulations. Adjustments were made for the partially enumerated Aboriginal communities.

References

Canada, INAC (Indian and Northern Affairs Canada) (2002) *Basic Departmental Data 2000*, Ottawa: INAC, Information Management Branch, Corporate Information Management Directorate, First Nations and Northern Statistics Section, 82 pages.

Canada, Statistics Canada (1989) *Revue Générale du Recensement de 1986*, Ottawa: Supply and Services Canada, Catalogue 99-137F.

— (1999) *1996 Census Dictionary. Final Edition Reference*, Ottawa: Industry Canada, Catalogue 92-351-UIE.

Clatworthy, S. (1994) "The Migration and Mobility Patterns of Canada's Aboriginal Population," Draft report of a study prepared by Four Directions Consulting Group for Indian and Northern Affairs Canada, Research and Analysis, 268 pages.

Crégheur, A. (1988) *Assessment of Data on Aboriginal Identity. 1986 Census of Canada*, Ottawa: Statistics Canada, Housing, Family and Social Statistics Division, 36 pages.

Eschbach, K. (1993) "Changing Identification among American Indians and Alaska Natives," *Demography*, 30(4): 635-652.

Goldmann, G. (1993) "The Aboriginal Population and the Census. 120 Years of Information – 1871 to 1991," Communication presented at the Congrès de l'UIESP, Montréal.

Guimond, E. (1999) "Mobilité ethnique et croissance démographique des populations autochtones du Canada de 1986 à 1996," in *Le rapport sur l'état de la population du Canada 1998-1999*, A. Bélanger, (ed.), Statistics Canada, Ottawa: Industry Canada, Catalogue #91-209-XPF, 187-200.

— (forthcoming 1) "L'explosion démographique des populations autochtones du Canada de 1986 à 1996," University of Montréal, Department of Demography, doctoral studies under the supervision of N. Robitaille.

— (forthcoming 2) "The Demographic Explosion of Aboriginal Populations: Looking at the Contribution of Ethnic Drifters," in *Aboriginal Conditions: Research Foundations for Public Policy*, J. White, P. Maxim, and D. Beavon, (eds.), Vancouver: UBC Press.

Guimond E, D. Beavon, M. Cooke, and M.J. Norris (2001) "Emerging Aboriginal Identities Moving into the New Millenium: The Canadian, American, Australian and New Zealand Experiences," Communication presented at the Population Association of America (PAA) meeting, Washington.

Lee, T. (1990) "Definitions of Indigeneous Peoples in Selected Countries," Ottawa: Indian and Northern Affairs Canada, Finance and Professional Services, Quantitative Analysis & Sociodemographic Research, Working Paper Series 90-4, 29 pages.

Nault, F. and M.V. George (1992) "New Estimates of the Mortality of Registered Indians, Canada, 1973-1990," Paper presented at the 1992 annual meeting of the Canadian Population Society, Charlottetown.

Nault, F., J. Chen, and M.J. Norris (1992) *Demographic Time Series Data on Births, Deaths and Population for Registered Indian Population, Canada, 1973-1990,* Report prepared for Indian and Northern Affairs Canada.

Norris, M.J., D. Kerr, and F. Nault (1995) *Summary Report on Projections of the Population with Aboriginal Identity, Canada, 1991-2016,* Prepared by Population Projections Section, Demography Division, Statistics Canada, for the Royal Commission on Aboriginal Peoples, Canada Mortage and Housing Corporation.

Norris M.J., D. Beavon, E. Guimond, and M. Cooke (2000) "Migration and Residential Mobility of Canada's Aboriginal Groups: An Analysis of Census Data," Communication presented at the Population Association of America (PAA) meeting, San Francisco.

Passel, J.S. (1996) "The Growing American Indian Population, 1960-1990: Beyond Demography," in *Changing Numbers, Changing Needs. American Indian Demography and Public Health,* G.D. Sandefur, R.R. Rindfuss, and B. Cohen, (eds.), Washington: National Academy Press, 79-102.

Perreault, J., L. Paquette, and M.V. George (1985) *Projections de la population indienne inscrite, 1982-1996.* Indian and Northern Affairs Canada.

Pressat, R. (1979) *Dictionnaire de démographie,* Paris. Presses Universitaires de France, pp. 245-247.

Robitaille, N. and R. Choinière (1987) "L'accroissement démographique des groupes autochtones du Canada au XXᵉ siècle," Cahiers Québécois de démographie, 16(1).

Robitaille, N. and E. Guimond (2001) "The Reproduction of Aboriginal Groups: Exogamy, Fertility and Ethnic Mobility," Communication presented at the Conference of the International Union for the Scientific Study of Population (IUSSP), Brazil.

Romaniuk, A. (1974) "Modernization and Fertility: The Case of the James Bay Indians," *Canadian Review of Sociology and Anthropology*, 11(4): 344-357.

Ross, K. (1996) *Population Issues, Indigenous Australians*, Australian Bureau of Statistics. Occasional Paper 4708.0, 88 pages.

Savard, R. and J.R. Proulx (1982) *Canada. Derrière l'épopée, les autochtones*, Montréal: l'Hexagone, 232 pages.

Siggner, A.J. and G. Brûlotte (1975) *The Methodology for a Population Projection Model for the Registered Indian Population by Place of Residence, for Canada and the Regions: 1973 to 1985*, Indian and Northern Affairs Canada.

Tapinos, G. (1985) *Éléments de démographie. Analyse, déterminants socioéconomiques et histoire des populations*, Paris, Armand Colin, collection U, 367 pages.

Aboriginal Mobility and Migration Within Urban Canada: Outcomes, Factors and Implications

Mary Jane Norris[1]
Research and Analysis Directorate
Indian and Northern Affairs Canada

Stewart Clatworthy
Four Directions Project Consulting

Within the larger context of mainstream society, Aboriginal mobility and migration reflect a myriad of relationships with the state including Aboriginal identity, culture, community, traditional lands, legal status, benefits, and services. The factors and reasons related to the decision to move provide some insight into the dynamics of the social and economic determinants underlying demographic patterns and outcomes. Thus far, the significance of population movements has been underestimated in the sociology of Aboriginal peoples and warrants serious consideration relating to the issues of programs and services in urban areas.

This study, which uses data largely from the 1996 Census and the 1991 Aboriginal Peoples Survey (APS), examines the role of migration in relation to the considerable growth of Aboriginal populations since the 1960s, especially in urban areas.

Four Aboriginal Populations

The mobility and migration patterns of four major groups – Registered Indian, Non-Status Indian, Métis and Inuit – are examined for census respondents who reported an Aboriginal identity (as North American Indian, Métis, or Inuit) and/or who indicated they were Registered under the *Indian Act* (799,000 respondents). Of these, the Registered Indian population (488,100) is the largest, followed by Métis (210,000), Non-Status Indians (90,400), and Inuit (41,100).[2]

Registered Indians and Non-Status Indians are generally people of North American Indian (First Nations) descent. People belonging to groups that had negotiated treaties with the Crown are generally Registered Indians.

Many of these treaties included establishing reserve lands where members of these groups have historically lived. There were 610,000 people on the Indian Register in 1996; however, the 1996 Census enumerated only about 488,000 Registered Indians due to high undercoverage and incomplete enumeration of reserves. Non-Status Indians are not registered under the *Indian Act*, and relatively few live in reserve communities. In many cases, Non-Status Indians are descendants of mixed (Registered and not registered) parenting combinations, who are not eligible to be registered.[3] Métis are also descendents of mixed parenting combinations (generally Aboriginal and non-Aboriginal), traditionally those descended from the historic Red River Métis community in western Canada. The Inuit are indigenous people of northern Quebec, the Northwest Territories, Nunavut and Labrador.

Four Geographies in Place of Residence

Four mutually exclusive categories for place of residence are used here to analyse migration patterns: reserves and settlements and three geographies excluding reserves that include urban census metropolitan areas (CMAs), urban non-CMA areas, and rural areas. An Indian reserve is legally defined in the *Indian Act* as a tract of land that has been set aside for the use and benefit of an Indian band or First Nation. While some reserves are in urban areas, the majority are located in rural areas. Settlements include Crown land and other communities with Aboriginal populations as defined by Indian and Northern Affairs Canada, but do not include all Métis and Inuit communities. Reserves and settlements are combined as one geography for origin-destination flows. A CMA, including urban and rural fringes, has an urban core population of at least 100,000. An urban non-CMA, a smaller urban centre, includes cities where the urban core contains at least 10,000 people. As defined for this analysis, both CMAs and census agglomerations (CAs) exclude rural fringes and any reserves in urban areas. Rural areas comprise sparsely populated lands lying outside urban areas, including the rural fringes of CMAs, but excluding reserves and settlements.

The distinction between reserves and other Aboriginal communities, as well as between Registered and Non-Status populations, is an important one for any demographic analysis of Aboriginal groups. Certain rights and benefits are associated with Registered Indian status, especially on reserves, where the majority of Registered Indians are located. These benefits include access to funding for housing, post-secondary schooling, and tax exemption status, as well as land and treaty rights. Aboriginal populations in other communities, such as Métis and Inuit, do not have legal access to the same rights and benefits. For these reasons, the distinction between reserve and non-reserve geographies is important in understanding the "push-pull" factors associated with the migration patterns of Registered Indians.

Mobility and Migration Data and Concepts

Census migration data used in this analysis are obtained from the five-year mobility question, which asks about an individual's residence five years earlier. While the results presented in this analysis use data based on the five-year mobility question, the census also includes a one-year mobility question. In this analysis, only internal migration (within Canada) is studied.[4] We use such terms as "migrants," which refers to those who have moved between communities; "residential movers," which refers to those who have moved between residences in the same community; and "mobility," which refers to all moves involving a change of residence.

Limitations of the Data

While the census provides the most complete picture of the patterns and trends of migration in Canada, there are several cautionary notes that one should consider with respect to the use of census data to measure Aboriginal migration and mobility patterns. First, census questions on ethnicity and mobility are only administered to a sample of the total census population. This does not include persons in institutions, such as prisons, chronic care facilities, or rooming homes. Consequently, the fact that persons in institutions such as prisons, chronic care facilities, or rooming homes are "missed" could be problematic given that the incarceration rates for Aboriginal people tend to be extremely high, and that in urban centres there tend to be very high concentrations of Aboriginal people who are either living in rooming houses, because of the lower rent, or who are homeless. This could imply then that with respect to destinations, urban areas may be understated as destinations of migrants, although the extent to which this is a factor is difficult to assess.

Second, patterns of underreporting, along with self-reporting of Aboriginal identity and status, may also differ by males and females, and therefore could possibly affect the interpretation of observed differences in the migration patterns of men and women. For example, a higher underreporting of adult males, because of incarceration, may contribute to observed gender differentials in-migration.

Third, a significant proportion of the reserve population is not captured in the census due to the incomplete enumeration of certain reserves, as well as high rates of undercoverage on reserve. This means that the unadjusted census-based residential distribution of Registered Indians, for percentages residing on-reserve are underestimated, while percentages off-reserve, including urban and rural areas are correspondingly over-estimated. In addition reserves may be understated as a destination in the migration data on Registered Indians because of higher undercoverage on reserves and incompletely enumerated reserves not being represented in the current destination data, although they are in the origin as place of residence five years ago. For purposes of analyzing the census data on migration flows, incompletely enumerated reserves were excluded as origins in their respective censuses.

Fourth, census data on mobility and migration itself have some conceptual limitations. For example, demographic, marital status, and socio-economic characteristics of migrants may not be the same as when they migrated. Also, moves of people who leave and return during an interval, who made several moves during the interval, as well as those who died during the interval, are not captured. While the one-year data provide a more accurate picture of migration patterns and characteristics for a given year, the limitation is that it could be an unusual or volatile time period and may not be typical of the longer trends. In this sense, the five-year question provides a more accurate portrayal of mobility trends.

Urban-Rural Composition

Aboriginal groups differ significantly in their degree of urbanization (see Figure 1). The most urbanized Aboriginal groups are the Non-Status Indians and Métis, with 73 percent and 66 percent respectively living in urban areas. Not surprisingly, the Inuit tend to be the least urbanized, with less than 30 percent residing in urban areas. Registered Indians are also distinct from the other Aboriginal groups, because at least half of their population resides on reserves (census figure of 48 percent understated)[5] with about 10 percent located in rural areas off reserve. Registered Indians are less urbanized than the Non-Status Indian and Métis groups, with some 37 percent (overstated) in urban areas off reserve.

Propensity to Move

The share of migrants or movers in a population signals the amount of mobility in a population, relative to its size, without necessarily referring to the origins or destinations of the moves. The amount of migration between communities and mobility within communities can have important consequences for the general stability and cohesion of a community as well as for ties between communities.

Analyses of census data suggest that certain patterns and trends in Aboriginal migration have persisted over the past couple of decades (Norris, 1990, 1996). More than half (55 percent) of the Aboriginal population changed residences within Canada between 1991 and 1996, compared to just 40 percent of non-Aboriginal people.

Mobility Status by Place of Residence

Census data show that Registered Indians living off-reserve tend to move more frequently than either their counterparts on-reserve or the Canadian population in general (Robitaille and Choinière, 1985; Norris and Pryor, 1984; Norris, 1985, 1990, 1996) (660 and 295 per 1,000). About 66 percent of Registered Indians residing off reserve had moved over the 1991-96 period, such that 29 percent of the population moved between communities, while the other 37 percent of residents moved within the same community off reserve. By comparison, movers, including migrants, account for a much smaller proportion of the Canadian population in general, with corresponding percentages of 43 percent (20 percent migrants and 23 percent residential movers). As well, there are greater shares of movers and migrants among other Aboriginal groups compared to the mainstream population, but still less than those observed for Registered Indians, except on reserve where movers and migrants make up much less of the population with corresponding percentages of only 38 percent total movers, with some 12 percent migrants and 16 percent residential movers. The higher mobility of the Aboriginal population, particularly off reserve, reflects not only migration from reserves and other Aboriginal communities, but also high levels of residential mobility (Norris, 2000).

The mobility of the Aboriginal population is especially high in Canada's large cities (CMAs.). The vast majority, about 70 percent, of Aboriginal residents in large urban areas had changed residences between 1991 and 1996, with more than 45 percent of the urban Aboriginal population moving within the same community. In sharp contrast, the non-Aboriginal residents of these cities moved considerably less often during the period, with just under half having moved, and in the case of residential movers, just over one in five (21 percent) of the population had changed residences within the same community (Figure 1).

Figure 1: Movers (Residential and Migrant) as a Percentage of Population, by Urban and Rural Areas, Canada, 1991-1996

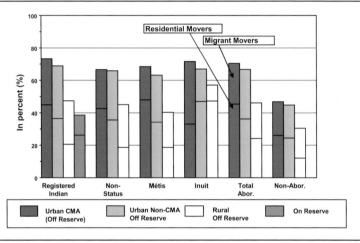

Source: Statistics Canada, 1996 Census of Canada (unpublished data).

While Aboriginal groups are similar in that all experience significantly higher mobility compared to the non-Aboriginal population, their mobility levels and patterns do differ by geography. At first glance, mobility rates over the 1991-96 period not broken down by residence would suggest that registered Indians, with 53 percent of their population having moved, tend to be less mobile than other Aboriginal populations (Non-Status Indians (61 percent), Métis (58 percent) and Inuit (60 percent). However, analysis by geographic areas reveals significant variations by residence for Aboriginal groups as well as for the non-Aboriginal population with generally higher mobility in urban than in rural areas. Off reserve, the registered Indian population tends to be the most mobile of the Aboriginal groups in urban areas. Aboriginal groups also differ among each other in their type of move, that is, in the extent to which they migrate from one community to another, or simply move within the same community. For example, within large cities, relocations within the same community accounted for 70 percent of all Métis moves, compared to 65 percent for Registered Indians, 62 percent for Non-Status Indians, 55 percent for non-Aboriginals and 46 percent for Inuit. In contrast with the situation in large urban areas, moves within the same community accounted for the vast majority (83 percent) of Inuit moves in rural areas. By way of comparison, residential movers formed about 50 percent of all movers from other Aboriginal groups and about 40 percent of all non-Aboriginal movers in rural areas. Some caution should be used in interpreting the mobility patterns of the Inuit in rural areas, as the CSDs used to define Inuit communities are likely to be much larger (geographically) than those of the communities of other Aboriginal sub-groups. The possibility exists that some Inuit moves within the same rural CSD could in fact involve quite distant relocations.

Propensity to Move by Age, Gender, and Origin-Destination

Mobility is a phenomenon that varies by age, tending to peak during young adulthood. Higher Aboriginal mobility compared to the general population, however, is not just a function of the younger Aboriginal age structure, it occurs across all ages, with differences especially pronounced in urban areas. For example, residential mobility rates are higher among Aboriginal youths and adults, compared to the non-Aboriginal population. The general pattern of mobility over age groups, however, is similar for the populations. Mobility rates tend to decrease over the school-age years, peak during the young adult years of 20-29, and then decline fairly steadily among older age cohorts (Figure 2). Young adult females tend to be the most mobile in any population, including the Aboriginal population (Norris, 1985, 1990, 1996).

Figure 2: Five-Year Residential Mobility Rates, Canada, 1991-1996

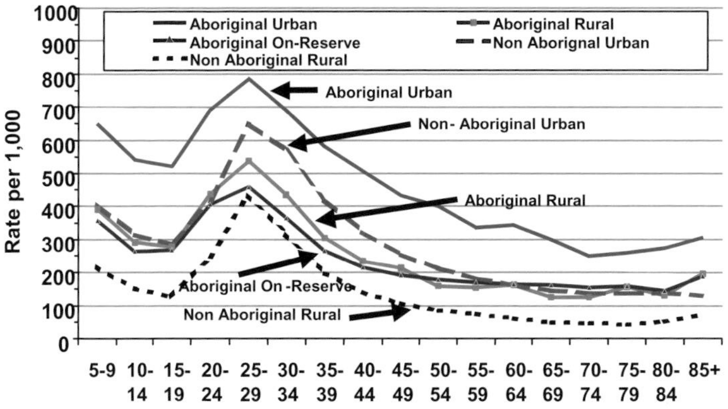

Note: residential rates are calculated for the non-migrant population only.

Source: "Aboriginal Mobility and Migration Within Urban Canada: Outcomes, Factors and Implications", Norris, M.J. and Stewart Clatworthy, 2003, DIAND.

For Registered Indians, women have higher rates of out-migration from reserves, while in the opposite direction men have higher rates of in-migration (i.e., to reserves). Within the context of migration between rural and urban areas, out-migration rates from rural to urban areas were higher among women than men for both Registered Indians and other Aboriginal individuals. For Registered Indians, this pattern is similar to that identified for migration from reserve to off-reserve areas. However, in the case of the flow from urban to rural areas, the pattern of higher migration rates for men, as observed in the flow to reserves, does not occur with other Aboriginal communities or groups (Norris et al., 2003).

Such variations in migration patterns by origin–destination and by gender, suggest that there are "push and pull" factors between reserve and non-reserve Aboriginal communities and cities that affect women differently than they do men.

Origin–Destination Flows

Except for the Inuit, migration between urban communities (i.e., urban-to-urban flows) accounts for the largest stream of Aboriginal migrants. This dimension of migration, however, varies among Aboriginal sub-groups. Migrants between urban areas formed a larger segment of total migrants for the Non-Status Indian and Métis populations (59 and 52 percent, respectively) than for the Registered Indian population (37 percent) These differences among Aboriginal sub-groups reflect, in part, sub-group differences in residential distribution and urbanization.

Movement to and from reserves distinguishes the mobility patterns of Registered Indians from those of other Aboriginal groups. That the stream of migration from reserves to cities is overshadowed by the flow from cities to reserves indicates that migration is a reciprocal process. Reciprocal moves between communities on and off reserve accounted for about a third of the 87,400 Registered Indians who migrated between 1991-96, while close to two thirds of migrants moved between communities located outside of reserves. Only three percent of all Registered Indian moves involved relocations between Indian reserves (see Table 1). Nearly two thirds of the 28,600 migrants who moved between on and off-reserve locations were moving to reserves, practically all of them coming from city locations. Among the 56,100 migrants who moved between off-reserve locations, well over half (58 percent) comprised moves between different cities. Seven out of ten Registered Indian migrants between 1991-96 can be classified into one of three major flows: urban-to-urban (37 percent),

Table 1: Distribution of Aboriginal Migrants by Origin-Destination Flows, Canada, 1991-1996 Migration Period

Origin/Destination Flows	Registered Indian		Non-Status Indian		Métis		Inuit	
	Number	%	Number	%	Number	%	Number	%
Urban to Urban	32,370	37.1	11,890	59.1	19,675	52.5	1,150	24.2
Urban to Rural	8,505	9.7	3,670	18.2	8,440	22.5	920	19.3
Rural to Urban	11,925	13.7	2,445	12.1	5,795	15.5	1,175	24.7
Rural to Rural	3,290	3.8	1,165	5.8	2,550	6.8	1,330	27.9
Urban to Reserve	17,155	19.6	470	2.3	535	1.4	15	0.3
Reserve to Urban	6,045	6.9	240	1.2	155	0.4	30	0.6
Reserve to Reserve	2,670	3.1	35	0.2	15	0.0	-	0.0
Reserve to rural	1,205	1.4	75	0.4	90	0.2	100	2.1
Rural to Reserve	4,175	4.8	140	0.7	205	0.5	40	0.8
TOTAL No. of Migrants Aged 5+	87,340	100.0	20,130	100.0	37,460	100.0	4,760	100.0
TOTAL Population Aged 5+	424,765		77,505		162,925		34,085	
% Migrants to Total Population Aged 5+	20.6		26.0		23.0		14.0	

Source: Statistics Canada, 1996 Census of Canada (unpublished data).

urban-to-reserve (20 percent) and rural-to-urban (14 percent). Flows from reserves to urban areas (CMA and non-CMA) accounted for only seven percent of the migration volume (Table 1).

The proportion of migrants moving from urban to rural areas is significantly higher for Non-Status Indians (18 percent) and Métis (23 percent) compared to Registered Indians (just 10 percent). Part of this difference is attributable to the urban-to-reserve flow of 20 percent for Registered Indians, representing their "city to First Nation" flow in that some of the "urban-to-rural" flow of other Aboriginal groups may be their equivalent of a "city to Aboriginal community" flow. Contrasts are even more pronounced with the Inuit, the least urbanized population, for which the rural-to-rural stream represents the largest share of Inuit migrants at 28 percent. For all four Aboriginal groups, about 20 percent of migrants are contained in the flow that could include movement best described as "from city to Aboriginal community."

Net Migration Flows

Reserves and settlements combined gained more than 14,000 migrants between 1991 and 1996, mainly through their exchange of migrants with larger cities (with CMAs losing 5,065 migrants to reserves); smaller urban areas (4,405 migrants), and to a lesser extent from rural areas (2,970). Rural and smaller urban areas saw total net out-flows of 6,385 and 4,405 migrants. While some of this net out-flow was to CMAs, and from rural to small urban areas, the largest net flows were to reserves and settlements (see Figure 3).

Figure 3: Five-Year Net Migration Flows
Registered Indians Aged 5+, Canada, 1991-1996

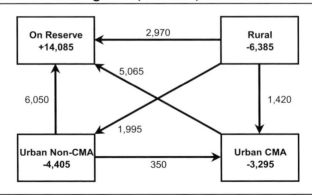

Source: Statistics Canada, 1996 Census of Canada (unpublished data). From Norris et al 2002.

Urban areas also experienced net losses of Métis and Non-Status Indian populations, similar to Registered Indians.[6] Unlike Registered Indian migrants, however, most of this was through the exchange with rural areas rather than reserves such that rural areas gained, rather than lost population through migration. For example, rural areas gained 1,155 Non-Status Indian migrants in their exchange with cities, both large (660 migrants from CMAs) and small (560 migrants from non-CMAs). As with Non-Status Indians, among the Métis, rural areas gained population through net in-migration, while large cities experienced the greatest net losses. In the case of the Inuit, patterns of net migration contributed little to the redistribution of population,[7] such that small urban areas recorded a small net inflow of 245 migrants, with no measurable change for the larger CMAs (see Norris et al., 2003).

Net Migration Rates

The significance of the impact of migration is captured in the net migration rates, which vary by both geography and Aboriginal group. For example, in the case of Registered Indians, the impact of net migration on population was most pronounced in rural areas, which experienced significant population loss. While reserves did gain population as a result of net in-flows of migrants, the impact, although positive on the growth of reserve population, was relatively small. Thus, while the major focal points in Registered Indian migration continue to be urban areas and reserves, the impact in terms of net gain or loss of population is felt most significantly in rural areas, which have lost Registered Indian population through migration mainly to urban areas (Figure 3). Conversely, while net migration to urban areas was also negative due to net losses to reserves, the impact was small relative to the population in urban areas. In rural areas, the high rate of population loss for Registered Indians contrasts sharply with the rate of population gain for Non-Status Indians and Métis. All groups in large cities experienced a low rate of net out-migration.

Figure 4: Net Migration Rates By Place of Residence Canada, 1991-1996

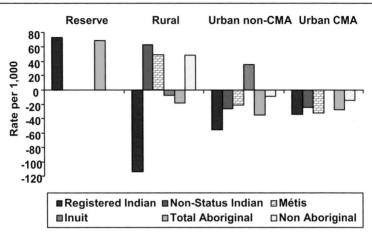

Source: Statistics Canada, 1996 Census of Canada (unpublished data). From poster presentation: "Migration and Residential Mobility of Canada's Aboriginal Groups: An Analysis of Census Data", Norris, M.J., Beavon D., Guimond E, and Cooke M. 2000, DIAND.

Most of the patterns identified for the 1991-96 time period represent a continuation of earlier trends. For example, Census data suggest that there has been a consistent net in-flow or gain of Registered Indian migrants to reserves, although relatively small in relation to the reserve population. Throughout the 1970s and 1980s, a pattern of positive net migration to both reserves and cities continued. The migrants to reserves from urban areas outnumbered those leaving reserves (Norris, 1992). Both rural (non-reserve) areas and smaller urban areas experienced a continued net loss of Registered Indian migrants between 1986 and 1991, as well as over earlier documented five-year periods from 1966-71 on. The patterns of net gains and losses observed for reserves, rural and small urban areas over the 1991-96 period were largely similar to previous Census observations of five-year net migration flows. In the case of the larger urban areas (CMAs), these large cities did in fact experience net gains of migrants in previous periods, 1986-91, 1981-86, (with the exception of 1976-81 characterized in general as a period of "metropolitan turnaround" with respect to migration) and most significantly during 1966-71 when there appeared to be significant urbanization and high net in-migration rates of Registered Indians to CMAS.

Migration as a Component of Growth

Migration can play either a significant or a negligible role in the population growth of any geographic area, depending on the net impact of the migration flows to and from that area, relative to the population size of that area. The size of the Aboriginal population in Canada, and its distribution between rural and urban areas and Aboriginal communities, has changed considerably since the 1960s. The total population of Aboriginal ancestry has increased dramatically, and most of this growth appears to have occurred in urban areas.

As the preceding analysis of net migration patterns demonstrates, migration is currently not a major contributing factor to positive growth of the Aboriginal population in any of the geographical areas under study (see also Guimond). In the case of Registered Indians, migration has been a significant contributor to population change only in rural areas, which have experienced large net losses. With respect to reserves and major urban centres, migration does not appear to have played a significant role in the observed population increases. The fact that *both* reserves and larger urban areas (until the 1996 Census) have been consistent net gainers of migrants undermines popular notions of a continuing exodus from reserves. It is important to consider all factors that can affect growth generally and those specific to the different Aboriginal groups themselves. These other factors (see Guimond, 1999; Clatworthy et al., 1997) include fertility, natural population growth, legal changes including legislative reinstatements and status inheritance under the *Indian Act,* and ethnic identification change or ethnic mobility/drift, intermarriage and family formation. Any one of these factors could result in differential growth rates between reserves and cities. However, over the past decade the largest increase in the Registered Indian population off reserve has been due to legislative reinstatements, some 120,000 to date, resulting from changes to the *Indian Act* in 1985 (also known as Bill C-31). The fact that almost 85 percent of the Bill C-31 registrants continue to reside off reserve has meant that from 1985 to 1995, a dramatic shift in the on/off-reserve population split has occurred. That the census counts of the on-reserve population also increased significantly between 1991 and 1996, further substantiates that reserves are not experiencing a mass exodus of their population to urban areas (Norris, 2000).

We cannot ignore the high rates of two-way migration both "into and out of cities," as well as high mobility "within cities," given the implications of residential instability for the well-being of Aboriginal people in cities. However, it is likely that this high rate of "churn," especially for Registered Indians has contributed to the impression that cities are gaining population through migration. Reserves increase the churn to and from cities. Whereas other Aboriginal communities experienced net out-migration during the period, reserves posted net gains of Registered Indian migrants.

Migration to and from Cities

As shown for the top 10 CMAs based on Registered Indian population in Figure 5, Registered Indians consistently have the highest rates of both in- and out- and consequently gross-migration, followed by other Aboriginal groups (including Métis and Non-Status Indians) and then by Canadians in general. Most of these CMAs over the 1991-96 period generally posted net losses of population through migration for all three groups, with the notable exceptions of Saskatoon and Thunder Bay which experienced net gains of Registered Indian and "other Aboriginal" migrants.

As seen in Figure 5, variations exist among CMAs in terms of their gross (in plus out) and net migration rates. Different urban areas may have different "push or pull" factors associated with them, including the presence of sizeable urban Aboriginal populations (such as in Regina and Winnipeg) or educational institutions (such as in Thunder Bay), or other economic and social characteristics of individual urban areas. However, without further analysis, one can only speculate as to the range of factors that affect migration patterns across cities. It could be that restrictive changes in provincial social welfare policies introduced during the early 1990s in Alberta and Ontario affected migration patterns in major cities in those provinces. On the other hand, other forces in the larger urban and provincial economies would likely also have affected these migration patterns. Similarly, the role that cities play as primary service centres (such as Thunder Bay) can also be expected to influence migration patterns.

With respect to migration into and out of cities, reserves themselves can contribute significantly to higher rates among Registered Indians than other Aboriginal people, in that reserves provide a unique set of factors for potential migrants such as housing, a major reason for moving (Clatworthy, 1996). Whereas other Aboriginal communities (e.g., Métis, Inuit) experienced net out-migration during the period, reserves posted net gains of Registered Indians migrants (Norris et al., 2003). Moving back to a reserve is an alternative that is generally only available to Registered Indians. As well, the higher rates of in-migration to reserves among males is not a pattern seen in migration to other Aboriginal communities, nor for that matter in the migration from urban to rural areas among Registered Indians.

Figure 5: Five-Year Gross Migration Rates for Top 10 Cities, Canada, 1991-1996

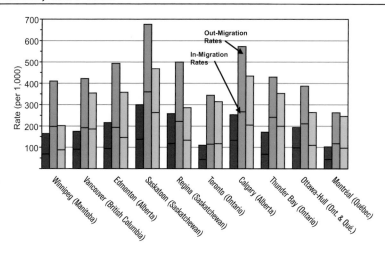

Net Migration Rates for Top 10 Cities, Canada, 1991-1996

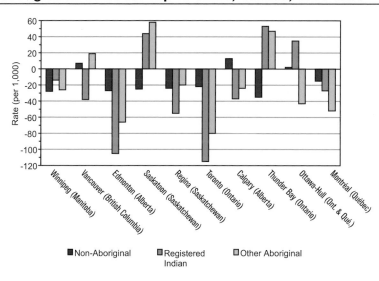

■ Non-Aboriginal   ▣ Registered   ☐ Other Aboriginal
Indian

Source: Statistics Canada, 1996 Census of Canada (unpublished data). From Norris et al, forthcoming 2002.

In their roles as both origins and destinations, reserves serve to increase the churn to and from cities, as demonstrated in the case of the Winnipeg CMA which saw rates of in- and out-migration for Registered Indians twice those of other Aboriginal populations. Between 1991 and 1996, 27 percent of Registered Indian migrants moving to Winnipeg during this period came from reserves, while some 47 percent of Registered Indians who left Winnipeg had moved to reserves. Clearly, if the flows between Winnipeg and reserve communities were removed, the rates of Registered Indian migration into and out from Winnipeg would be more similar to the other Aboriginal populations.

Push-Pull Factors

The literature has tended to focus on the "pushes" and "pulls" that contribute to the migration between cities and reserves. For example, the various "push" factors from reserves include lack of employment opportunities and resulting difficult social conditions (Trovato et al., 1994: 15), poor economic conditions on reserves (Hawthorn, 1966; McCaskill, 1970; Falconer, 1985; Trovato et al., 1994), marriage and family formation, boredom, quality of life, lack of housing, health facilities, educational opportunities, institutional completeness (Gerber, 1984; Trovato et al., 1994), and band politics (Cooke, 1999). Corresponding to these "pushes" are the "pulls" of the city that attract migrants, such as the "bright lights" of the city in the case of young adults (Krotz, 1990) or better access to housing.

Migration from cities to reserves has generally been attributed mainly to return migration (Frideres, 1974; Siggner, 1977; Norris, 1990), characterized as resulting from an inability of people who have moved from reserve communities to find employment or to otherwise adjust to life in the city (Trovato et al., 1994: 287). In addition, a major "push" factor from cities is a lack of access to affordable housing (Trovato et al., 1994: 28; Cooke, 1999). For those who are able to secure housing in reserve communities, returning home to a reserve may be preferable to remaining in the city, where affordable housing is often located in impoverished inner-city areas (RCAP, 1996).

As destinations, reserves or Aboriginal communities present "pulls" in their roles as a home base and "cultural hearth" to which return is possible and relatively easy (Lurie 1967). Reserves provide friends, extended family support, and culturally appropriate activities and services that may not be available off reserve. Accordingly, people may perceive their reserve communities as offering a better quality of life than urban centres for raising children: lower crime rates and less alcohol and drug abuse. Others have suggested that retirement to reserve communities is a desirable option (Cooke, 1999).

Also, compared to other Aboriginal communities, reserves provide a unique set of factors for potential migrants (legal status, benefits, access to funding for housing) as suggested by the high levels of mobility of Registered Indians between reserves and urban areas, the unique pattern of higher male in-migration to reserves, as well as the net in-flows of migrants to reserves.

Reasons for Migration

Until recently, relatively little analytical research has been undertaken on the reasons for moving among Aboriginal populations. For example, the common belief that the primary reason for migration from reserves to cities is to search for employment has not had much empirical testing due to the absence of data until the 1991 Aboriginal Peoples Survey (APS), which included questions on reasons for moving (Statistics Canada, 1993). The major reasons for migration were found to be family and housing, regardless of destination, followed by education in the case of leaving reserves, and employment in moves between urban communities.

Figure 6: Reasons for Migration, by Origin-Destination Flow, registered indians, Canada, 1991

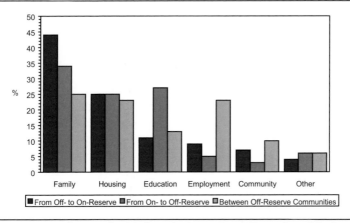

Source: Statistics Canada, 1991 Aboriginal Peoples Survey, From Clatworthy and Cooke, 2001.

Individual and Community Characteristics in the Decision to Migrate

Migration can be viewed as an outcome of the interplay of individual, community, and destination characteristics. Peters (1994) has suggested that Aboriginal women (who are over-represented in the Aboriginal migrant population according to studies by Gerber (1977), Clatworthy (1996) and Norris (1985, 1990, 1996)) tend to move in a family context, whereas men may tend to move as lone, "economically motivated" individuals (Clatworthy and Hull, 1983). The 1991 APS indicates that males were more likely than females to cite housing factors and education as reasons for leaving reserve communities, whereas females were much more likely to identify family-related issues.

In communities located either "near to" or "distant from" urban centres, people are more likely to leave and less likely to return. (Gerber 1977, 1984; Clatworthy and Cooke, 2001). For example, communities nearest (within 60 km) to urban service centres, and those furthest (more than 300 km) from urban centres, have higher predicted out-migration rates and lower in-migration rates than do communities at more moderate distances. Other findings suggest communities with higher rates of participation in traditional cultural activities tend to have lower rates of out-migration. High levels of economic development in communities may actually promote out-migration from reserves due to the interconnectedness with the off-reserve labour market and broader economy (Clatworthy, forthcoming).

Residential Mobility within Cities

As we saw earlier, within large cities, residential movers comprise a significantly larger share of movers among Aboriginal populations as compared to non-Aboriginals, with Métis movers maintaining the highest share of residential movers (Figure 1). On the other hand, if we consider the rate of residential mobility relative to the non-migrant population (that is, excluding migrants from the denominator/population at risk) we find that while Aboriginal residential rates continue to be significantly higher than those of the non-Aboriginal population in urban areas (Figure 2) it is Registered Indians in both large and small cities who display somewhat higher rates of residential mobility compared to other Aboriginal groups (with the exception of Inuit in small cities)8 (Figure 7). Generally though, within urban areas the extent of differences in residential mobility rates among Aboriginal groups is not as pronounced as differences in rates of migration to and from cities noted earlier (where

Registered Indians demonstrated consistently higher rates of migration to and from cities). The high rates of residential mobility identified for all Aboriginal groups in urban areas suggest that factors that lead to residential instability (e.g., housing deficiencies, low incomes, and low rates of homeownership) are encountered by all sub-groups.

Figure 7: Residential Mobility Rates by Place of Residence, Canada, 1991-1996

Between 1991-1996, 55 percent of Aboriginal population moved (22 percent migrants & 33 percent residential) versus 43 percent for non-Aboriginals (20 percent migrants & 23 percent residential). (Note: residential rates are calculated for the non-migrant population only).

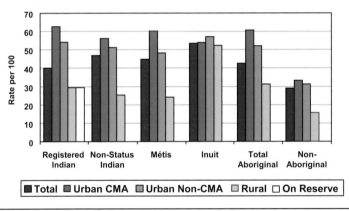

Source: "Aboriginal Mobility and Migration Within Urban Canada: Outcomes, Factors and Implications", Norris, M.J. and Stewart Clatworthy, 2003, DIAND.

For now the most important consideration of Aboriginal mobility is not redistribution of the population, but rather the high rate of movement or churn both "to and from" and "within" cities. In particular, very high levels of residential mobility suggest the possibility that many Aboriginal moves may not lead to "constructive" or "positive" outcomes.

Implications of Aboriginal Mobility within the Urban Context

The outcomes and factors associated with Aboriginal mobility have significant implications for the well-being of Aboriginal people in urban areas. The urban Aboriginal population is in a high state of flux. Statistics suggest it is one that is highly mobile, characterized by family instability and dissolution, with a high proportion of female lone-parent families; economically marginalized with low incomes and experiencing high victimization and crime rates. Many of these factors have the potential to affect delivery of services, including schooling and housing. Housing is a major reason for moving not just from reserves, but also to reserves, as well as for the high rates of residential mobility in urban areas. Aboriginal people tend to live in older and often deficient housing (Clatworthy, 1996: 24) and have greater difficulty finding suitable housing because of discrimination as well as lower average incomes.

Implied in the myth that urban growth is largely due to migration from reserves to urban areas is the belief that characteristics of urban Aboriginal populations are those largely associated with migrants. These misunderstandings could adversely affect policy development. Demographic and socio-economic characteristics and correspondingly, needs and services, tend to differ among non-movers, residential movers, and migrants, and for the latter, by origin of previous residence, be it another city or reserve. The phenomenon of ethnic mobility is also implicated in the compositional effects of migrant and non-migrant characteristics in urban areas including the impact of "new Aboriginals" (those who did not identify as Aboriginal in previous censuses, who may have also migrated earlier from Aboriginal communities).

Residential movers, who represent half of the Aboriginal population in urban CMAs, are more likely than non-movers to experience housing affordability problems as well as at least one housing need or housing deficiency (Clatworthy, 2000). In relation to their non-migrant counterparts, Aboriginal migrants, who represent about 20 percent of the urban CMA Aboriginal population and who have moved mainly from city to city, tend to be younger, with females forming the majority (and at different stages in family development), characterized by younger families and hence fewer children, with lone parents more common. In general, Aboriginal migrants possess higher educational attainment and have a higher incidence of school attendance, but even though they are more likely to be active in the labour market in their new community, they do have higher rates of unemployment, especially among youth. Characteristics of migrants moving to urban areas would likely vary according to their residence of origin, be it another city, a reserve or other Aboriginal community, with accordingly different needs and services. The implication of frequent mobility in urban areas is not so much change in population size, but rather high population turnover and changing composition with attendant disruptive effects on individuals, families, communities, and service providers. Thus, programs that deliver social services to urban Aboriginal populations by neighbourhoods, for health, employment and education, are particularly liable to be affected.

Adverse Effects of High Mobility on Student Performance

The example of providing educational services illustrates the challenges and implications for well-being associated with high levels of mobility and residential instability. Clatworthy (2000) found a strong positive relationship between the Aboriginal share of population and school turnover rates in central Winnipeg neighbourhoods. A 10 percent increase in the Aboriginal share of neighbourhood population results in a 14 percent increase in student turnover. While considerable anecdotal evidence suggests that student performance is adversely affected by high turnover, one American study clearly documents the significance of mobility on student performance in examining the link among children's mobility and housing situations with educational outcomes. The report from the *Journal of Housing and Community Development* on "The Link between Housing and Education" indicates that the relationship between student mobility and academic performance (including behavioural problems) warrants significant attention, as demonstrated by a 1994 Government Accounting Office (GAO) study which recommends that U S educational policy recognize and measure this phenomenon of mobility as a key-contributing factor to student academic underachievement.

> The GAO Study …revealed that of the nation's third graders who have changed schools frequently, 41 percent are below grade level in reading, compared with 26 percent of third graders who have never changed schools. …Results are also similar for math…. Children who have moved often were also more likely to have behavioural problems.

The issue of low educational achievement among Aboriginal people in Canada is a growing concern in Canada, and the implications of high population turnover on student performance cannot be ignored, especially when we recall that education is one of the main reasons people leave reserves. In fact, in their note on considerations arising from the report on the "Over-Representation of Aboriginal Students Reported with Behaviour Disorders" the Ministry of Education in British Columbia (2001: 4) acknowledges the significance of mobility as a barrier to student success, both externally and as an unintended consequence of the school system itself.

> There are barriers to the success of Aboriginal children identified with severe behaviour disorders and one of these barriers is mobility. In some cases, family mobility and instability can be problematic. …What the study does not

mention is that mobility created by the school system can be equally disruptive to a student. When students have behavioural problems, part of the problem is that they are sometimes removed from the regular class and placed in an alternate setting or special class. ...When Aboriginal students feel alienated they may become discouraged and no longer try to learn or even want to attend school.

It is this latter point that also raises the challenges of delivering culturally appropriate services in urban areas, not only in schooling but also in many other areas such as health and family services, and reminds us again that reserves remain attractive destinations as "a cultural hearth" for Aboriginal people in urban areas who feel socially or culturally isolated, if not economically marginalized.

Social Isolation and Social Cohesion

A major challenge of Aboriginal people living in urban areas is maintaining cultural identity and developing urban institutions that reflect Aboriginal values (RCAP, 1996). To the extent that urban institutions conflict with Aboriginal cultural values, the experiences of Aboriginal migrants in an urban environment can be considered from a social isolation perspective as discussed by Yang (2002), such that social isolation is characterized by a lack of contact or of sustained interaction with the individuals and institutions that represent mainstream society. "Being cut off from the mainstream society both socially and residentially, individuals are deprived of exposure to role models for social behavior and access to opportunities, which leads to economic marginalization, further exacerbating their social isolation" (Yang, 2002).

Social isolation and economic marginalization has implications for increased mobility, and for the needs and challenges facing Aboriginal people in establishing their own institutions and developing social cohesion within the urban context. Beavon and Norris (1999) proposed that high mobility (or churn) could lead to weaker social cohesion in communities and neighbourhoods and, as a consequence, people living in these areas could exhibit greater social problems (e.g., poorer educational attainment, divorce, crime, suicide), which in turn could lead to even greater levels of churn.

Conclusion and Postscript

To conclude, future research about the mobility of Aboriginal people clearly needs to focus on the turbulence in urban communities caused by high rates of residential instability, as well as the turnover between reserves and urban areas. A constant turnover of population between two areas is with little doubt socially disruptive, depending on the length of time people spend away. In the case of the urban Aboriginal population, this pattern can affect service delivery, and have negative implications for the development of strong urban Aboriginal community institutions. For reserve communities, high population turnover may also affect community institutions and social cohesion. Looking ahead, for reserves, the shortage of functional housing and job opportunities in First Nation communities could potentially increase pressures to migrate from reserves, especially against a background of projected rapid growth in the working-age population. On the other hand, these same projections point to an aging Aboriginal population. This process may increase residential stability because people have less inclination to relocate at older ages. As for the present, it is the frequency of population movement between reserves and cities, and within cities, not an exodus from the former, that has the greatest implications for the well-being of Aboriginal people and communities.

Results from the recent 2001 Census release would also suggest a continuation of similar mobility and migration patterns with the following highlights being reported by Statistics Canada: "More people move to Indian reserves than leave"; and in reference to the again observed high mobility: "This high turnover of population...creates challenges on the health care, housing and social services, and the local school systems."

A preliminary analysis of 2001 Census data for Registered Indians suggests a continuation of their previous migration patterns, with small net inflows to reserves (of some 10,000 migrants) while major urban areas continue to post relatively small net losses over the 1996-2001 period, but small net inflows over the one-year period (2000-01). Patterns of five-year net migration among the Métis are somewhat similar to those observed in the 1996 Census. Rural areas gained migrants in the exchange with urban areas, large cities posted a net inflow (relatively small) instead of a net outflow as in 1996, and smaller cities continued to experience net out-flows. The migration patterns of Non-Status Indians during the 1996-2001 period differed the most from previous patterns. The overall level of net migration for rural areas was practically nil during the period, in comparison to large net inflows to rural areas of the previous five-year period. In fact, the net effect of 1996-2001 migration for Non-Status Indians was practically nil with respect to the redistribution of population, as was also the case for Inuit, although for the latter this was also the situation in 1996.

With respect to migration to and from cities, analysis of five-year data thus far clearly indicates higher rates of in, out, and gross migration for Aboriginal populations, at least twice those of non-Aboriginals. As well, for most of the cities studied, rates of Registered Indian migration continued to be larger than those of other Aboriginal groups, although not to the same extent as in the previous five-year period.

In the case of ethnic mobility, 2001 Census results would support the continuation of this phenomenon particularly in the case of the Métis, which according to the Census had the largest population gain of the three Aboriginal groups (North American Indian, Métis, and Inuit) with a 43 percent increase from five years earlier, and a largely urbanized population, with more than two thirds living in urban areas. As noted in the release itself and as supported by 2001 migration data, not all the growth can be attributed to demographic factors.[9] Clearly, migration is not a major component of growth.[10]

These findings from the 2001 Census again indicate that migration is still currently not a major factor to the positive growth of the Aboriginal population in any of the areas under study, particularly with respect to reserves and major urban centres. Furthermore, they continue to reinforce the case that for now the most important considerations of Aboriginal mobility are not redistribution of the population, but the high rate of movement or churn both to and from, and within cities, which has the greatest implications for the well-being of Aboriginal people and communities.

Notes

1   The views expressed in this paper are those of the authors and do not necessarily represent the views of Indian and Northern Affairs Canada (INAC). The authors would like to acknowledge with thanks technical support provided by Lucette Dell'Oso of the Research and Analysis Directorate, INAC and Gerry Ouellette of Statistics Canada.

2   Defining Aboriginal populations is a multi-dimensional phenomenon involving overlapping concepts of ethnic affiliation and legal status. Accordingly, the separate counts shown here include multiples. For example, some Métis have legal Indian status.

3   In 1985, amendments to the *Indian Act* restored Registered Indian status to those who had lost status as a result of provisions of earlier versions of the Act.

4 External migrants, those persons who were living outside Canada five or one year earlier) are not considered to be a significant factor in Aboriginal migration. Furthermore, the census cannot measure external out-migration because Canadians whose usual place of residence is outside Canada do not participate in the census.

5 We estimate that it is more likely closer to 60 percent based on adjusted 1991 APS data and the Indian Register.

6 There was minor activity involving reserves and settlements which resulted in a small net in-migration.

7 Caution should be used when interpreting the patterns given the small numbers involved.

8 Caution should be used when interpreting rates given the small numbers involved.

9 Increased awareness of Métis issues coming from court cases related to Métis rights, and constitutional discussions, as well as better enumeration of Métis communities have contributed to the increase in the population identifying as Métis (Census release, January 2003).

10 It is also worth noting that from an international perspective both the patterns of Aboriginal migration and the phenomenon of ethnic mobility are not unique to Canada's censuses, having also been observed in the censuses of other countries such as Australia.

References

BC (British Columbia), Ministry of Education (2001) "Over-Representation of Aboriginal Students Reported with Behaviour Disorders," McBride Management, Commissioned for the Ministry of Education.

Beavon, D. and M.J. Norris (1999) "Dimensions of Geographic Mobility and Churn in Social Cohesion: The Case of Aboriginal Peoples," Presentation, Indian and Northern Affairs Canada, Research and Analysis Directorate, November.

Bostrom, H. (1984) "Government Policies and Programs Relating to People of Indian Ancestry in Manitoba," in *Dynamics of Government Programs for Urban Indians in Prairie Provinces*, R. Breton and G. Grant, (eds.), Montréal: Institute for Research on Public Policy.

Canada, INAC (Indian and Northern Affairs Canada) (1997) *Gathering Strength: Canada's Aboriginal Action Plan*, Ottawa: Indian and Northern Affairs Canada.

Canada, Statistics Canada (1993) *User's Guide to 1991 Aboriginal Data*, Ottawa: Statistics Canada.

—— (1998) *Mobility and Migration: 1991 Census*, Cat no. 93-322, Ottawa: Statistics Canada.

Chapman, M. (1978) "On the Cross-Cultural Study of Circulation," *International Migration Review*, 12(4): 559-569.

Clatworthy, S.J. (1996) "The Migration and Mobility Patterns of Canada's Aboriginal Population," Report prepared for the Royal Commission on Aboriginal Peoples, Ottawa: Canada Mortgage and Housing Corporation, and the Royal Commission on Aboriginal Peoples.

—— (2000) "Patterns of Residential Mobility Among Aboriginal Peoples in Canada: An Urban Perspective," Presentation made at the Aboriginal Strategy Federal Workshop, Regina, Saskatchewan, May 11-12, 2000.

—— (2001) "Re-Assessing the Population Impacts of Bill C-31," Report prepared by Four Directions Project Consultants for Indian and Northern Affairs Canada, Research and Analysis Directorate.

—— (forthcoming) "Registered Indian Migration between On- and Off-Reserve Locations, 1986-1996: Summary and Implications," Report prepared by Four Directions Project Consultants for Indian and Northern Affairs Canada, Research and Analysis Directorate.

Clatworthy, S.J. with M. Cooke (2001) "Reasons For Registered Indian Migration," Report prepared by Four Directions Project Consultants for Indian and Northern Affairs Canada, Research and Analysis Directorate.

Clatworthy, S.J. and J. Hull (1983) *Native Economic Conditions in Regina and Saskatoon*, Winnipeg: Institute of Urban Studies.

Clatworthy, S.J., J. Hull, and N. Loughren (1997) "Implications of First Nations Demography," Report prepared by Four Directions Consulting Group for Indian and Northern Affairs Canada, Research and Analysis Directorate.

Cooke, M.J. (1999) "On Leaving Home: Return and Circular Migration between First Nations and Prairie Cities," Unpublished master's thesis, University of Western Ontario.

Falconer, P. (1985) "Urban Indian Needs: Federal Policy Responsibility and Options in the Context of the Talks on Aboriginal Self-Government," Unpublished discussion paper, Winnipeg: Institute of Urban Studies.

Frideres, J.S. (1974) "Urban Indians," in *Canada's Indians: Contemporary Conflicts*, J.S. Frideres, (ed.), Scarborough: Prentice-Hall.

Gerber, L.M. (1977) "Community Characteristics and Out-Migration from Indian Communities: Regional Trends," Paper presented at Indian and Northern Affairs Canada.

—— (1984) "Community Characteristics and Out-Migration from Canadian Indian Reserves: Path Analyses," *Canadian Review of Sociology and Anthropology*, 21(2): 46-54.

Guimond, E. (1999) "Ethnic Mobility and the Demographic Growth of Canada's Aboriginal Population from 1986-1996," *Report on the Demographic Situation in Canada*, 1998-1999, Ottawa: Statistics Canada.

Hanselmann, C. (2001) "Urban Aboriginal People in Western Canada: Realities and Policies," Calgary: Canada West Foundation

Hawthorn, H. B., (ed.), (1966) *A Survey of the Contemporary Indians of Canada*, Ottawa: Indian Affairs Branch.

Howes, C. (2000) "The New Native Tycoons," *National Post*, January 27: D05.

Krotz, L. (1990) *Indian Country: Inside Another Canada*, Toronto: McClelland and Stewart.

Lee, E.S. (1966) "A Theory of Migration," *Demography*, 3: 45-67.

Loh, S., R. Verma, E. Ng, M.J. Norris, M. V. George, and J. Perreault, (1998) "Population Projections of Registered Indians, 1996-2021," Unpublished report prepared by Statistics Canada, Population Projections Section, Demography Division, for Indian and Northern Affairs Canada.

Lurie, N.O. (1967) "The Indian Moves to an Urban Setting," *Resolving Conflicts- A Cross-Cultural Approach*, Winnipeg: University of Manitoba Extension and Adult Education Department.

McCaskill, D.N (1970) "Migration, Adjustment, and Integration of the Indian into the Urban Environment," Unpublished master's thesis, Carleton University.

Melting Tallow, P. (2001) "A Place to Hang Your Headdress," *Aboriginaltimes*, 10(5): 31-34.

Norris, M. J. (1985) "Migration Patterns of Status Indians in Canada, 1976-1981," Paper prepared for the Demography of Northern and Native Peoples in Canada session at Statistics Canada, June, 1985.

—— (1990) "The Demography of Aboriginal People in Canada," in *Ethnic Demography: Canadian Immigrant*, Racial and Cultural Variations, S.S. Halli, F. Trovato, and L. Driedger, (eds.), Ottawa: Carleton University Press.

—— (1992) "New Developments and Increased Analytical Possibilities With Mobility and Migration Data From the 1991 Census," Paper prepared for the annual meeting of the Canadian Population, Charlottetown, Prince Edward Island, June 2-5, 1992.

—— (1996) "Contemporary Demography of Aboriginal Peoples in Canada," in *Visions of the Heart: Canadian Aboriginal Issues*, D.A. Long and O.P. Dickason, (eds.), Toronto: Harcourt Brace Canada.

—— (2000) "Aboriginal Peoples in Canada: Demographic and Linguistic Perspectives," in Visions of the Heart: Canadian Aboriginal Issues, second edition, D.A. Long and O P. Dickason, (eds.), Toronto: Harcourt Brace Canada.

Norris, D.A. and E.T. Pryor (1984) "Demographic Change in Canada's North," *Proceedings – International Workshop on Population Issues in Arctic Societies*, Gilbjerghoved, Gilleleje, Denmark, May 2-5, 1984.

Norris, M.J., D. Kerr, and F. Nault (1995) "Projections of the Population with Aboriginal Identity in Canada, 1991-2016," Report prepared by Statistics Canada, Population Projections Section, Demography Division for the Royal Commission on Aboriginal Peoples, Ottawa: Canada Mortgage and Housing Corporation and the Royal Commission on Aboriginal Peoples.

Norris, M.J., Marty Cooke, and Stewart Clatworthy (2003) "Aboriginal Mobility and Migration Patterns and the Policy Implications," in Aboriginal Condition: The Research Foundations of Public Policy, J. White, P. Maxim, and D. Beavon, (eds.), Vancouver: UBC Press.

Peters, E. (1994) Demographics of Aboriginal People in Urban Areas, in Relation to Self-Government, Ottawa: Indian and Northern Affairs Canada.

Ponting, J.R., (ed.) (1997) First Nations in Canada: Perspectives on Opportunity, Empowerment, and Self-Determination, Toronto: McGraw-Hill Ryerson.

RCAP (Royal Commission on Aboriginal Peoples) (1996) People to People, Nation to Nation: Highlights from the Report of the Royal Commission on Aboriginal Peoples, Ottawa: Royal Commission on Aboriginal Peoples.

Reeves, W. and J. Frideres (1981) "Government Policy and Indian Urbanization: the Alberta Case," Canadian Public Policy, 7(4): 584-595.

Robitaille, N. and R. Choinière (1985) An Overview of Demographic and Socio-Economic Conditions of the Inuit in Canada, Ottawa: Indian and Northern Affairs Canada.

Siggner, A.J. (1977) Preliminary Results from a Study of 1966-71 Migration Patterns among Status Indians in Canada, Ottawa: Department of Indian Affairs and Northern Development.

Sjaastad, L.A. (1962) "The Costs and Returns of Human Migration," Journal of Political Economy, 70: 80-93.

Trovato, F., A. Romaniuc, and I. Addai (1994) On- and Off-Reserve Migration of Aboriginal Peoples in Canada: A Review of the Literature, Ottawa: Indian and Northern Affairs Canada.

Yang, X. (2002) Migration, Socioeconomic Milieu, and Migrants HIV Risk-Taking Behavior: A Theoretical Framework, Department of Sociology and Criminal Justice, Paper presented at Population Association of America, Atlanta, Georgia, May.

Young, T.K., J. Reading, B. Elias, J.D. O'Neil (2000) "Type 2 Diabetes Mellitus in Canada's First Nations: Status of an Epidemic in Progress," Canadian Medical Association Journal, 163(5): 561-566.

Urban Residential Patterns of Aboriginal People in Canada

Paul S. Maxim
Department of Sociology
University of Western Ontario

Carl Keane
Department of Sociology
Queen's University

Jerry White
Department of Sociology
University of Western Ontario

Introduction

There is a long tradition of research, in North American sociology, on residential settlement patterns. Much of the impetus for this research comes from the Chicago School that focused on the ecological patterns of urban settlement of immigrants in America's large cities in the early 20th century. That research broadened, especially after World War II, when the United States experienced high rates of internal migration. Canadian sociologists conducted similar research, but to a lesser extent. In both the United States and Canada, however, almost none of that research has focused on the indigenous population. The settlement dynamic of First Nations peoples in urban areas is of particular interest in the Canadian context as we have seen both a revitalization of reserves (First Nations communities) and an apparent increase in movement to urban centres.

Recent research suggests that, while the First Nations populations on reserves have been growing at rates faster than the general Canadian population, the number of people declaring themselves as Aboriginal has been increasing in the urban areas at even faster rates. In 1951 only seven percent of the Aboriginal population lived in an urban area (more than 1,000 persons) while the 1991 Census shows that 42 percent of those defined as single origin North American Indians are in such communities (Statistics Canada, 1994: Table 1; Drost et al., 1995: 13). Despite this geographic shift, little analysis has been done on the living patterns of Aboriginal people in urban centres.

Furthermore, much of the research on urban residential patterns is of American origin, so generalizing from these studies is difficult since the patterns of settlement in the United States and Canada are quite different (Fong, 1996). American cities remain highly segregated by race, particularly regarding African- and Asian-Americans; the situation is not as pronounced in Canada.

Although the research on residential segregation in Canada is significant (Balakrishnan, 1976, 1982; Balakrishnan and Hou, 1995; Balakrishnan and Krault, 1987; Bourne et al., 1986; Darroch and Marston, 1971; Kalbach, 1987) most of it is directed toward the comparison of residential patterns among Canadians of European origin. Some of the more recent studies do highlight issues relating to visible minorities (Balakrishnan and Hou, 1995; Balakrishnan and Krault, 1987) but, again, little attention is focused on people of Aboriginal ancestry.

The reasons for residential segregation or concentration are numerous (Balakrishnan and Krault, 1987: 139). On the one hand, voluntary segregation takes place when groups of people of similar ancestry choose to live close to one another to maximize social interaction. Close physical proximity often helps to foster or maintain social institutions, such as ethnic clubs, schools, stores, or churches, and to foster the maintenance of group norms and values. Cohesive neighbourhoods found in Toronto, such as "Chinatown," "Little Italy," or "Greektown," are seen by many as positive ethnic enclaves that contribute as much to the broader society as to the specific ethnic communities that they comprise. This wish to form cohesive co-ethnic neighbourhoods is known as the "cultural proximity model."

For many groups, a unique cultural heritage is easier to maintain through ethnic residential concentration than when the group is more broadly dispersed throughout the community. Economic drivers may also result in voluntary concentration. If one is a migrant (either internal or external), finding suitable housing and work opportunities is often easier by moving to a neighbourhood where friends, relatives, and compatriots reside. Research also suggests that ethnic entrepreneurship is assisted through the existence of a cohesive and centralized ethnic market. Some researchers see ethnic enclaves as incubators that allow small businesses to develop during their formative years. The unique aspects of ethnic communities, such as language and culturally determined tastes and preferences, serve to insulate small ethnic businesses from larger and more established enterprises. Once past the development stage, these businesses can use the ethnic community as a springboard for expansion into the larger marketplace.

Much of the literature on ethnic mobility suggests a common model for many groups that migrate; they initially find lodging in neighbourhoods of co-ethnics. With time, however, most ethnic groups achieve economic, social, and geographic mobility and integrate, in varying degrees, into the larger mainstream community. This pattern also exists beyond traditional definitions of "ethnicity." Similar patterns appear with internal migrants when people move from one locality to another. For example, we would expect to see similar trends among rural-urban migrants or interregional migrants.

The other side to voluntary segregation, however, is involuntary segregation. Involuntary segregation can also occur for several reasons. Co-ethnics who share a paucity of human capital and economic resources may find that they have little alternative than to reside in lower rent districts or in neighbourhoods closer to certain types of employment.

A less benign reason for involuntary segregation results from discrimination. Historically, some religious groups – such as Jews in Europe – and some racial groups – such as African-Americans – were legally relegated to specific neighbourhoods. While overt discrimination is no longer legally nor culturally sanctioned in most nations, a more insidious form of discrimination can exist when people are informally restricted in their access to certain neighbourhoods and institutions. This is typical of much non-white segregation in both the United States and Europe.

Focusing on Aboriginal segregation in Canada, Drost et al. (1995: 48) concluded that, "the relatively higher residential concentration of Aboriginals[1] in the core city areas of the western CMAs may have lead to ghetto effects that exacerbate the already low degree of integration of Aboriginals…."

Explanations and Dimensions of Segregation

Researchers have developed several explicit hypotheses or models to explain residential segregation. The ecological model predicts that cultural proximity among ethnic groups follows temporal patterns of succession. This is perhaps most likely with immigrants who migrate in successive waves, with one immigrant group geographically supplanting another in neighbourhoods where immigrants traditionally land. The pattern appears most pronounced when little variation occurs in human capital among immigrants, as happened in 19th and early 20th century Canada and the United States. With a greater diversity in human capital, however, the strict ecological successionist model is likely to be less obvious. Newer migrants with higher levels of capital – whether monetary, educational, or linguistic abilities – are able to merge more rapidly into existing communities.

Thus, even under the ecological succession model, we would expect internal migrants such as Aboriginal peoples to be less residentially concentrated than immigrants, since some reasons that have traditionally led to extreme patterns of concentration do not exist. Specifically, as indigenous peoples, Aboriginal people are more likely to have friends and relatives who have lived in urban centres for a longer period. We may see these networks as a form of social capital. Furthermore, these contacts, who may act as a residential "draw," are probably more widely dispersed (assuming they have realized increases in their human or financial capital). Similarly, some human capital aspects that create co-ethnic clumping (such as language ability) do not serve as structural barriers for most Aboriginal people.

On the other hand, the "social distance hypothesis" suggests that despite all else, groups with more similar cultural backgrounds are more likely to coexist in similar neighbourhoods. Thus, for example, we would not be surprised to see people of Mediterranean origin residing together. On the other hand, the co-residence of people of Chinese and Italian origin would be considered less likely under this model. While we may operationalize social distance in several ways, this hypothesis implicitly assumes that cultural affinity is more important in determining group-level social relationships than economic and other factors. The classic work in this area is that of Bogardus (1928) who developed his "social distance scale." More recently, Canadian research by Pineo (1977) and others (e.g., Balakrishnan, 1982) has used measures of "social standing" and found that in Canadian metropolitan areas, residential segregation increases with social distance.

Apart from the reasons for segregation occurring, several indicators can be used to detect its existence and extent. The indicators we examine include, evenness, concentration, and centralization. Massey et al. (1996: 173) describe these indicators as follows.

> Evenness is the degree to which the percentage of minority members within residential areas approaches the minority percentage of the entire urban area; as areas depart from the ideal of evenness, segregation increases. Concentration is the relative amount of physical space occupied by a minority group; as segregation increases, minority members are confined to a small and geographically compact area. Finally, centralization is the degree to which minority members settle in and around the centre of an urban area, usually defined as the central business district.

The Data

The source of data included in this analysis is the 1996 Census of Canada. Ethnicity is a complex issue. To capture some of that complexity, recent censuses have asked Canadians about both their origins and their identity. Origin refers to people's ancestry while identify refers to the cultural group with which people feel they most closely belong. While considerable overlap exists between these two concepts among most recent immigrants, the two diverge the longer people live in Canada and as populations merge and people acquire multiple origins. Many Canadians have such a varied ancestral mixture that the origin question either has little meaning as a social concept or is simply too complex for any meaningful analysis. Part of the solution to the multiple origin issue has been simply to ask people with which group they identify. Identity, however, is socially constructed. Consequently, many people chose not to identify with any of their ethnic origins. Also, many increasingly describe themselves simply as "Canadians."

Both indicators of origin and identity are based on self-identification. From the perspective of the Census, people are whom they say they are. Occasionally, this can lead to the problems illustrated in Ryder's (1955) classic study of the discrepancy in the recording of Canadians of German origin before and after World War II. Without doubt, the policy shifts of the Government of Canada to emphasize multiculturalism in the mid to late 1960s led to a greater acceptance of diversity within the Canadian matrix. This has resulted in many Canadians, including Aboriginal people, reporting origins that they previously refused to proclaim in public. The increased willingness to self-identify among Aboriginal peoples confounds many of our estimates. For example, many sources conclude that the rate of migration of Aboriginal people into our major cities increased from the 1950s through to the 1990s. Peters (2000: 247) suggests that the absolute increase between 1981 and 1991 was greater than the increase between 1971 and 1981. How much of that increase is due to actual migration and how much is simply due to changes in self-identification is open to debate.

The complexity involved in origin and identity is just as evident for Aboriginal people as anyone else living in Canada. To make matters more difficult for social analysts, we also impose a legal element to definitions that go beyond the issues involved in origin and identity. Thus, not only do we have people with Aboriginal origins and identity, we also have those the government legally recognizes as Registered Indians under the *Indian Act* and the recognition of Métis and Inuit people in the *Canadian Charter of Rights and Freedoms*.

Depending upon the area we choose to examine, there are varying degrees of overlap across all three types of definitions. In some cities, distributions of people by origin and identity are almost perfectly correlated; in other areas substantial divergence exists. Due to space limitations, we will limit our current discussion to those people who claim North American Indian origin in the 1996 Census. It is possible to identify those who claim single North American Indian origin and those who claim multiple origins, one of which is North American Indian. Again, for illustrative purposes, we will combine both those with single and multiple origins. Data are available for 22 census metropolitan areas (CMAs) in Canada. For readers who are interested, similar information by other definitions is available on our Web site <www.ssc.uwo.ca/sociology/firstnations/Profiles.html>.

Residential Segregation

As mentioned earlier, the sociological literature has a long tradition of analyzing residential segregation. The issue came to the forefront in the 1930s when the Chicago School examined residential distribution patterns to test hypotheses relating to social ecology (e.g., Park, 1925, 1936a,b; Park and Burgess, 1921). More recent analysts have concerned themselves with processes of socio-economic development and discrimination.

The empirical reality for most communities is that many interesting sociological characteristics, such as ethnicity, are not evenly distributed across a community. Instead, we find population "clumping" where some groups concentrate more in certain geographical areas than others. This concentration can be depicted graphically, which we have done for urban Aboriginal peoples. However, since people of Aboriginal origin form only a small proportion of the population of Canada, our first step involved an examination of the data to ensure that enough variance exists throughout the target CMAs. As a by-product of that analysis, we produced a series of maps presenting the distribution of total-origin North American Indians by census tract. While many studies of residential segregation use enumeration areas as their basic geographical unit of analysis, we use the larger agglomeration of census tracts. We take this approach because Aboriginal people often form a small proportion of the population in any given neighbourhood. Consequently, many enumeration areas have zero observations for this group.

For space reasons, the maps are not reproduced here (available at www.ssc.uwo.ca/sociology/firstnations/Profiles.html). We further limit this discussion to eight CMAs (Vancouver, Edmonton, Regina, Saskatoon, Winnipeg, Toronto, Montréal, and Halifax), which have been selected based on their population size and to provide regional representation. This approach follows the work of Drost et al. (1995) who show that concentration of Aboriginal and non-Aboriginal people vary from city to city. The maps provide some information on the degree of concentration. The maps also provide an indication of centralization. Recall that centralization refers to the degree to which a group is segregated near the centre of a city. We often see the phenomenon of centralization in the United States, where minorities concentrate in declining city centres, often occupying inadequate housing (Massey and Denton, 1988: 291).

The maps are informative, in that while some concentration may be occurring, the patterns vary among cities. Virtually no concentration appears in Halifax, while Winnipeg, Regina, and Saskatoon do exhibit some evidence of concentration. In brief, the maps show a lack of consistency with respect to concentration. Likewise, with centralization, city-centre concentration varies among cities and is not pronounced in any one city, although Winnipeg, Regina, and Edmonton exhibit some degree of centralization.

There are also other ways of depicting residential segregation other than graphically. One way is to consider a single group and to examine its statistical distribution across subdistricts, such as neighbourhoods or census tracts, within a community. The Gini Index is one of the most commonly used measures of distribution.

Within Group Distributions

Using the Gini Index, we can obtain a measure of how evenly distributed a group is across census tracts. There are several ways of understanding the Gini Index. Here we are focusing on the proportion of Aboriginal people within each census tract compared with the total population of the census tract. Used this way, the Gini Index provides an indication of how much dissimilarity exists among the proportions of Aboriginal peoples compared with the total possible dissimilarity across the census tracts. If each census tract has the same proportion of Aboriginal people, then the value of the Gini Index is 0. The maximum value of the Gini coefficient is 1.0 and this occurs when everyone in the target group lives in the same area. Put another way, the more uneven the spatial distribution, the larger the value of the Gini coefficient.

Table 1 displays Gini indices for several ethnic groups. The column labelled North American Indian Total contains people who report any North American Indian origins. The North American Indian Single column, however, represents only those people who report being North American

Indian only. For comparative purposes, we have also included people who belong to a visible minority group and those who report being of any Canadian, French, English, or Italian origin. The Canadian, French, and English columns include both multiple and single origins, thus allowing for potential overlap in group membership. To illustrate the impact of examining single and multiple origins, we have also included Gini indices for those who report single Italian origin only and those who report any Italian origin. People of Italian origin provide an excellent example of how residential indices can change when we change our focus from single to mixed origin. There is a large population in Canada reporting either single or multiple Italian origin and, unlike many other ethnic groups, they are widely disbursed across CMAs.

While there is a considerable amount of information presented in Table 1, there are two important trends that are worth noting. First, if we compare both people of North American Indian and Italian origin, the measures of concentration vary considerably based on whether we use total or single origin. In general, people of single origin tend to be more concentrated in their residential patterns than people who report multiple ethnic origins. In general, people reporting single North American Indian origins are slightly more residentially concentrated than single origin Italians. While the indices for single North American Indians may appear high (indicating high levels of residential segregation) they are lower than some other groups such as those reporting single Vietnamese, Greek, Portuguese, or East Indian origin. On the other hand, they are higher than people reporting other single European origins such as Polish, German, or Dutch.

The other point worth noting is that there is considerable variation across CMAs whether we focus on measures of total or single origin. Focusing on people reporting any North American Indian origin shows that variation across cities is substantial. Sudbury has the lowest overall measure of residential segregation at 0.278, followed by such cities as Halifax (0.281), Montréal (0.389), Vancouver (0.394), Edmonton (0.412),Toronto (0.466), Regina (0.510), Saskatoon (0.548) and Winnipeg with the highest value of 0.553. In brief, the Gini indices, representing the evenness in residential location, vary across the country with the mid-western cities generally having the highest levels of segregation.

Although these indices are informative, it is also interesting to compare segregation indices across groups. For example, Table 1 also includes the Gini coefficients for total visible minorities. The Gini coefficients for the visible minorities are higher than those for total North American Indian in all but four of the cities. That is, visible minorities are more

Table 1: Gini indices for selected ethnic groups by census metropolitan area

Census Metropolitan Area	No. of Census Tracts	GINI INDICES							
		North American Indian Total	North American Indian Single	Visible Minority	Canadian Total	French Total	English Total	Italian Total	Polish Total
Halifax	75	0.281	0.684	0.476	0.190	0.133	0.086	0.268	0.379
Quebec	152	0.357	0.719	0.531	0.181	0.174	0.349	0.472	0.743
Montreal	756	0.389	0.722	0.617	0.386	0.298	0.545	0.576	0.585
Sherbrooke	31	0.297	0.718	0.407	0.129	0.123	0.554	0.238	0.605
Trois-Rivieres	34	0.303	0.700	0.474	0.137	0.139	0.265	0.425	0.681
Ottawa-Hull	214	0.288	0.608	0.534	0.294	0.346	0.374	0.414	0.363
Oshawa	49	0.309	0.683	0.357	0.098	0.141	0.091	0.269	0.234
Toronto	804	0.466	0.793	0.569	0.355	0.320	0.403	0.547	0.448
Hamilton	162	0.431	0.726	0.449	0.163	0.178	0.193	0.375	0.248
St.-Catherines-Niagara	83	0.321	0.615	0.357	0.109	0.274	0.129	0.363	0.208
Kitchener	81	0.316	0.720	0.364	0.145	0.127	0.159	0.258	0.246
London	87	0.379	0.620	0.436	0.131	0.133	0.136	0.281	0.259
Windsor	59	0.339	0.674	0.465	0.133	0.237	0.158	0.350	0.237
Sudbury	37	0.278	0.536	0.387	0.180	0.266	0.124	0.464	0.273
Thunder Bay	31	0.381	0.493	0.304	0.109	0.109	0.107	0.242	0.156
Winnipeg	157	0.553	0.733	0.532	0.222	0.349	0.244	0.350	0.264
Regina	49	0.510	0.608	0.345	0.135	0.140	0.122	0.305	0.180
Saskatoon	50	0.548	0.670	0.406	0.124	0.132	0.128	0.378	0.142
Calgary	153	0.357	0.587	0.461	0.141	0.135	0.161	0.283	0.183
Edmonton	187	0.412	0.688	0.505	0.175	0.171	0.174	0.394	0.145
Vancouver	298	0.394	0.684	0.530	0.271	0.232	0.301	0.338	0.234
Victoria	65	0.358	0.637	0.389	0.135	0.149	0.104	0.244	0.204

residentially segregated than people of Aboriginal origin in such cities as Halifax, Montréal, Toronto, Edmonton, and Vancouver. On the other hand, people of Aboriginal origin are residentially more concentrated in Thunder Bay, Winnipeg, Regina, and Saskatoon. The same is not true, however, when we consider people reporting single North American Indian origin. In all instances, these single origin people are more residentially concentrated than people of visible minority origins in all of the CMAs examined.

Discussion

This study has focused on the concepts of evenness, concentration, and centralization as indicators of urban residential segregation of Aboriginal people. Population distribution maps that are the foundation of this study reveal some evidence of concentration, but little evidence of centralization. With respect to evenness, Table 1 reveals considerable variation in the Gini coefficients. Aboriginals in Winnipeg, Regina, and Saskatoon may experience some residential segregation, but again the degree of evenness varies across Canada. In fact, as noted earlier, Canadian Aboriginal peoples may be more evenly distributed overall than some other ethnic groups.

It is possible to take this analysis one step further and ask what are some of the determinants of residential concentration? The sociological literature suggests that there are many reasons why people choose to live where they do. One of the primary correlates of housing choice for most people is cost. Focusing only on people of Aboriginal origin, people of multiple North American Indian origin tend, on average, to earn more than people of single origin. Thus, it perhaps comes as no surprise that one of the factors most closely correlated with the proportion of people of single North American Indian origin is the cost of housing within a neighbourhood. Housing costs appear to be a major determinant of where single origin Aboriginal people live; it is less a factor with people of multiple Aboriginal origins (Maxim et al ,2000a,b).

The examination of residential patterns of Aboriginal people in urban areas provides some insight into an important issue. Nevertheless, many of our most interesting hypotheses surround the dynamic aspects of settlement. That is, the analysis conducted here is static since it reflects the situation at one point in time. Residential settlement patterns, however, are dynamic and they change over time. For example, Clatworthy's (1996, 2000) research addressing on-off-reserve migration to major urban centres suggests a substantial flow between First Nations communities and urban centres and between one urban centre and another. Not only does that dynamic need examination in greater detail, but the patterns of intra-urban migration need addressing. The classical successionist model suggests that much movement is of the "up and out" variety, following a general pattern of upward economic and social mobility. It is an empirical question whether this pattern holds for any or all of Canada's Aboriginal peoples who choose to live in major urban centres.

Further research exploring neighbourhood dynamics would also be beneficial. Knowing the degree to which existing institutions and organizations servicing Aboriginal communities act as a draw would be useful. Migration research focusing on both internal and international migrants has led to the notion of "chain migration." This means that people are drawn to neighbourhoods already settled by family, friends, and co-ethnics since established residents often ease the search for housing and jobs. Chain migration might be a large factor underlying the settlement patterns of Aboriginal peoples. An interesting question is whether this process is more pronounced among Aboriginal peoples than other Canadians. The conventional wisdom surrounding the importance of extended family and community within First Nations communities suggests that this might be the case.

We are also unaware, except through anecdotal evidence, of the systematic role that proximity to reserves and connecting transportation routes play in urban settlement. Our analyses of residential segregation suggest that Aboriginal peoples in most major communities are reasonably well integrated into the geographical urban landscape. On the other hand, it is clear that some Aboriginal people are more segregated in some cities. It would be interesting to know what circumstances underlie those differences, and to what degree those differences are due to "pull" factors and to what degree they are influenced by "push" factors. It is the "push" factors that have important policy implications. That is, if segregation is occurring involuntarily, the relevance of a housing policy providing affordable housing, available in various parts of a city, is obvious. Identifying these correlates of residential patterns is beyond the scope of this article. Distinguishing the "pull" and "push" factors of urban residential patterns will guide our future research.

Note

1   There is no evidence that Drost, Crowley, and Schwindt actually investigated the concentrations of Aboriginal populations in the core of cities. It seems they took this as a given.

References

Balakrishnan, T.R. (1976) "Variations on Two Themes: Racial and Ethnic Patterns in the Attainment of Suburban Residence," *Demography*, 28: 431-53.

—— (1982) "Changing Patterns of Ethnic Residential Segregation in the Metropolitan Areas of Canada," *Canadian Review of Sociology and Anthropology*, 19: 92-110.

Balakrishnan, T.R. and F. Hou (1995) *The Changing Patterns of Spatial Concentration and Residential Segregation of Ethnic Groups in Canada's Major Census Metropolitan Areas, 1981-1991*, Discussion paper 95-2, Population Studies Centre, University of Western Ontario.

Balakrishnan, T.R. and J. Krault (1987) "Segregation of Visible Minorities in Montréal, Toronto and Vancouver" in Leo Driedger, ed., *Ethnic Canada: Identities and Inequalities*, Toronto: Copp-Clark.

Bogardus, E.S. (1928) *Immigration and Race Attitudes*. New York: J. S. Ozer.

Bourne, L.S., A.M. Baker, W. Kalbach, R. Cressman, and D. Green (1986) Canada's Ethnic Mosaic: Characteristics and Patterns of Ethnic Origin Groups in Urban Areas, Report no. 26. Toronto: Centre for Urban and Community Studies, University of Toronto.

Canada, Statistics Canada (1994) "Profile of Urban and Rural Areas, Canada, Provinces and Territories – Part B (1991 Census of Population)," Cat. #93-340XPB.

Clatworthy, S.J. (1996) "The Migration and Mobility Patterns of Canada's Aboriginal Population," *Royal Commission on Aboriginal People: People to People Nation to Nation*, Ottawa: Minister of Supply and Services Canada.

—— (2000) "Factors Influencing the Migration of Registered Indians Between On and Off Reserve Locations in Canada," Ottawa: Research and Analysis Directorate, Indian and Northern Affairs Canada.

Darroch, A.G. and W.G. Marston (1971) "The Social Class Basis of Ethnic Residential Segregation: The Canadian Case," *American Journal of Sociology*, 77: 491-510.

Drost, H., B. Crowley, and R. Schwindt (1995) *Market Solutions for Native Poverty*, Toronto: C.D. Howe Institute.

Fong, E. (1996) "A Comparative Perspective on Racial Residential Segregation: American and Canadian Experiences," *Sociological Quarterly*, 37: 192-226.

Kalbach, W.E. (1987) "Growth and Distribution of Canada's Ethnic Populations," in L. Driedger, (ed.), *Ethnic Canada: Identities and Inequalities*, Toronto: Copp-Clark.

Massey, D.S. and N.A. Denton (1988) "The Dimensions of Residential Segregation," *Social Forces*, 67: 281-315.

Massey, D.S., M.J. White, and V. Phua (1996) "The Dimensions of Residential Segregation Revisited," *Sociological Methods and Research*, 25: 173-205.

Maxim, P., J. White, P. Whitehead, and D. Beavon (2000a) "An Analysis of Wage and Income Inequality Dispersion and Polarization of Income among Aboriginal and Non Aboriginal Canadians," London: Population Studies Centre, University of Western Ontario.

—— (2000b) "Patterns of Urban Residential Settlement among Canada's First Nations Communities," London: Population Studies Centre, University of Western Ontario.

Park, R.E. (1925) "The Urban Community as a Spatial Pattern and Moral Order," *Publications of the American Sociological Society*, 20: 1-14.

—— (1936a) "Human Ecology," *American Journal of Sociology*, 42: 3-49.

—— (1936b) "Succession: an Ecological Concept," *American Sociological Review*, 1.

Park, R.E. and E.W. Burgess (1921) *Introduction to the Science of Sociology*, Chicago: University of Chicago Press.

Peters, E., (2000) "Aboriginal People in Urban Areas," in *Visions from the Heart: Canadian Aboriginal Issues*, D. Long and O. P. Dickason, (eds.), Toronto: Harcourt Canada.

Pineo, P.C. (1977) "The Social Standing of Ethnic and Racial Groupings," *Canadian Review of Sociology and Anthropology*, 14: 147-57.

Ryder, N. (1955) "The Interpretation of Origin Statistics," *Canadian Journal of Economics and Political Science*, 21: 466-79.

Aboriginal Languages in Canada's Urban Areas: Characteristics, Considerations and Implications

M.J. Norris
Research and Analysis Directorate
Indian and Northern Affairs Canada

L. Jantzen[1]
Strategic Policy and Management
Heritage Canada

Canada's indigenous languages and cultures are generally associated with Aboriginal communities and reserves. Yet, in the 1996 Census nearly 40,000 persons, or close to one in five persons who reported an Aboriginal mother tongue were residing within the boundaries of major cities across Canada. This study contrasts the situation between Aboriginal communities (including reserves) and areas off reserve and, for the first time, presents the size, characteristics, and composition of different Aboriginal languages for Canada's major cities. The results provide useful insights into, first of all, the demographics, viability, and geography of Aboriginal languages within Canadian cities, and then, some of the considerations and implications associated with these findings. The authors discuss the implications of the status and diversity of Aboriginal languages for the urban Aboriginal population relating to cultural identity, First Nation affiliation and governance, program and service delivery, and geographical mobility, as well as the issue of supporting Aboriginal languages and cultures in urban areas. The research demonstrates the challenges faced by Aboriginal people in maintaining their language outside of their communities, and raises considerations associated with maintaining the connection with language and culture within an urban milieu.

Background

The variety in Aboriginal culture and identity is reflected in Canada's Aboriginal languages. According to Statistics Canada's classification system, there are 50 individual Aboriginal languages or isolates (languages that cannot be related to any of the major families) that belong to 11 Aboriginal language families – 10 First Nations and Inuktitut. The range in population size is considerable. According to the 1996 Census, the three largest families – Algonquian (147,000), Inuktitut (28,000), and Athapaskan (20,000) – represented 93 percent of persons with an Aboriginal mother tongue. The other eight language families and isolates account for the remaining seven percent.

Geography is an important contributor to the diversity, size, and distribution of Aboriginal languages: the population bases of the Salish, Tsimshian, Wakashan, Haida, Tlingit and Kutenai languages in British Columbia were never as widely dispersed (due to the province's mountainous geography), as were the Algonquian and Athapaskan languages that developed in the open central plains and eastern woodlands (Priest, 1983; Grubb, 1979). The languages with the largest mother tongue population also tend to be widespread, such as the Algonquian family of languages extending from the Atlantic to the Rockies.

Many of Canada's Aboriginal languages are endangered and have already suffered great losses due to the forces of modernization, discouragement in residential schools, the influence of dominant languages, and possibly the fact that many Aboriginal languages are predominantly oral. At the time of European contact, there were probably many more languages spoken in Canada.

According to 1996 Census data, only a small proportion of the Aboriginal population speaks an Aboriginal language. While in 1996 some 800,000 people reported an Aboriginal identity, only 207,000 (26 percent) reported an Aboriginal language was their mother tongue (or first language learned and still understood). Even fewer, 145,000 (18 percent) reported an Aboriginal language as that being spoken most often in the home, implying that learning an Aboriginal mother tongue does not guarantee continued use. However, some 233,000 Aboriginal respondents (30 percent) (239,000 total respondents) reported that they could speak and understand an Aboriginal language well enough to conduct a conversation. Clearly, then, while some people shift from an Aboriginal language to another home language, others may be either learning indigenous languages or beginning to use the language later in life, a phenomenon that appears to be especially pronounced in urban areas. The data suggest, especially for endangered languages, that although younger generations may not be learning their indigenous language as a mother tongue, there nevertheless seems to be some interest in learning it as a second language (Norris, 1998).

Size and Transmission Critical

The transmission of a language from one generation to the next, as well as population size, are both important considerations in the viability of a language. Only three Aboriginal languages (Cree, Inuktitut, and Ojibway) have sufficiently large population bases for long-term language survival. These three languages are highly likely to be passed on to the next generation, as indicated by high Continuity Indexes that measure the ratio of home language speakers to the population with that particular language as a mother tongue. The use of a language at home has important implications for the prospects of transmission to the next generation, and hence its continuity. A language no longer spoken at home cannot be handed down as a mother tongue to the younger generation. For example, Inuktitut has a relatively high Continuity Index of 86 persons speaking Inuktitut at home for every 100 with an Inuktitut mother tongue, followed by Continuity Indexes of 72 and 55 for Cree and Ojibway, respectively. The state of these three languages can be classified as viable (Table 1).

In sharp contrast, many of the smaller languages, often with far fewer than a 1,000 speakers, especially in British Columbia, have very low prospects for continuity and can be considered endangered. For example, Table 1 shows that as of 1996, there were only 240 persons with a Haida mother tongue, and the Continuity Index is only 6. On the other hand, even with only a few thousand people, some of the smaller languages elsewhere in Canada appear viable when home usage is taken into account, such as Attikamek in Quebec with a mother tongue population of only 4,000 persons, but a Continuity Index of 97. Other small-sized languages such as Montagnais-Naskapi, Mi'kmaq, Dene, and Dogrib are considered viable, tending to be spoken in isolated or well-organized communities with strong self-awareness, where language is considered one of the important marks of identity (Kinkade, 1991).

"Young" and "Old" Languages

The average age of those who have an Aboriginal mother tongue or speak it as a home language indicates the extent to which the language has been transmitted to the younger generation. The higher the average age, the relatively fewer young people have learned or still understand the language and the older the people who still speak it. If the language is not transmitted to the younger generations, then as these older persons continue to age and then die, so will the language. Viable languages such as Attikamek, Inuktitut, and Dene are characterized by relatively young

Table 1: Selected Indicators* for Aboriginal Language Vitality, Total Population, Canada, 1996

Aboriginal Languages	Mother Tongue	Index of Continuity	Percent of children in mixed marriages	Index of Ability	Average age of Population with:			Viability Status of Language
					Knowledge of Aboriginal Language	Aboriginal Mother Tongue	Aboriginal Home Language	
Algonquian Family	**146,635**	**70**	**34**	**117**	**30.5**	**30.9**	**28.8**	**mostly viable**
Cree	87,555	70	31	117	29.9	30.2	27.9	viable large
Ojibway	25,885	55	47	122	34.9	36.2	34.4	viable large
Montagnais-Naskapi	9,070	94	19	104	25.1	25.2	24.8	viable small
Micmac	7,310	72	43	111	29.5	29.9	29.2	viable small
Oji – Cree	5,400	80	27	114	25.7	26.3	26.8	viable small
Attikamek	3,995	97	7	103	21.8	21.9	21.5	viable small
Blackfoot	4,145	61	50	135	36.4	39.7	40.6	viable small
Algonquin	2,275	58	50	119	29.8	30.7	31.4	viable small
Malecite	655	37	83	148	40.5	44.0	44.8	viable small
Algonquian NIE	350	40	75	159	47.2	52.2	46.7	uncertain
Inukitut Family	**27,780**	**86**	**19**	**109**	**23.9**	**23.9**	**23.3**	**viable large**
Athapaskan Family	**20,090**	**68**	**41**	**117**	**31.4**	**32.5**	**30.0**	**mostly viable**
Dene	9,000	86	28	107	24.4	24.8	24.1	viable small
South Slave	2,620	55	45	124	35.6	37.8	38.4	viable small
Dogrib	2,085	72	29	118	28.3	29.8	30.6	viable small
Carrier	2,190	51	70	130	37.5	41.4	40.5	viable small
Chipewyan	1,455	44	82	128	39.4	40.2	40.7	viable small
Athapaskan, NIE	1,310	37	70	129	41.6	44.7	44.2	uncertain
Chilcotin	705	65	55	130	32.2	37.0	36.9	viable small
Kutchin-Gwich'in (Loucheux)	430	24	67	114	53.0	53.1	56.8	endangered
North Slave (Hare)	290	60	36	116	38.3	39.1	39.8	endangered
(Dakota)Siouan Family	**4,295**	**67**	**49**	**111**	**31.0**	**31.9**	**28.0**	**viable small**

Salish Family	**3,200**	**25**	**79**	**132**	**42.0**	**48.7**	**47.2**	**endangered**
Salish NIE**	1,850	24	80	130	43.0	49.7	48.5	endangered
Shuswap	745	25	80	134	38.7	46.3	42.9	endangered
Thompson	595	31	80	135	43.1	48.6	48.3	endangered
Tsimshian Family	**2,460**	**31**	**71**	**132**	**43.2**	**48.0**	**49.6**	**mostly endangered**
Gitksan	1,200	39	76	123	41.4	45.2	45.7	viable small
Nishga	795	23	70	146	41.8	47.5	57.6	endangered
Tsimshian	465	24	83	132	50.5	55.9	52.7	endangered
Wakashan Family	**1,650**	**27**	**79**	**118**	**47.3**	**51.3**	**51.1**	**endangered**
Wakashan	1,070	24	88	129	47.7	53.0	53.2	endangered
Nootka	590	31	69	99	46.5	48.1	48.4	endangered
Iroquoian Family***	**590**	**13**	**88**	**160**	**36.4**	**46.5**	**52.0**	**uncertain**
Mohawk	350	10	100	184	36.6	46.1	60.5	uncertain
Iroquoian NIE	235	13	80	128	35.8	47.0	41.4	uncertain
Haida Isolate	**240**	**6**	**100**	**144**	**46.7**	**50.4**	**64.6**	**endangered**
Tlingit Isolate	**145**	**21**	**100**	**128**	**45.5**	**49.3**	**41.6**	**endangered**
Kutenai Isolate	**120**	**17**	**67**	**200**	**37.1**	**52.3**	**41.2**	**endangered**
Aboriginal Ln.nie	**1,405**	**28**	**68**	**176**	**43.0**	**47.0**	**45.8**	**endangered**
Total Aboriginal Languages	**208,610**	**70**	**34**	**117**	**30.4**	**31.0**	**28.3**	**mix of viable and endangered**

Source: Adapted from Norris, 1998. Statistics Canada, Census of population, 1996

* The indicators – Index of Continuity, Index of Ability and average age of Mother tongue and Home language – are based on single and multiple responses (of Mother Tongue and Home Language) combined. The Index of Continuity is a ratio of the number of persons with a given Home Language to the number of persons with that particular Mother Tongue times 100. The Index of Ability is a ratio of the number of persons reporting knowledge of a given language to the number with that particular Mother Tongue times 100.

** The viability "status" of the individual languages is based on a classification from M.Dale Kinkade's "The Decline of Native Languages in Canada" in *Endangered Languages*, edited by R.H. Robins and E.M. Uhlenbeck, Berg Publishers Limited, 1991.

*** Data for the Iroquoian family is not particularly representative due to the significant impact of incomplete enumeration of reserves for this language family. Other languages such as those in the Algonquian family may be affected to some extent by incomplete enumeration.

mother tongue populations (average ages between 22 and 24 years) and corresponding high Continuity Indexes (between 86 and 97) (Table 1). In contrast, the endangered languages such as Haida, Kutenai, and Tlingit have typically older mother tongue populations (average ages between 40 and 65) combined with extremely low Continuity Indexes of 20 or less.

In general, the population with an Aboriginal mother tongue is older than the overall Aboriginal population – seniors are much more likely to have an Aboriginal mother tongue than younger generations. In 1996, only 20 percent of children under 5 had an Aboriginal mother tongue. In comparison, 60 percent of those 85 years and over and 30 percent of those aged 40 to 44 had an Aboriginal mother tongue.

A Second Language Instead of a Mother Tongue

As noted earlier, although younger generations may not be learning their indigenous language as a mother tongue, it appears they are at least learning it as a second language, as evidenced by the Ability Index. For example, the Kutenai language family has the smallest and one of the oldest mother tongue populations, and one of the lowest Continuity Indexes, yet for every person with a Kutenai mother tongue there are two people (generally younger) who are able to speak it, suggesting that younger generations are more likely than older generations to learn Kutenai as a second language than as a mother tongue (Table 1). These patterns of second language are even more pronounced off reserve, especially among the younger generations (Norris, 1998).

Stage of Life Affects Use

Analysis of past census data (1981-96) shows that the use of an Aboriginal language at home relative to the mother tongue population is related to stages in life. For example, the decline in home language usage is significant as youth leave home and enter the labour force, marry, start families, or move to a larger urban environment, especially for women. Women are more likely than men to leave their reserves and move to other locations where the chances of marrying non-Aboriginal individuals are higher, and the exposure to the dominant language is much greater (Norris, 1998). Furthermore, linguistic intermarriage, more prevalent in larger urban populations, poses challenges to transmitting Aboriginal language as a mother tongue, especially among endangered languages that are characterized by a high degree of mixed marriages (Table 1). Children in mixed (Aboriginal-non-Aboriginal languages) marriages, however, are much less likely to have an Aboriginal mother tongue than children in marriages where both parents have an indigenous mother tongue (Norris and MacCon, 2003).

Language and Community

In 1996, practically all (99 percent) of the populations with an Aboriginal mother tongue or home language or knowledge of Aboriginal languages (98 percent), reported an Aboriginal identity. Registered Indians living on reserve comprise well over half (58 percent) of the total identity population that reported an Aboriginal mother tongue. Relatively high proportions of Registered Indians residing on reserve (52 percent) and Inuit (67 percent) reported an Aboriginal mother tongue compared to the more urbanized non-Status Indian (six percent) and Métis (eight percent) identity populations (Figure 1). (Please refer to Siggner for definitions of different Aboriginal populations.) Clearly the reserve environment of Registered Indians and the northern communities of the Inuit tend to support the maintenance and transmission of Aboriginal languages. Many of the challenges, however, confronting Aboriginal languages are exacerbated in an urban environment (RCAP, 1996: Vol. 3, pp. 614-617).

Figure 1: Percentage of Identity Population with an Aboriginal Mother Tongue by Aboriginal Group and Place of Residence, Canada, 1996

Clearly, northern communities and reserves tend to support the maintenance and transmission of Aboriginal languages. In contrast, the off-reserve environment poses major challenges to the survival of Aboriginal languages.

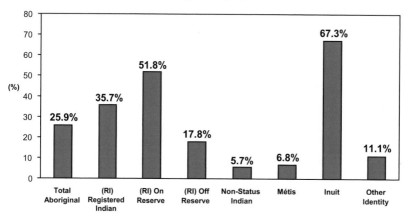

Language Demographics

In 1996, 48 percent of those reporting an Aboriginal identity resided in cities[2] throughout Canada, numbering about 382,000 people (about 21,000 of whom were living on reserves within these areas).

While city residents represent 15 and 19 percent of the populations with either an Aboriginal mother tongue or knowledge of an Aboriginal language, they represent only seven percent of the population who speak an Aboriginal language at home (Table 2). The latter statistic suggests serious problems for the intergenerational transmission of Aboriginal languages within an urban environment.

According to the 1996 Census, only nine percent of Aboriginal people in census metropolitan areas/census agglomerations (CMAs/CAs), excluding reserves, reported an Aboriginal mother tongue, compared to 26 percent of the total Aboriginal population, while 40 percent of the Aboriginal population residing outside cities reported an Aboriginal mother tongue. Although the proportion of Aboriginal people in cities reporting knowledge of an Aboriginal language is higher at 12 percent than the share with an Aboriginal mother tongue, it is still much less than half of the overall percentage of 29 percent, and significantly lower than the 43 percent of people outside cities who reported knowledge of an Aboriginal language. The greatest gap between Aboriginal populations within and outside cities is in terms of language use in the home: only three percent of Aboriginal city residents report that an Aboriginal language was used most often in the home, compared to 31 percent of the population outside of cities and 18 percent overall (Table 2).

Of course, the state of Aboriginal languages in cities contrasts even more sharply when compared to Aboriginal communities, as evidenced by low continuity in cities with only 40 persons speaking an Aboriginal language at home for every 100 persons with an Aboriginal mother tongue as compared to a ratio of 80 among the Registered Indian population on reserve. As well, people in cities who report knowledge of an Aboriginal language are much more likely to have gained it as a second language rather than as a mother tongue, as demonstrated by an Ability Index of 132 persons able to speak an Aboriginal language for every 100 with an Aboriginal mother, in contrast to an Ability Index of close to 100 among Registered Indians on reserve where practically all speakers have learned their language as their mother tongue.

Table 2: Aboriginal Identity Population by Language Counts, by Place of Residence, Canada, 1996 Census

	Canada – Total number of people (1)	On Reserve (2)		Off Reserve (3)		Cities – CMA/CAs (includes reserves within CMA/CA boundaries) (4)		Cities – CMA/CAs Adjusted (excludes reserves within CMA/CA boundaries) (5)		Population Outside CMA/CAs (includes reserves within CMA/CA boundaries) (6) = (1) - (5)	
		Total number of people	% of Canada total (2)/(1)	Total number of people	% of Canada total (3)/(1)	Total number of people	% of Canada total (4)/(1)	Total number of people	% of Canada total (5)/(1)	Total number of people	% of Canada total (6)/(1)
Total Aboriginal*	799,000	232,145	29%	88,940	43%	381,645	48%	360,600	45%	438,400	55%
Mother Tongue	207,045	118,105	57%	51,270	35%	39,600	19%	31,600	15%	175,445	85%
Home Language	145,390	94,120	65%	105,765	45%	15,200	10%	9,500	7%	135,890	93%
Knowledge	233,900	128,135	55%	105,765	45%	52,500	22%	43,400	19%	190,500	81%
% of Aboriginal Identity Population with Aboriginal Mother Tongue, Home Language or Knowledge by Residence											
Mother Tongue	26%	51%		16%		10%		9%		40%	
Home Language	18%	41%		9%		4%		3%		31%	
Knowledge	29%	55%		19%		14%		12%		43%	

* Included in the Aboriginal population are those persons who reported identifying with at least one Aboriginal group, i.e., North American Indian, Métis or Inuit (Eskimo) and/or who reported being a Treaty Indian or a Registered Indian as defined by the *Indian Act of Canada* and/or who reported they were members of an Indian Band or First Nation.

The transmission of Aboriginal languages as a mother tongue from parent to child is clearly jeopardized in an urban environment given the small share of Aboriginal persons speaking an Aboriginal language at home. About 28 percent of people aged 65 and over, residing in cities, reported an Aboriginal mother tongue compared to just over five percent of young adults (15-24). Overall, the average age of the population reporting an Aboriginal mother tongue is about 30.7 years, whereas for many cities, their Aboriginal mother tongue populations tend to be even older, especially in British Columbia where there are already many endangered languages. The average age of Aboriginal mother tongue populations in many B.C. cities is over 40, in Prairie cities it ranges from 30-35 years, while cities that have a reserve within their CMA/CA boundaries, such as Québec City, have lower average ages (Figure 2).

These figures and the fact that Aboriginal languages are being spoken relatively little in the homes of urban residents, especially among Aboriginal women in the childbearing ages, demonstrate the challenges of language maintenance within urban environments, with serious implications for the intergenerational transmission of Aboriginal languages. It also suggests that urban Aboriginal youth will not likely learn an Aboriginal language as a mother tongue, but rather as a second language. According to the 1996 Census, among urban children aged 5-14, there are 160 who have an ability to speak an Aboriginal language for every 100 with an Aboriginal mother tongue, suggesting that 60 of the 160 must have learnt it as a second language. In contrast, among children on reserve, the number reporting an ability to speak the language is closer to the number with an Aboriginal mother tongue, as indicated by an Ability Index of about 115.

Thus, the less the language is spoken at home, the less it is transmitted as a mother tongue to the younger generation. The association between low continuity and aging mother tongue populations is reflected in cities (Figure 2). For example, in Vancouver, where Aboriginal languages are spoken relatively little as a home language, as illustrated by an extremely low Continuity Index of just over 10, the average age of the population with an Aboriginal mother tongue is 45. In contrast, in Prince Albert, where a Continuity Index of close to 50 indicates that Aboriginal languages are being spoken more in the home, the average age of persons reporting an Aboriginal mother tongue is just over 30.

While the urban environment poses a challenge to Aboriginal languages in general, it should be remembered that some of the inter-city differences seen here also reflect differences in diversity and viability among the individual languages themselves. For example, Cree, which is the largest and most viable indigenous language in Canada, is the major Aboriginal language in Prince Albert, representing close to 90 percent of the mother tongue population; whereas in Vancouver, language composition is much more diverse, with several languages represented and many of which, apart from Cree and Ojibway, are considered endangered. Also, remember that some cities contain reserves within the CMA/CA boundaries, some of which represent a significant share of the CMA/CA mother tongue population.

Figure 2: Continuity Index by Average Age of Aboriginal Mother Tongue Population, for Selected CMA/CAs, Canada 1996

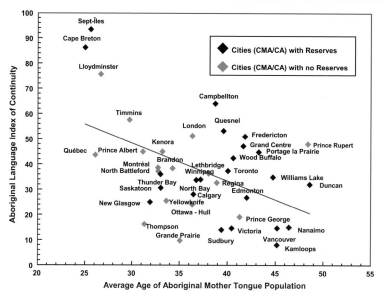

Different Rates of Urbanization

The considerable diversity and extensive distribution of Aboriginal languages throughout Canada is reflected in the country's cities. The language composition of the urban population is not proportionately representative of the country overall, given that not all Aboriginal languages are similar in their degree of urbanization. For example the share of Ojibway in urban areas is disproportionately higher, with about 26 percent of the Ojibway mother tongue population residing in urban areas, compared to 17 percent for Cree. On the other hand, while Inuktitut is the second largest mother tongue population after Cree in Canada and accounts for 13 percent of the total mother tongue population, it represents only two percent of the urban population reporting an Aboriginal mother tongue, because just under three percent of people with an Inuktitut mother tongue reside in cities.

Table 3: Aboriginal Identity Population in CMA/CAs Reporting an Aboriginal Mother Tongue*, Canada, 1996

Aboriginal Languages	Total Mother Tongue Population	Mother Tongue Population in CMA/CA	% of Total Mother Tongue in CMA/CA	CMA/CA Mother Tongue Population (excludes reserves within boundaries)	% Mother Tongue in CMA/CA (excludes reserves within boundaries)
Total Aboriginal Languages	207,050	39,545	19.1%	31,545	15.2%
Algonquian Family	**145,845**	**30,700**	**21.0%**	**24,285**	**16.7%**
Cree	87,055	15,300	17.6%	14,725	16.9%
Ojibway	25,775	7,205	28.0%	6,630	25.7%
Montagnais-Naskapi	9,065	2,230	24.6%	540	6.0%
Micmac	7,240	3,715	51.3%	460	6.4%
Oji – Cree	5,355	340	6.3%	340	6.3%
Attikamek	3,975	285	7.2%	285	7.2%
Blackfoot	4,140	970	23.4%	970	23.4%
Algonquin	2,250	220	9.8%	220	9.8%
Malecite	650	255	39.2%	115	17.7%
Algonquian NIE	340	180	52.9%	180	52.9%
Inukitut Family	**27,615**	**735**	**2.7%**	**735**	**2.7%**
Athapaskan Family	**19,925**	**3,060**	**15.4%**	**2,610**	**13.1%**
Dene	8,950	570	6.4%	570	6.4%
South Slave	2,570	205	8.0%	205	8.0%
Dogrib	2,080	270	13.0%	270	13.0%
Carrier	2,185	560	25.6%	465	21.3%
Chipewyan	1,440	950	66.0%	615	42.7%
Athapaskan, NIE	1,300	160	12.3%	155	11.9%
Chilcotin	705	255	36.2%	240	34.0%
Kutchin-Gwich'in (Loucheux)	425	55	12.9%	55	12.9%
North Slave (Hare)	270	35	13.0%	35	13.0%

(Dakota)Siouan Family	4,270	710	16.6%	495	11.6%
Salish Family	**3,190**	**1,485**	**46.6%**	**560**	**17.6%**
Salish NIE	1,850	1,050	56.8%	390	21.1%
Shuswap	740	380	51.4%	115	15.5%
Thompson	600	55	9.2%	55	9.2%
Tsimshian Family	**2,445**	**850**	**34.8%**	**800**	**32.7%**
Gitksan	1,195	285	23.8%	285	23.8%
Nishga	785	330	42.0%	325	41.4%
Tsimshian	465	235	50.5%	190	40.9%
Wakashan Family	**1,655**	**515**	**31.1%**	**440**	**26.6%**
Wakashan	1,065	235	22.1%	200	18.8%
Nootka	590	280	47.5%	240	40.7%
Iroquoian Family	**585**	**505**	**86.3%**	**505**	**86.3%**
Mohawk	355	290	81.7%	290	81.7%
Iroquoian NIE	230	215	93.5%	215	93.5%
Haida Isolate	**235**	**65**	**27.7%**	**65**	**27.7%**
Tlingit Isolate	**145**	**30**	**20.7%**	**30**	**20.7%**
Kutenai Isolate	**120**	**20**	**16.7%**	**20**	**16.7%**
Aboriginal Ln.nie	**1,255**	**870**	**69.3%**	**870**	**69.3%**

* Mother Tongue = Mother Tongue Population (Single and Multiple Responses)
NIE = not included elsewhere

Urbanization appears to pose a challenge as demonstrated in the case of Ojibway. While still viable as one of the three largest languages, it is the most urbanized and has the lowest continuity of the three (with an overall index of 55 compared to 72 for Cree). For smaller endangered languages, a higher degree of urbanization probably exacerbates an already difficult situation. Some caution must be used in interpreting the role of urbanization with respect to language maintenance and transmission. It can also vary by language, region, and situation, especially in relation to reserve communities that may be located near or within a CMA or CA (e.g., Montagnais-Naskapi).

City Profiles

Winnipeg, Edmonton, and Vancouver account for the largest share of Canada's Aboriginal identity non-reserve populations in cities, with 12 percent, eight percent, and eight percent respectively; followed by Saskatoon (four percent), Toronto (four percent) and Calgary (four percent). Regina, Ottawa-Hull, Prince Albert and Montréal are also in the top 10 cities with three percent of the total Aboriginal identity population living off reserve in cities (Figure 3).

To some extent, the cities with the largest share of the urban Aboriginal population also have the largest proportion of the urban population with an Aboriginal mother tongue. Winnipeg and Edmonton represent the highest proportions, with 14 percent and eight percent. Seven cities place in the "top 10" in terms of their mother tongue and Aboriginal identity populations: Saskatoon, Vancouver, Prince Albert, Calgary, Edmonton, Toronto, and Winnipeg. On the other hand, larger Aboriginal populations do not always correspond to larger mother tongue populations. Some urban centres with smaller Aboriginal populations have disproportionately higher shares of Aboriginal language counts, such as Thunder Bay, Thompson, and Grand Centre, which are in the "top 10" Aboriginal language cities.

Figure 3: Cities With Aboriginal Mother Tongue Population Over 200+ by Residence On and Off Reserve, 1996 Census

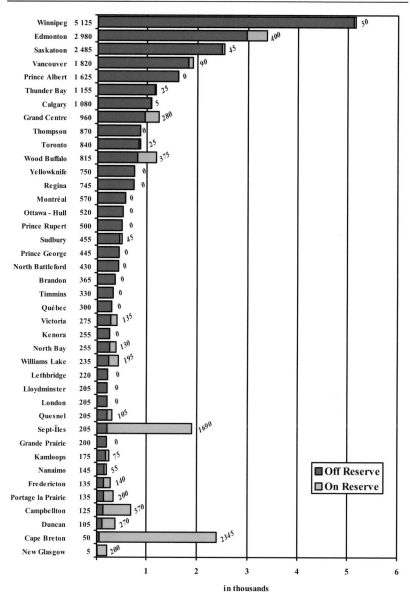

in thousands

Mother Tongue Population = Single and Multiple Responses

Specific Cities

The sheer size of the Aboriginal population within a city is important, but to provide a more complete picture of the state of Aboriginal languages, other factors must be considered: the proportion of a city's population that reported an Aboriginal identity, the proportion of the Aboriginal population that reported an Aboriginal mother tongue, home language, or knowledge of an Aboriginal language, as well as other measures of language viability, including "continuity" (language in the home), and "ability" (second language acquisition). Other demographics, such as the average age of the city's mother tongue population, the extent of linguistic diversity within the city and the presence of a reserve within or near cities are also important considerations when comparing different cities. When taken together, all these factors can give a sense of how Aboriginal languages are faring from city to city. Figure 4 profiles the linguistic diversity of the "top 7" cities in terms of the largest populations reporting an Aboriginal mother tongue, providing a distribution of these populations by different languages. (For purposes of comparison, distributions are based only on the population within CMA/CA boundaries, and exclude any reserve populations within city boundaries.)

Obviously, individual cities differ significantly from each other with respect to the state of Aboriginal languages. Ranking cities by the absolute size of the Aboriginal identity population (Figure 3) does not necessarily reflect the viability of Aboriginal languages within the city. On the other hand, a relatively high share of Aboriginal persons comprising a city's population, combined with more homogenous Aboriginal language composition, tends to co-exist with younger mother tongue populations and relatively more home speakers (i.e., greater continuity). For example, even though the population reporting an Aboriginal mother tongue in Vancouver, of some 1,900 persons, represents the fourth largest such population among Canada's cities, it does not appear to be viable, characterized as it is by an extremely low Continuity Index of just over 10 and an "old" population with an average age of 45. This may be reflective of the fact that people reporting an Aboriginal identity made up just two percent of Vancouver's population and that its population with an Aboriginal mother tongue is significantly diverse, consisting of at least 10 different languages (Figure 4). The picture is very different in Prince Albert where although the population reporting an Aboriginal mother tongue is smaller at 1,600 and ranks fifth, it exhibits the highest Continuity Index of 45 and the youngest average age at 31 years among urban populations off reserve. This suggests that among cities, Aboriginal languages are faring the best in Prince Albert, where in sharp contrast to Vancouver, a significant proportion of residents, practically one in four, report an Aboriginal identity and an extremely homogenous linguistic composition with practically 90 percent of the population with an Aboriginal mother tongue speaking Cree and the remaining 10 percent, Dene. However, even though Prince Albert paints a more positive picture than other cities, nevertheless, in all cities, the likelihood of people transmitting their Aboriginal language from one generation to another through the home is extremely low compared to the situation in Aboriginal communities, and suggests that within urban areas, the use and maintenance of Aboriginal languages must rely on support outside the home.

Figure 4: Distribution of Aboriginal Mother Tongue Population[i] Within CMA/CAs by Aboriginal Languages for Top Seven CMA/CAs, Canada, 1996

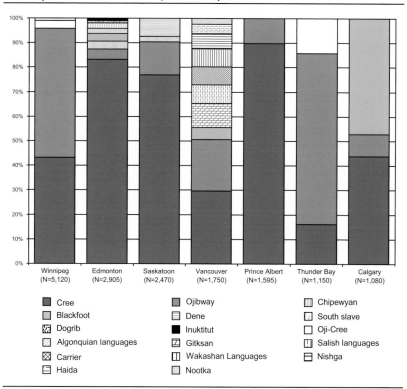

i. Reported for the population with Aboriginal Identity and excludes reserve population within CMA/CA boundaries.

Discussion And Implications

The preceding analysis demonstrates the significant presence of indigenous languages within Canada's urban areas and a resilience that persists even in the face of almost overwhelming odds. Yet at the same time, the findings suggest that urban Aboriginal people continue to be confronted with considerable challenges in maintaining that presence. This is a concern that should not be ignored given the role of identity in adapting to an urban environment.

Aboriginal identity includes a number of elements: spirituality, language, a land base or ancestral territory, elders, traditional values, family, and ceremonial life (RCAP, 1996: Vol. 4, p. 524). In urban areas, language can play an important and tangible role for Aboriginal people in contributing to developing and maintaining a strong sense of identity. In their interaction with the larger dominant cultures in cities, many Aboriginal migrants experience culture shock, alienation, confusion, perhaps racism, unemployment – experiences that raise the salience of their own identity and distinctiveness (RCAP, 1996: Vol. 4, p. 522). Some, however, successfully adapt to their urban environment by blending aspects of both cultures, whereby they maintain a strong Aboriginal identity, while integrating elements of non-Aboriginal culture (RCAP, 1996: Vol. 4, p. 524).

Challenges to Language Use in Cities

Although urban Aboriginal people may want to participate in the mainstream dominant society without undermining their own cultural identity, clearly there are obstacles. Isolation from family and home community, lack of culturally relevant resources and activities and the necessity to deal with non-Aboriginal institutions and agencies for programs and services create tensions and difficulties in maintaining Aboriginal identity in general, and even more so for Aboriginal language.

Compared to their counterparts in Aboriginal communities, Aboriginal children and youth in urban areas face significant challenges in learning and using an Aboriginal language, as our findings reflect: Aboriginal languages are not spoken the most often in urban households. Often, Aboriginal populations with an indigenous mother tongue in cities tend to be the older generations, and only a precariously small proportion (about five percent) of urban youth have an Aboriginal mother tongue. Nor do they have many opportunities to learn, study or even play with classmates in Aboriginal languages even though many want to (RCAP, 1996: Vol. 4, p. 529). For both those growing up in cities and those who are making the transition from reserve to city, the Royal Commission on Aboriginal Peoples (RCAP) recommended that youth centres be established in urban communities, and that cultural programs could be used to help develop and sustain Aboriginal identity in ways such as bringing youth and elders of the city together so that elders could share their knowledge of the language and culture. The Commission recognized that Aboriginal language immersion programs were especially important within urban settings (RCAP, 1996: Vol. 4, p. 534), given that language was not being transmitted in urban Aboriginal homes. As the findings indicate, it is the younger generation, especially outside Aboriginal communities, who are increasingly likely to learn an Aboriginal language as a second language.

Ties between City and Community

The Commission also addressed the role of community, in the context of both home community and within the city, noting that urbanization tends to include Aboriginal people making frequent returns to their home communities as part of reinforcing cultural and family ties, and maintaining a sense of group cohesion (RCAP, 1996: Vol. 4, p. 537). Often, this mobility reflects the absence of a strong sense of community in the city and the lack of access to culturally relevant institutions, programs, services, or resources.

In documenting the high mobility or "churn," characterized by high rates of movement to and from, as well as within cities, it has been noted that in the case of migration to and from cities Registered Indians experience significantly higher rates in comparison to the other more urbanized Aboriginal groups of Métis and non-Status Indians. Furthermore, it has been shown that for Registered Indians reserves are associated with this higher churn which reflects a number of elements, not only economic, but as noted earlier, frequent moves to maintain family and cultural ties with the home community (Norris and MacCon, 2003). The importance of community, social cohesion, and cultural belonging within urban settings cannot be overlooked in the implications of this churn between city and community which, while having negative implications in terms of service delivery within urban areas, may in fact contribute to an increased sense of well-being for the individual in maintaining a strong sense of cultural identity.

A study of Registered Indian migration based on data from the 1991 Aboriginal Peoples Survey (APS) revealed that family considerations, followed by housing, are the major reasons for moving to and from reserve communities and, moreover, the ability to speak an Aboriginal language increases the likelihood (more than double the rate) of migrating (likely back) to reserves. "Language ability may reflect a closer attachment to the culture and community that exists on reserve and a greater desire among this group to return to a familiar cultural and social environment." (Clatworthy, 2002a).

Also, in his study of First Nation affiliation in cities, Clatworthy (2002b) notes that those First Nations with larger urban populations experience higher rates of migration into the city with lower rates of out-migration to reserves in comparison to those First Nations with small numbers of members residing in the city. These findings suggest that the presence of a relatively large cultural community within the city may reduce the need to move back home as frequently, thereby serving to engender a sense of social cohesion, belonging, and increased cultural relevance within the city itself.[3]

Within the city, the presence of a relatively sizable Aboriginal population also seems to correspond to a healthier state of Aboriginal languages, as suggested by the findings of this study. Those cities with larger shares of Aboriginal population tend to exhibit younger populations reporting an Aboriginal mother tongue, and relatively greater use of an Aboriginal language in the home. However, some caution must be used in this interpretation, because the viability of individual languages and the linguistic diversity varies from city to city, as do other factors, such as location of and distance to reserves.

Cultural Diversity in Urban Areas

In his study of census data on the affiliation of urban Aboriginal people with First Nations, Clatworthy found considerable variation in the First Nation composition of different cities. Of the six cities studied, Edmonton was the most diverse in its composition, with the 20 largest First Nations residing in Edmonton accounting for less than one half of the city's total First Nation population. In contrast, Thunder Bay and Regina were the least heterogeneous of the cities, with each of their 20 largest First Nation populations accounting for roughly three quarters of their First Nation populations, while Winnipeg, Saskatoon, and Calgary were in between with a corresponding figure of 60 percent. These findings attest to the challenges of developing and delivering culturally and linguistically appropriate programs and services to urban Aboriginal populations.

In urban areas, significant diversity of Aboriginal cultures may also create barriers to social cohesion, community development, and cultural retention; limit opportunities for institutional and political development; and the extension of First Nations governance and administered services to urban off-reserve populations (because many of the urban First Nations often represent small minorities of their total First Nation population, most of whom are on reserves) (Clatworthy, 2002b: xiii).

In some more linguistically homogenous urban centres, the presence of one or two major languages can play a potentially unifying role in bringing different First Nations together. For example, although Edmonton has 167 different First Nations residing within its boundaries, most of this Aboriginal population shares the same Cree language. Although some of these Cree respondents may speak different dialects, this is an opportunity to enhance co-operation among nations and communities of the same language group to promote support for developing and maintaining their Aboriginal language within an urban centre, an approach similar to part of the language strategy recommended by RCAP (1996: Vol. 3, p. 618).

The demographics of Aboriginal languages also present another challenge given that it is the elderly, and perhaps to some extent students from reserves, among the urban Aboriginal population who may require and desire services the most in their own language as well as culturally and linguistically appropriate programs.

Enhancement and Support

The Commission noted that a number of initiatives supporting Aboriginal languages in urban areas have begun in cities across Canada, such as teaching languages in friendship centres, in cultural survival schools, and in child-care centres. The Commission had recommended that school boards and all levels of government support the development of Aboriginal-controlled early childhood programming delivered in Aboriginal languages (RCAP, 1996: Vol. 4, p. 534). For example, Health Canada's Head Start Program off reserve incorporates language as one of its components.

Supporting Aboriginal languages in urban areas requires an effort by many organizations and institutions to promote use and increase awareness, for both Aboriginal and non-Aboriginal populations – an important first step in revitalizing and maintaining Aboriginal languages. Cultural industries can play a significant role in increasing awareness through broadcasting and the arts. The Commission also recommended granting special status to Aboriginal languages and guaranteeing their use in public places, at least within Aboriginal communities, if not the broader community. In the sense of validating language in the larger society, status is best signalled through use in institutions, in both written and oral communications, as well as in public spaces and in many areas of daily life.

Conclusion and Postscript

To conclude, while Aboriginal languages are very much present in their distribution and diversity in urban areas throughout Canada, the results of this study suggest that Aboriginal people are confronted with many challenges in maintaining that presence. In fact, the findings attest to the concerns of the Commission surrounding the survival of Aboriginal language and culture in urban areas and at the very least, help reinforce the Commission's recommendations toward supporting and enhancing Aboriginal culture in urban areas.

Furthermore, it should be remembered that language outcomes of children are critical to the long-term survival, maintenance, and revival of Aboriginal languages, and that nowhere are these outcomes more jeopardized than in cities. In 1996, while the proportion of Aboriginal children in Canada that had an Aboriginal mother tongue was only 20 percent, it was significantly lower in cities at only five percent.

Given UNESCO's caution that a language is endangered if it is not learned by at least 30 percent of the children in that community, it becomes apparent that any prospect of increased urbanization of Aboriginal populations is worrying in that it is liable to contribute to further erosion of Aboriginal languages being spoken in the home, something that is critical for children in maintaining their language and for future generations of speakers. The findings of this study suggest that increased urbanization can only serve to accelerate the process of language erosion, such that Aboriginal languages that are currently considered viable may experience growing problems of continuity with younger generations and in the case of already endangered languages hasten their extinction which appears to be only a generation away.

Postscript 2001

While it is difficult to predict future outcomes, a preliminary analysis of more recent 2001 Census data suggests a continued erosion of Aboriginal languages and similar patterns of contrast in their viability between communities and cities. Although there appears to be relatively little change between the two censuses with the population reporting knowledge of, or ability to speak, an Aboriginal language, remaining at about 239,000, the population reporting an Aboriginal mother tongue in Canada declined from some 208,600 in 1996 to 203,900 in 2001. Such a decline attests to the impact of lessening continuity (i.e., transmission of Aboriginal languages to the younger generation), which seems to be no longer offset by still relatively high levels of Aboriginal fertility. Correspondingly, among the population reporting an Aboriginal identity, the proportion with an Aboriginal mother tongue dropped from some 26 percent in 1996 to just 20 percent in 2001 (although caution is required in comparing Aboriginal populations between censuses owing to ethnic mobility – fluidity in self-identity, see Guimond). In any case these figures would also imply similar declines among Aboriginal children.

In the case of home language use, intercensal comparisons are not straightforward, since in 2001 a second part to the home language question was introduced. Information was given for languages spoken "most often" at home and for languages spoken "regularly" at home. Overall, in 2001 about 129,300 respondents reported speaking an Aboriginal language "most often" in the home (which while not directly comparable to 1996 is a drop from the 145,000 persons in 1996 who reported speaking an Aboriginal language "most often" at home) and in some ways is consistent with the long-term decline in speaking Aboriginal languages at home. However, more encouraging is that an additional 52,000 respondents indicated using an Aboriginal language "regularly" at home.

This additional element provides new insight into the use of Aboriginal languages within the home, especially in the contrasting patterns between Aboriginal communities and cities. Among the population residing on reserves who report using an Aboriginal language at home, 75 percent speak an Aboriginal language "most often"; the other 25 percent use an Aboriginal language on a "regular" basis. In contrast, the pattern is practically reversed in cities outside of reserves, where only 41 percent of respondents who report home use speak an Aboriginal language "most often," while the majority (59 percent) speak an Aboriginal language on a "regular" basis.

From the viewpoint that it is difficult to maintain use of an Aboriginal language at home especially in urban areas, these findings that people are at least using an Aboriginal language on a "regular" basis are encouraging. On the other hand, it seems that the language used "most often" at home would still most likely be the one transmitted to the next generation (although further analysis of these data is necessary and advised to understand the impact of "regular" use). To some extent, similar comparisons are mirrored in the individual languages. For example, the vast majority (82 percent) of people speaking Inuktitut at home report it as their language spoken "most often," whereas among the more urbanized Cree and Ojibway, these languages are reported as spoken "most often" among 69 and 56 percent of home users respectively; and in the case of endangered languages, only a minority of home language users report their language as spoken "most often" (e.g., Haida at only 10 percent).

From the perspective of intergenerational transmission, measures of continuity based on language used "most often" at home, as well as ability, imply patterns for 2001 similar to those already identified in this study for 1996. Continuity, while generally lower than 1996 (to the extent that it is comparable) remains significantly higher on reserves, with an estimated index of 70 in 2001, compared to just 27 for urban populations off reserve. Similarly, persons residing in these urban areas are more likely to learn an Aboriginal language as a second language compared to persons residing on reserves, as evidenced by Ability Indexes of 135 and 113 respectively. In the case of individual languages, comparisons are analogous to those observed in 1996. For example, in 2001 the Continuity Index for the more viable Inuktitut language is estimated at 82, compared to lower indexes of 62 and 45 for Cree and Ojibway respectively, and only 6 for the endangered Haida language. The Ability Indexes for these languages, while generally higher are also like their 1996 patterns in 2001 with respective values of 110, 121, 130, and 172. This brief analysis would suggest if anything, continuing declines in the intergenerational transmission of Aboriginal languages as a mother tongue, accompanied by a growing likelihood that Aboriginal languages will increasingly be learnt as second languages.

While further analyses of 2001 data are required, a preliminary assessment suggests a continuation of trends and similar implications and issues as identified in this study concerning the challenges confronting the survival and maintenance of Aboriginal languages within Canada's urban areas.

Notes

1   The views expressed in this paper are those of the authors and do not necessarily represent the views of Indian and Northern Affairs Canada (INAC) or of Canadian Heritage. The authors would like to acknowledge with thanks technical support provided by Lucette Dell'Oso of the Research and Analysis Directorate, INAC and Gerry Ouellette of Statistics Canada.

2   The term "cities" is used interchangeably with census metropolitan area (CMA) and census agglomeration (CA). A CMA is a very large urban area, including urban and rural fringes and reserves, with an urban core population of at least 100,000. A CA is a large urban area, including urban and rural fringes and reserves, with an urban core population of at least 10,000. In this analysis, the presence of reserves is controlled for – any reserves in urban areas are excluded in comparisons across "cities."

3   It has been proposed that high mobility or churn is thought to lead to weaker social cohesion in communities and neighbourhoods, with potentially negative implications for the development of strong urban Aboriginal community institutions.

References

Clatworthy, S.J. (2002a) *Registered Indian Migration between On- and Off- Reserve Locations*, 1986-1996: Summary and Implications, Report prepared by Four Directions Project Consultants for Research and Analysis Directorate, Indian and Northern Affairs Canada.

—— (2002b) *First Nation Affiliation Among Registered Indians Residing in Select Urban Areas*, Report prepared by Four Directions Project Consultants for Research and Analysis Directorate, Indian and Northern Affairs Canada.

Grubb, David McC. (1979) "Languages of British Columbia," in *The Languages of Canada*, J.K. Chambers, (ed.), Didier, Canada.

Harrison, B.R. (1997) "Languages Integration: Results of an Intergenerational Analysis," *Statistical Journal of the United Nations ECE*, 14: 289-303.

Kinkade, M.D. (1991) "The Decline of Native Languages in Canada," in *Endangered Languages*, Robert H. Robins and Eugenius M. Uhlenbeck, (eds.), published with the authority of the Permanent International Committee of Linguists (CIPL), Berg.

Norris, M.J. (1998) "Canada's Aboriginal Languages," *Canadian Social Trends*, 51 (Winter), Statistics Canada, Cat. No. 11-008.

—— (2000) "Aboriginal Peoples in Canada: Demographic and Linguistic Perspectives," in *Visions of the Heart: Canadian Aboriginal Issues*, D.A. Long and O.P. Dickason, (eds.), second edition, Toronto: Harcourt Brace Canada.

Norris, M.J., and K. MacCon (2003) "Aboriginal Language Transmission and Maintenance in Families: Results of an Intergenerational and Gender-Based Analysis for Canada, 1996," in *Aboriginal Conditions: The Research Foundations of Public Policy*, Jerry White, Paul Maxim, and Dan Beavon, (eds), Vancouver: UBC Press.

Norris, M.J., D. Beavon, E. Guimond, and M. Cooke (2002) *Registered Indian Mobility and Migration: An Analysis of 1996 Census Data*, Indian and Northern Affairs Canada.

Ponting, J.R. (1997) *First Nations in Canada, Perspectives on Opportunity, Empowerment, and Self-Determination*, Toronto: McGraw-Hill Ryerson Limited.

Priest, G.E. (1983) *Aboriginal Languages in Canada, Statistics Canada*, Housing, Family and Social Characteristics Division.

RCAP (Report of the Royal Commission on Aboriginal Peoples) (1996) Volume 3, Gathering Strength and Volume 4, *Perspectives and Realities*, Minister of Supply and Services Canada.

Tait, Heather (2000) "Aboriginal Women," in *Women in Canada*, Statistics Canada, Cat. No. 89-503, XPE. pp. 253-254.

UNESCO (1996) *Atlas of the World's Languages in Danger of Disappearing* Stephen A.Wurm, (ed), Paris, Canberra: UNESCO Publishing and Pacific Linguistics.

The Challenge of Measuring the Demographic and Socio-Economic Conditions of the Urban Aboriginal Population

Andrew J. Siggner
Housing, Family & Statistics Division
Statistics Canada

This article will focus on the Aboriginal population living in urban areas and examine a series of demographic and socio-economic characteristics of the Aboriginal and non-Aboriginal populations. However, one of the first questions for policy-makers, planners, and researchers is to determine, from a statistical or analytical perspective, how Aboriginal peoples are defined. There are macro-historical, sociological, and legal events, which are affecting the demographic size and growth of the Aboriginal population, making it even more challenging to understand why socio-economic patterns are changing. The traditional demographic components of growth, namely, fertility, mortality, and migration, are not the only factors affecting the population.

Another phenomenon has been occurring in recent years, which is also affecting the size and growth of the Aboriginal population. This phenomenon, which we have dubbed the "ethnic mobility" factor of growth, is defined in terms of people changing their ethnic or cultural affiliations on the census form, from one census to the next. There are various Aboriginal concepts used in the census and the ethnic mobility factor can affect the counts according to these different concepts. Furthermore, significant differences can occur in the socio-economic characteristics of a given Aboriginal population, depending on which Aboriginal definition is used. Philip Kreager is right when he states:

> For members of a given collectivity, from the family to the state, deciding who is and who is not included in the group generally determines its capacities. The estimated capacities of one group in comparison with others have a direct bearing on courses of action for all collectivities that may be implicated.

The fact that people may report their ethnic, religious and other identities differently from one census to the next...to suit preferred statuses, is significant not only as a potential source of bias affecting the analysis of trends, but as evidence of active adjustment of population composition and structure to changing circumstances.[1]

This phenomenon has actually been occurring in Canada, as measured by our census, for at least two decades. The Aboriginal population has been growing so fast that the usual demographic growth factors, namely fertility, mortality, and net migration cannot explain the rapid growth in this population. The bulk of this rapid growth has occurred in urban areas, and in particular east of the Manitoba/Ontario border. Furthermore, the extent of the growth varies according to which definition of the Aboriginal population is chosen. Guimond also found the most rapid growth in the Aboriginal origin-based population to have occurred between 1986 and 1991.[2] He attributes this growth to more than the impact of natural increase (the difference of births and deaths). In fact, the growth is assumed to be coming from "ethnic mobility" (i.e., from those who changed their ethnic affiliation between censuses).[3]

Why has this occurred? It is likely due to an important legislative amendment to the *Indian Act* in 1985 (Bill C-31), where former Status Indian women who married men without legal Indian status (and their children) were allowed to regain their legal Indian status. In 1991, almost 70 percent were living in urban areas. This change in the *Indian Act* led to an increase in the total Status Indian population in the 1985-91 period of over 80,000 people, while many more than that who were ineligible to regain Indian status applied for reinstatement. The change in the *Indian Act* likely induced a large number of people, who may not have even been reporting themselves as North American Indian in the census, to do so following the amendment. Interestingly, the North American Indian growth rate between 1991 and 1996 slowed down considerably compared to the 1986-91 period. This was likely due to the bulk of "C-31s" having applied in the earlier period. What this does suggest is that public policy and legislation can have significant demographic impacts on the size and growth of the population.

The Indian population is not the only Aboriginal population affected by this rapid growth phenomenon. Between 1991 and 1996, the Métis population had the most growth among the three Aboriginal groups, with an average annual growth rate of 6.7 percent per year (see Table 1).[4] In this five-year period, there were important political and legal milestones for the Métis. Métis received significant recognition in the final report of the

Royal Commission on Aboriginal Peoples (1996). Discussion of a Métis enumeration process during the Charlottetown constitutional process (1992), which was one of the most significant political and jurisdictional issues affecting the Métis, also raised awareness of Métis issues. In more recent years, the Métis have won important lower court hunting rights cases and greater land rights recognition in provinces like Saskatchewan. As most Métis live in urban areas, the ethnic mobility factor may tend to affect the size of the Métis in urban areas more so than in rural areas. Indeed, this has already been observed in the 1996 Census. It remains to be seen what further demographic impact these other events will have on the growth of the Métis in the most recent 2001 Census. The 2001 Census results for the Aboriginal populations were released in January 2003 (see Update).

Table 1: Growth Rates for the Aboriginal Origin and Aboriginal Identity Populations, Canada, 1986-96

Aboriginal Origin, Aboriginal Identity, Aboriginal Group	Average Annual Growth Rate 1986-1991 (%)	Average Annual Growth Rate 1991-1996 (%)
Aboriginal Origin (total)	7.0	1.9
• Aboriginal Identity (total)	6.6	2.3
- North American Indian	7.1	0.9
- Métis	5.1	6.7
- Inuit	3.4	2.3
• No Aboriginal Identity	7.8	1.2

Note: Rates adjusted for incompletely enumerate Indian reserves in all three censuses.

Source: 1986, 1991 and 1996 Census, taken from Guimond, E. (1999) "Ethnic Mobility and the Demographic Growth of Canada's Aboriginal Populations from 1986 to 1996," in *Current Demographic Trends*, Ottawa: Statistics Canada December, p. 190.

Population Size and Distribution

Because of the limitations on the length of this article, only two major definitions of Aboriginal peoples are explored from the census for the remainder of this study: those with Aboriginal origin and those reporting an Aboriginal identity.[5] The size and percentage share of the Aboriginal origin population residing in urban areas was about 625,000 (or 55 percent), while the Aboriginal identity population, was 395,000 (or 47 percent) (Figure 1).[6] Why the difference? It is because within the Aboriginal origin population, there is a group who report on their 1996 Census questionnaire that they have an Aboriginal origin, but do not self-identify as an Aboriginal person, and they are much more urban than their Aboriginal identity group counterparts. In fact, this former group shows almost the same percentage residing in urban areas (75 percent) as the non-Aboriginal population (78 percent) (see Figure 1).

Figure 1: Per Cent of Population by Various Aboriginal Definitions, Residing On-Reserve, or in Urban & Rural Residence, Canada, 1996

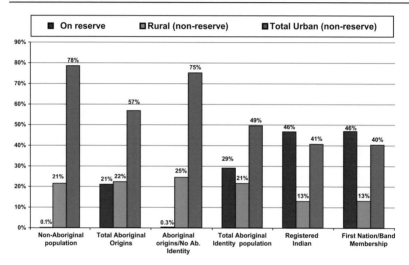

Within all urban areas, 61 percent of the Aboriginal origin-based population lives in larger urban areas or census metropolitan areas (CMAs), and 39 percent are in smaller urban non-CMAs.[7] The equivalent data for the Aboriginal identity population is 56 percent in urban CMAs and 44 percent in urban non-CMAs. Thus, based on the definition of the Aboriginal population used, the distribution within urban areas varies. Of course, there are differences in these distributions across Canada. In the Prairies, for example, there is not much difference in the geographic distributions between the Aboriginal origin and identity-based populations, because there is not much difference in two counts according to the two definitions of Aboriginal population. East of Manitoba, the geographic differences are greater partially due to the difference in the size of the Aboriginal-origin based population which is 40 percent larger than the Aboriginal identity population. In Montréal and Toronto, for example, among those reporting an Aboriginal origin, only 18 percent and 35 percent, respectively, also said they self-identified as an Aboriginal person. In contrast, 86 percent and 83 percent of the Aboriginal origin population in Regina and Saskatoon said they self-identified as an Aboriginal person (see figures 2a and 2b).

Figure 2a: Aboriginal Origin & Aboriginal Identity Populations for Selected CMAs, 1996

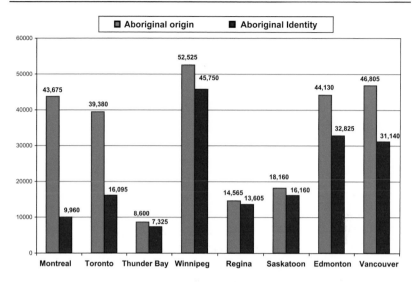

Figure 2b: Total Aboriginal Origin Population Who Self-Identify Those Who Do Not, Selected CMAs, 1996

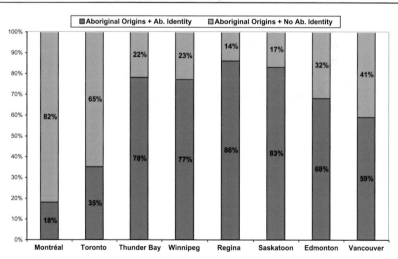

Other Socio-Economic Characteristics

Let us look at the characteristics of the urban Aboriginal populations using both the origin and identity-based definitions of "Aboriginality." The remainder of the analysis will group the Aboriginal population into those living in all urban areas, and present the data for selected regions. Ontario is chosen as an example of an eastern region with a much higher share of people reporting an Aboriginal origin compared to those reporting an Aboriginal identity. The remaining provinces have lesser degrees of difference in their respective origin and identity counts.

Female Lone Parents

The first variable we examine is the percentage of persons in families who are female lone parents. From Figure 3, overall, more than one in five persons in families[8] with Aboriginal identity are female lone parents in urban areas. There are sharp differences by region. For example, in Saskatchewan the percentage is 27 percent female lone parents compared to only 19 percent in Ontario, using the Aboriginal identity definition. However, compared to the non-Aboriginal population in urban areas throughout Canada, the percentage of female lone parents is seven percent, or three times smaller than their Aboriginal counterparts.

The gap between the percentage of female lone parents using the Aboriginal identity definition compared to the origin definition is not as great as with other characteristics, as we will see. Interestingly, the number of Aboriginal women far exceeds the number of men using both Aboriginal definitions. The Aboriginal identity population does make up a significant portion of the Aboriginal origin population and more women than men using the Aboriginal identity definition live in urban areas. The question is, do the women who have an Aboriginal origin, but report no Aboriginal identity in the census, outnumber the men in the same situation? The answer is, yes. There were 138 such women for every 100 men in urban areas in 1996. While the percentage of female lone parents in this group is about one third lower compared to the Aboriginal origin population, as a whole, their share is still nearly double that of the non-Aboriginal population. Is understanding the above-noted phenomena an important research question from a policy and planning perspective? It could be if it helps to explain why the Aboriginal origin and identity populations are growing so much faster than would be expected from natural increase (the difference between births and deaths). For example, are Aboriginal women out-marrying more than Aboriginal men and thus tending to lose their Aboriginal identity or at least report it less in the census? Is there a relationship between the loss of their Aboriginal identity and their duration of marriage/partnership with their non-Aboriginal spouse? Is this group one which would tend to declare an Aboriginal identity in the future, especially if they are separated or divorced from their non-Aboriginal spouse? In other words, is this group of women, in particular, part of the reason why the Aboriginal population has been growing so rapidly in recent years?

Figure 3: Female Lone-Parents as a Per Cent of All Persons in Families by Aboriginal Identity and Origin, in Urban Areas, Canada & Regions, 1996

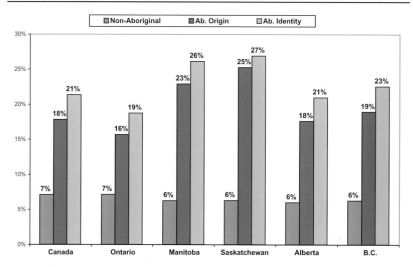

Highest Level of Schooling

One key issue facing Aboriginal peoples especially in relation to economic development and self-governance is their preparation for participation in the so-called "knowledge economy." The data on educational achievement points to some serious gaps between the non-Aboriginal population and the Aboriginal population, using both definitions of Aboriginality.

In 1996, the percentage of the Aboriginal population aged 15 years and over, with a university degree (nine percent) living in urban areas, using the origin definition, was half the non-Aboriginal population's (18 percent), and two thirds smaller using the Aboriginal identity definition (six percent) (see Figure 4). Although there has been much discussion in the media about the lack of education among the Saskatchewan Aboriginal population (eight percent), the gap with their non-Aboriginal counterparts is not as great as in other provinces, and their percentage is actually slightly better than the Aboriginal urban populations in the three other western provinces.

Figure 4: Population Aged 15+, with University Degree by Origin & Identity, in Urban Areas, Canada & Regions, 1996

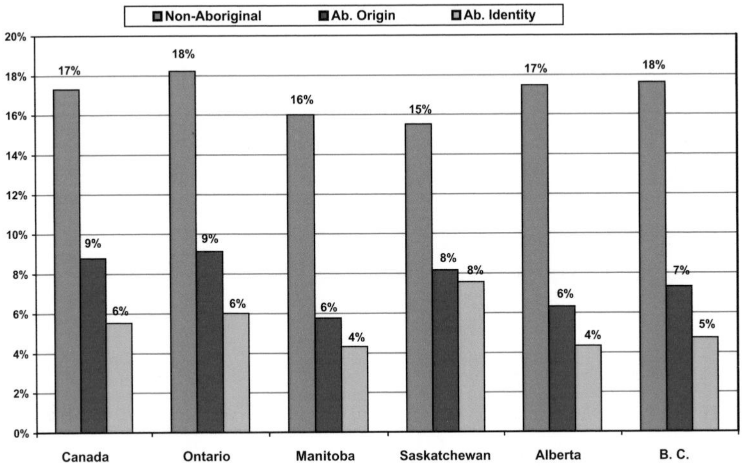

It is important to note, however, that level of education has been improving in the Aboriginal origin and identity population in recent years. Nevertheless, part of this improvement has stemmed from a portion of the population, who already have high levels of education, changing their ethnic affiliation. It is not easy with available statistical data to discern how much is due to real gains in education and how much to a more well-educated population now declaring their Aboriginality, either in terms of origin or identity. In an earlier study by the author, which examined the growth of those with a university degree for the age cohort 25+ years old in 1986 to age 35+ in 1996, it was found that:

> ...the [average annual] growth [rate]in the cohort with a university degree was nearly 9 percent per year for the Aboriginal identity population, compared to the 1 percent per year average in the total population of Canada. Thus, even if we allowed that half of the growth in...the Aboriginal identity cohort with a university degree was due to improved levels of educational attainment within this cohort, it would still leave the other half of the growth due to "ethnic mobility" into the Aboriginal population by those with already high levels of schooling.[9]

Labour Force

Part and parcel with the preparedness of the Aboriginal population for the labour force is their actual participation in it. The data from Figure 5 demonstrate that for the Aboriginal identity population aged 15 and over, less than half the population (48 percent) is working in urban areas. This contrasts with a much higher 55 percent among those reporting Aboriginal origins, which, in turn, is closer to their non-Aboriginal counterparts at 59 percent. In Ontario, the employment ratio is much closer between the Aboriginal origin population and Non-Aboriginal population, while in Manitoba and Saskatchewan, the ratios are much closer between the Aboriginal origin and Aboriginal identity populations. The reader will recall, that the counts among those reporting Aboriginal origins and Aboriginal identity are closer to begin with in these two provinces. It is on this economic indicator that the higher employment ratio among those persons reporting an Aboriginal origin but no Aboriginal identity is observed on the overall Aboriginal origin population (which includes both this population and the Aboriginal identity population).

Figure 5: Employment: Population Ratio for Age 15+, by Origin & Identity, in Urban Areas, Canada & Regions, 1996

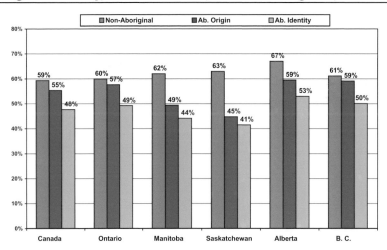

This is one of the main points of the article, namely that policy makers and planners need to be very cautious of who their target population is when assessing Aboriginal economic conditions, as very misleading indicators result, depending on the Aboriginal definition chosen.

The Urban Poor

The last economic indicator to be examined is the measure known as the low income cut-off (LICO). The LICO measures a household's ability to maintain a basic standard of living, allowing it to meet its shelter, food, and other costs in relation to the income received. Using the Aboriginal identity definition, overall in Canada, nearly half (47 percent) of the urban Aboriginal population lives below the LICO. This percentage is much lower using the Aboriginal origin definition (39 percent), in contrast to 21 percent among the non-Aboriginal population (see Figure 6). The percentage below the LICO varies hugely across regions, with the worst situation in urban Manitoba and Saskatchewan, no matter which Aboriginal definition is used. In both provinces, over half the Aboriginal population is living below the LICO, around three times the percentage for the non-Aboriginal urban populations. Urban Ontario shows the lowest rate relative to the other regions. Here the influence of the Aboriginal origin population reporting no Aboriginal identity is affecting the lower rates because they tend to be better off than their Aboriginal identity counterparts and represent an overall much larger share of the total Aboriginal origin population, in comparison to the other selected regions.

Figure 6: Percentage of the Population below the Low Income Cut-Off, by Origin & Identity, in Urban Areas, Canada & Regions, 1996

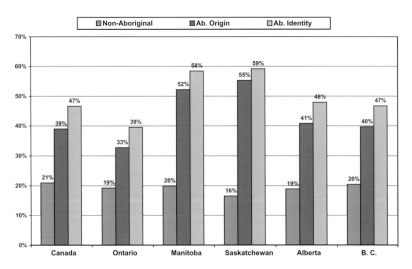

Conclusion

This article has used two broad definitions of Aboriginality contained in the 1996 Census to demonstrate the importance for policy-makers, planners, and other decision makers of picking their definitions of the Aboriginal population carefully, when undertaking their analyses. There are, in fact, four concepts altogether in the census. The other two, which are not explored here, include Registered Indian status and Indian Band/First Nation membership. While the article does not explore differences among Aboriginal groups such as the Métis, Indians without legal Indian status, or the Inuit, data for these other Aboriginal groups can be obtained from the census. This analysis has focused on the urban Aboriginal situation relative to the urban non-Aboriginal situation, rather than comparing the former to the Indian reserve and rural non-reserve conditions. The latter type of analysis may be relevant for assessing overall need among Aboriginal groups throughout Canada. The intent, here, is to give the reader an appreciation of Aboriginal conditions broadly across all urban areas in Canada and of the importance of the definition chosen to measure those differences, especially if the focus is a "needs-based" one, rather than a "rights-based" analysis. It would appear that the Aboriginal identity definition is a better basis for measuring the socio-economic conditions of Aboriginal people in urban areas, especially east of Manitoba and west of Saskatchewan. We found that there are not huge differences in socio-economic conditions in these two Prairie provinces using either the Aboriginal origin or identity definitions. This is because, for a variety of reasons, the total counts of the origin-based and identity-based Aboriginal populations in these two provinces are quite close.

Overall, in urban areas, Aboriginal peoples' conditions lag behind those of the non-Aboriginal population, usually by two to three times on the selected indicators, with the exception of the employment ratio where the gap is not as great. Of course, the real measure is how these conditions have changed over time. Starting in January 2003 and continuing throughout that year and the next, data from both the 2001 Census and the 2001 Aboriginal Peoples Survey will be released. These two new sources of information should shed considerably more light on current urban conditions and allow for greater historical comparisons.

Notes

1   Kreager, P. (1997) "Population and Identity," in *Anthropological Demography: Toward a New Synthesis*, D. Kertzer and T. Fricke, (eds.), Chicago: University of Chicago Press, p. 148.

2   Guimond, E. (1999) "Ethnic Mobility and the Demographic Growth of Canada's Aboriginal Populations from 1986 to 1996," *Current Demographic Trends*, Ottawa: Statistics Canada, December, pp.190-191.

3   Ibid., pp. 198-199.

4   Ibid., p. 190.

5   The Aboriginal identity population is largely a subset of the Aboriginal origin population. However, there were about 67,000 people who reported no Aboriginal origins, yet stated they had an Aboriginal identity or were legal Status Indians. These people have been added to the Aboriginal identity population.

6   The total Aboriginal origin and Aboriginal identity populations have been adjusted to include an estimated 44,000 living on Indian reserves, which were incompletely enumerated in 1996.

7   Urban CMAs are large urban areas with 100,000 or more population, while urban non-CMAs are those under 100,000 with a minimum population density of 400 persons per square kilometre.

8   All persons in families include husbands, wives, common-law partners and lone parents, but excludes children.

9   Siggner, Andrew J. (2000) "Impact of Ethnic Mobility on Socio-Economic Conditions of Aboriginal Peoples," Presented at the Canadian Population Society Annual Meetings at the University of Alberta, Edmonton, June.

The Marginalization of Aboriginal Women in Montréal

Mylène Jaccoud
Renée Brassard
Centre international de criminologie comparée
Université de Montréal

Introduction

Urbanization, high demographic growth, and precarious living conditions characterize the socio-economic and demographic conditions of Canada's First Nations. In Canada, the migration of Aboriginal people to urban centres began at the end of the 1960s. While this phenomenon emerged somewhat later in Quebec, it is no less real. According to the 2001 Census, Montréal has an Aboriginal identity population of 11,085, including 5,755 women. Officially, Aboriginal residents only represent 0.3 percent of the Montréal population. In 1996, 9,960 people identified as Aboriginal, including 5,185 women. Aboriginal organizations argue, however, that this is a serious underestimate: Partenariat Mikimon[1] estimates that the number is somewhere between 25,000 and 30,000.

In general, very little is known about the migratory experience of Aboriginal people living in urban centres, particularly the experiences of women. The earliest Canadian studies on the urbanization of Aboriginal people date back to the 1970s. Researchers at that time focused on what was viewed as the problems Aboriginal people experienced in adapting to living in western Canadian cities. These studies reduced these problems to issues of poverty, criminality, and alcoholism.[2] In the 1980s, the research focus shifted to living conditions, in an effort to identify the needs and adaptation strategies of this population.[3] Research in Quebec tended to follow these trends, highlighting living conditions and the needs of Aboriginal women in urban areas.[4] Only one study used life trajectories to examine urban migration, in this instance of Algonquin and Métis men and women migrating to the city of Val d'Or, a small Abitibi community located in central-western Quebec.[5] This chapter aims to understand the role of urbanization in the life trajectories of Aboriginal women, particularly those living in very precarious circumstances.

Marginalization and Exclusion

The growth of poverty that has characterized Western societies over the last 20 years has led to the emergence of the concept of exclusion/marginalization. This notion is used to describe the relative absence of certain social groups from the labour market and, more generally, from participation in society's core institutions. Exclusion and marginalization are, therefore, one aspect of social isolation, poverty, and economic insecurity. The literature also speaks in terms of rupture, distancing, marginality, social disqualification, and disintegration. The most common factor in social exclusion is economic in nature. Socio-economic data on Aboriginal people in Canada and Quebec confirm their disadvantaged position with respect to the Canadian population in general, despite recent socio-economic indicators that show an improvement in their living conditions. In 1996, the unemployment rate among Registered Indians was 27.2 percent, compared to 10 percent for the Canadian population in general. The average household income also remained inferior. In 1995, the average income was $25,602 for Registered Indians and $41,898 for the general Canadian population. The percentage of families with an income equal to or less than the low-income threshold was 41 percent for Registered Indians and 16.5 percent for Canadian households. Life expectancy among Registered Indians was also below that of the general Canadian population with a recorded 6.6-year gap. (In 1996, life expectancy for Registered Indians was 72 years and 78.6 for the Canadian population.) Infant mortality rates are close to two times higher, while suicide rates are three times greater within the Aboriginal population. The rate of violent deaths, victimizations, criminalization, and incarceration are proportionately higher among Aboriginal people than non-Aboriginal people.[6]

Economic indicators, however, are not the only criteria for defining exclusion and marginalization. The 1876 *Indian Act* has contributed to instituting borders within the borders of the nation state and, as a result, has confined and reduced the First Nations to the margins of state structures. This reduction has had political, economic, and social repercussions as well as an impact on identity. La Prairie's (1989) socio-structural model is certainly one of the most elaborate in its attempt to explain how this reduction has contributed to the psychosocial and economic disintegration of Aboriginal communities. According to La Prairie, colonization contributed to displacing Aboriginal people from productive to less fertile lands, maintaining Aboriginal communities in a state of underdevelopment. La Prairie believes that socio-economic transformations have altered the structure of traditional roles. In the traditional economy, the family constituted the main unit of production and consumption, a unit in which women and men played distinct functions and roles. Colonization destabilized the traditional male function of provider, while largely preserving women's roles within the family. This transformation led to tension and frustration, and led directly to family and conjugal violence. In fact, it is argued that women's efforts to escape the violence in Aboriginal communities is one of the main reasons for their overrepresentation in the migratory phenomenon.

On a macro-sociological level, the marginalization of Aboriginal people is explained not by a distancing from the centre but, to the contrary, an incorporation into the nation state. This incorporation is the result of a policy of internal reduction and segregation that made possible the expropriation of lands to which the First Nations were linked both materially and symbolically. The exclusion of Aboriginal peoples therefore does not involve a rupture from centre, but rather a rupture from historicity and Aboriginal processes of production and social reproduction. Instead, they experienced incorporation through spatial reduction, leading to limited or no access to the land's resources. In addition, exclusion and marginalization are understood as a process rather than a state – a dynamic and multi-dimensional process that is articulated around socio-economic, psychosocial (disintegration of the relational fabric), and symbolic (system of collective standards and representations out of which individual and collective identities are forged) dimensions.[7] Since structures and actors are inseparable, exclusion and marginalization must be understood as the product of the interaction between players and systems.

When all is said and done, the marginalization of Aboriginal people has been characterized largely in macro-sociological and historical terms. The theoretical works which we have briefly outlined yield identification markers for marginalization (economic, psychosocial, and symbolic) and a theoretical framework (particularly the dynamic character of the components of marginalization), but they do not portray clearly the microsocial dynamics which are at work. The qualitative approach, particularly the analysis of the life stories of the participants, are precious tools when attempting to reconstruct the life trajectories of the actors, because they mark key events and their impact, and thus allow a better rebuilding of those processes as well as a better understanding of the development of marginalization.

The Marginalization of Aboriginal Women in Montréal: A Case Study[8]

We analyzed the life trajectories of 10 Aboriginal respondents living in conditions that fall within the theoretical framework of exclusion and marginalization.[9] We contacted our respondents through Aboriginal community organizations, who partnered with us for this research, and non-Aboriginal resources in the Montréal area. We also directly solicited Aboriginal women who did not use official assistance resources by visiting certain parks, streets, metro entrances, and other areas in Montréal. The population studied was broken down on the basis of general criteria, such as age, civil status, religion, number of dependent children, First Nation of origin, and the period of time spent in Montréal.

Since our study focuses on the process of exclusion and marginalization experienced by Aboriginal women who have temporarily or permanently migrated to Montréal, we favoured a life narratives methodology.

Reconstructing our respondents' life narratives involved two to four interviews of one to two hours each. During these meetings, we encouraged our respondents to recount different stages of their lives: their life experience in their communities of origin, their departure from their communities, their various moves, their arrival in Montréal, and their movements since their arrival in Montréal. Our objective has been to trace chronologically the urban movements of Aboriginal women by collecting information on locations, spaces (health, work, housing, leisure, etc.), key events, processes, actions, barriers and difficulties, strategies employed to deal with difficulties, the role of various players and institutions to which these women tend to gravitate, and the reasons and factors that prompted these women to migrate to the city in the first place. In short, we were seeking a better understanding of the conditions and factors that brought these women to Montréal and to identify the place and role of Montréal in this journey. What are their living conditions in Montréal? How are their lives organized? Does life in an urban setting maintain, reinforce, or attenuate their living conditions?

The Respondents' Profiles

The majority of the 10 respondents were North American Indian (eight); while two were Inuit.[10] Study participants came from many different nations.[11] With the exception of one, all the respondents came from remote communities. Three respondents came from other provinces or territories

(Alberta, British Columbia, and Nunavut). At the time of the interviews, the majority of respondents were over 30 years of age (four were between 40 and 49; five were between 30 and 39). One respondent was 19.

Living Conditions in the Communities of Origin

Over half the respondents came from families in which both parents are Aboriginal (%). Although it was not always possible to identify clearly the socio-economic status of the parents, we were able to establish that one parent was generally the breadwinner, usually the father, while the mother did not tend to have paid work (homemaker). Most of the fathers worked as labourers (in factories, construction). With the exception of two respondents, all experienced conjugal violence in their homes, conflict between their parents, or a difficult relationship with one of their parents. Close to one half (%) of the respondents had personal experiences with alcoholism, with their father, mother, both parents, or a caregiver. In addition to family context, other situations (separation of parents, deterioration of economic conditions following the death of a spouse, criminal activity, etc.) led to the removal of close to half of our respondents from their homes for placement with members of their extended family (grandparents, sisters, brothers), foster families, or formal institutions such as rehabilitation centres. Whatever the arrangement, these women experienced separation from their birth parents for more or less extended periods of time during their childhood or adolescence. The general portrait of their living conditions in their communities of origin highlights the precariousness and fragile living conditions facing Aboriginal women.

Living Conditions at the Time of the Interviews

At the time of our interviews, the majority (60 percent) of our respondents were in a marital relationship, while three respondents were single and one was a widow. Of those in a marital relationship, four lived with their spouses. All the Aboriginal women we interviewed, except two, had between two and six children. Six of these had children placed by the Direction de la protection de la jeunesse (DPJ – youth protection services). Despite a number of attempts and strategies employed by the respondents to reclaim their children, none had succeeded in obtaining legal guardianship at the time of the interviews.

Data collected on socio-economic conditions revealed that a large majority of the respondents were receiving income security payments (%). Only one had a private income, while another worked as a translator. Three respondents had health problems, namely diabetes, anemia, and HIV. While most of the women we interviewed had been dependent on drugs and alcohol at some time in their lives, only three stated that they were still dependent. In terms of housing, half the women lived in an apartment or house, while the other half lived in women's shelters.[12] As for reliance on community resources, half the respondents had never or rarely relied on this form of assistance, while the other half regularly used these resources. The over-use of these resources was so pronounced in some cases that it was impossible for us to determine how often a respondent turned to these resources over the course of her trajectory. Note that the respondents who relied heavily on community resources tended to be those who for the most part had not managed to build an informal network in Montréal, thereby turning to an institutional network in its place.

Comparison between Initial and Present Conditions

Given the uneven quality of the information gathered, it is difficult to compare the conditions our respondents left behind in their communities of origin to those at the time of the interviews.[13] We were nonetheless able to identify two basic scenarios.

In the first scenario, the initial living conditions and those at the time of the interviews are different but equally precarious. In fact, precarious living conditions in the community of origin were replaced by other, equally precarious living conditions at the time of the interviews. For example, a respondent may have left behind a childhood context of family violence and parental alcoholism, and successive transfers from foster home to foster home, only to find herself, at the time of the interviews, reliant on social assistance, experiencing problems with youth protection services, and having to resort to food banks. In this scenario, certain Aboriginal women have remained on the same "track," but in different precarious conditions.

The second scenario is somewhat more vague in that, with the exception of two respondents whose living conditions had clearly improved in Montréal, our comparison reveals that for the majority of our respondents, *certain* living conditions were maintained and reproduced, others had improved and still others had deteriorated. In certain trajectories, for example, some respondents were more stable in terms of their housing situation at the time of the interviews compared to an earlier period in their lives (improvement), but their socio-economic situation continued to be precarious, and they had reproduced the alcohol abuse which characterized their family and community life (maintenance) or were experiencing serious health problems (deterioration). This scenario makes it difficult to identify a general trend in the life trajectories of our respondents.

Migration Patterns and the Lure of Montréal

Two types of mobility co-exist: extra-territorial mobility (moves from one community or city to another) and intra-territorial mobility (moves within a particular area). It is important to note the existence of this dual mobility, because a woman can experience relatively little extra-territorial mobility but extensive intra-territorial mobility. This is true of four respondents who, prior to settling in Montréal, moved only once (one respondent), four times (one respondent), and six times (two respondents) but who, once resident in Montréal, moved numerous times. In fact, these four respondents moved an average of 15 times within the Montréal area. Certain respondents had trouble recalling precisely when and where they moved after coming to the city (further evidence of their increased mobility) or resorted to living in shelters with such frequency that it is very difficult to retrace their movements. The intensity of this mobility must of course be weighted based on the number of years spent in Montréal. Taking this variable into account reveals that our respondents moved an average of once a year, with the exception of one Mi'kmaq woman who moved an average of once every two years. It is also important to bear in mind that intra-territorial mobility is extremely difficult to assess and that the average number of moves within Montréal has undoubtedly been underestimated.

If the atypical patterns of two respondents are excluded (the first pattern is not truly migratory, because although the woman in question lived in Montréal on numerous occasions she maintained her residence in her community of origin; while the second, a 41-year-old woman, moved only once, from her community of origin to Montréal), the average number of extra-territorial moves is 11. The extra-territorial mobility of the respondents aged 41 and up is 10 moves,[14] which is lower than that of respondents aged 30 to 39, who made an average of 13 extra-territorial moves. The sole 19-year-old respondent had made six extra-territorial moves by the time of the interview.

The data on the migration patterns of the Aboriginal women in our sample thus reveal a high degree of extra- and intra-territorial mobility. These findings concur, in this regard, with those of the study of the employability patterns of Aboriginal women in Montréal.[15] The frequent moves typical of the respondents in our sample are related to, but also quite certainly contribute to, the vulnerability and marginalization of the population studied.

The position of Montréal in the migration pattern varies. Three scenarios emerge from our analysis. The first involves a migration pattern in which Montréal becomes a destination at an early age (between the ages of 0 and 4). The second corresponds to the experience of two respondents who first came to Montréal during adolescence. The third scenario, the most common in our sample group, applies to five respondents who first moved to Montréal as adults aged 21 to 27.

Only rarely is arrival in Montréal part of a direct and linear trajectory. With the exception of the respondent who made only one direct move from her community of origin to Montréal and another whose first extra-territorial move was to Montréal, all the respondents moved to the city during a migration pattern that was already well under way. In fact, before moving to Montréal for the first time, the respondents had moved an average of six times. It is also interesting to note that Montréal is not necessarily a final destination for all Aboriginal women. Three respondents moved to Montréal temporarily, living there for periods ranging from one weekend to two, three, or four years.

Of the 10 women we met, two clearly said they had no intention of moving to Montréal permanently. One of them spends time in Montréal frequently but irregularly, while maintaining her residence in her community of origin. The other had been living in a Montréal shelter for Aboriginal women for a year at the time of the interview. Although waiting for public housing in the city, this respondent told us explicitly that this was a temporary or even strategic move designed to allow her to regain custody of her children, who had been placed by youth protection services. Although she has lived in Montréal for over 37 years, this woman still dreams of returning to her community of origin. It is interesting, and somewhat paradoxical, that the only respondent who moved directly from her community of origin to Montréal – at the early age of four – is the person who has had the most trouble adapting to life in the city, and after more than 37 years, still plans to return to her community of origin.

The earlier in their lives that the women move to Montréal, the more likely it is that the reasons for the move was beyond their control and thus imposed on them. In such circumstances, the move is usually associated with a family situation involving the separation of the parents and the subsequent decision of one of them to settle in the city. In a preponderance of these cases, the parent who moves to Montréal is non-Aboriginal. The combination of mixed parentage and the break-up of a marriage creates conditions that promote initial contact with Montréal, a move to the city or a decision to settle there. Two of the respondents moved to Montréal during adolescence. One teenager was attracted to the city because it offered a wealth of leisure activities and entertainment options. The other did not actively choose Montréal; it was one of a number of places she sought refuge after running away from a reception centre. Although the respondent did not say so, it is quite probable that, given her situation, Montréal was an attractive refuge, because it offered the anonymity and secrecy of a large urban centre. As for the women who moved to Montréal as adults, their reasons for doing so are quite varied, so much so that it is impossible to establish a generic profile. Some respondents chose Montréal as their destination for conjugal reasons (to be with a partner or husband) or employment purposes (relocation of an office), while others first became acquainted with the city during activities organized by their community (conference) or moved there to seek the assistance of relatives who already lived in the city (one woman lived with relatives following a fire in her home). We also noted that despite the violence experienced by Aboriginal women, no respondent said she chose Montréal as a refuge from the violence of a spouse or relative, contrary to the findings of existing research on the migration of Aboriginal women to urban centres.

Processes of Marginalization

The comparison of the living conditions of our respondents during their early years with the situations they found themselves in at the time of our interviews reveals that it is difficult to generalize about the direction of the marginalization process. As noted above, at the time they were interviewed, some problems the Aboriginal women encountered as children persisted (for example, socio-economic insecurity); others had dissipated (e.g., conjugal violence), and new problems had emerged (e.g., disputes with youth protection services regarding child custody). Furthermore, between the initial and final points of comparison, the conditions and problems fluctuated. We also concluded that several processes, rather than a single one, work to maintain, reinforce or offset the marginalization of Aboriginal women, and these processes are multidirectional rather than linear.

Generally, the paths followed by the Aboriginal women are, to a certain extent, determined by the living conditions of (and consequently the paths followed by) other people who impact their lives. These people include members of their immediate families (especially their parents) and their various partners and spouses. For example, certain women begin to take drugs when they become involved with a dealer and stop doing so when the relationship ends.

Living in a major urban centre does not have the same impact on all Aboriginal women. Although the anonymity and the weakening of social networks associated with life in a big city can make women more vulnerable, they also provide a measure of protection. The following examples illustrate these contrary effects.

Francine, 19 years old at the time of the interviews, is originally from an Aboriginal community in British Columbia. After her parents divorced, her father moved to Montréal and started a new family. Up to the age of 4, Francine would regularly visit her father, her only connection to Montréal. Following a legal dispute between the parents, Francine's mother was awarded custody of her. This judicial ruling led to a 10-year interruption in the relationship between father and daughter. Francine re-established contact with her father at the age of 14, and when she was 15, he invited her to spend the summer in Montréal. Francine accepted his invitation and met a boyfriend during her stay. She then decided not to return to her community. Alcohol abuse (a problem dating back to her community of origin) began to affect her school attendance, and when she broke up with her boyfriend, she decided to drop out of school. A conflict, which she describes as minor, arose between her and her stepmother during her father's absence. She was asked to leave the family home and ended up on the street. She then took refuge at the Native Women's Shelter of Montréal. (It should be noted that this situation eventually led to the separation of the father and stepmother. The respondent then moved back in with her father.)

Cora is a 31-year-old woman from Nunavut. She moved numerous times during her childhood (was adopted by her grandfather, returned to her mother's home, lived with her aunts, was placed in a foster home). Her childhood was marked by both domestic violence (she was beaten by her mother) and alcohol abuse (her grandfather's alcoholism). At 21, she met a Montréal man passing through Iqaluit. He asked her to come back to Montréal with him. Three months after her arrival in the city, the couple separated. She lived on the street for a week, working as a prostitute to make ends meet. To "get off the street," she decided "to find a boyfriend." She met a new partner but broke up with him a month later following another romantic encounter.

The experiences of Francine and Cora effectively illustrate how various kinds of ruptures (dropping out of school, break-ups with partners, breakdown of family relationships) can cause living conditions to deteriorate, when combined with the inability to form other social ties in Montréal. In Cora's case, this deterioration was exacerbated by a complete absence of social networks, which explains why she ended up living on the street and working as a prostitute. Francine, who was much more "integrated," found refuge at the Native Women's Shelter of Montréal.

By way of contrast, Linda's situation illustrates how the anonymity of life in Montréal and the city's multiethnicity can make the urban environment a relatively "protective" one. Linda comes from a mixed family background (non-Aboriginal birth father, Aboriginal birth mother; Aboriginal adoptive father, non-Aboriginal adoptive mother). Her mixed background made her subject to discrimination at school in her community of origin and at residential school, where she was called a "bastard" by the more visibly Aboriginal students and a "savage" by the non-Aboriginal students. This type of discrimination ended almost entirely once she arrived in Montréal, with the exception of her encounter with a landlord who refused to rent to Aboriginal or Black people. In fact, in this instance, the respondent used her status to her advantage, preferring to identify herself as Aboriginal rather than admit that she did not wish to live in substandard housing.

Generally, it is impossible to state unequivocally that Montréal is an environment that worsens, offsets or improves the living conditions of Aboriginal women. As we have seen, Aboriginal women are often born into family and community environments that are fraught with problems (ruptures, uprooting, socio-economic insecurity, violence, dependence on drugs and alcohol). These living situations determine the general outlines of the paths the Aboriginal women "follow." Although they remain on these paths throughout their lives, they experience periods of ascending and descending movement.

Louise's experience illustrates this idea of a path on which such movements can be observed. Louise is 40 years old. She was raised by her grandparents until the age of 13. When she was 15, a family tragedy had a profound impact on her life: during a family party in her community, her father was murdered. Her family held her responsible for his death. Though never charged with any crime, she was expelled from her community and placed in a foster home. After running away from this reception centre, she headed for Montréal. She was still just 15, and the only people she knew were friends of her father. To make ends meet, she began working as a prostitute on the day of her arrival in the city. At a metro station, she met a man who brought her home "to protect her from the dangers of the street." (This was the beginning of a long-term friendship.) The next day, she went to meet her father's friends, who were members of a motorcycle gang. With their help, she got a job as a dancer in a suburban club. For the next six years, a series of incidents and encounters brought her into regular contact with an environment associated with prostitution, stripping, drugs (cocaine), alcohol, and violence (including attempted murder).

From the age of 15 to 21, she moved back and forth between apartments (usually when involved in a relationship) and non-Aboriginal shelters for the homeless. She also spent time in detention facilities and hospitals (including a psychiatric hospital). At the age of 21, she visited her sister, who had just had a baby. Her contact with the newborn child was a turning point in her life: she decided to adopt the infant and to stop drinking alcohol. A female friend helped her apply for welfare benefits (her first application). She sought the assistance of a housing resource to furnish an apartment and moved in with her boyfriend. After someone apparently informed the welfare agency that she was living with a man, her monthly allowance was reduced. Three years later, for unknown reasons, the welfare agency withdrew her allowance. This decision was another turning point, because Louise was no longer able to pay her rent. She moved to the Native Women's Shelter of Montréal. She began working as a prostitute again and also resumed taking drugs and drinking alcohol. However, at age 27, she attempted to deal with her dependence on drugs and alcohol by undergoing two withdrawal treatments.

When Louise was 28, her sister came to Montréal to reclaim custody of her child, and Louise entered a period of depression. At age 29, she learned that she was HIV-positive. Over the next 11 years (up until the time of our interview), Louise's life was very much like it had been during her first years in Montréal: alcohol, drugs, prostitution, a series of relationships, conjugal violence, stays in shelters. At the time of our interview, Louise was living in a safe house and receiving welfare benefits.

Louise's experience is not necessarily representative of that of the other nine respondents, because she is clearly the most marginalized member of the group. However, the types of processes involved, particularly the ascending and descending movements, are representative of the paths followed by the other women. In many cases, a particular event (in Louise's case, the adoption of a child) creates a rupture in the course of the woman's life, leading to changes (the decision to stop consuming drugs and alcohol) and attempts to become more socially integrated (renting an apartment, giving up prostitution, applying for welfare). Louise's trajectory also shows how fragile these ascending movements can be. The cumulative impact of subsequent events (reduction then withdrawal of welfare benefits combined with the loss of custody of her nephew) led to a second rupture that brought the ascending movement to an end and precipitated the resumption of the lifestyle preceding this movement.

The respondents' trajectories are affected by encounters with people (often future partners or spouses) who significantly alter the women's life circumstances. Ultimately, the structure of their lives in the urban environment is determined from day to day. Most of the women said they had no long-term plans for their lives, other than regaining custody of their children. Although the daily restructuring of their lives in Montréal is clearly a reflection of the vulnerable situations they find themselves in, it also greatly contributes to their vulnerability. On the other hand, the women quickly form strong bonds with some of the people they meet, which at least temporarily provides them with a safety net.

Conclusion

Unlike existing research on the migration of Aboriginal women and their lives in urban settings, our findings do not allow us to conclude that migration to the city – in this case, Montréal – is in itself a marginalizing factor. The marginalization process begins in early childhood and is rooted in a much broader social context associated with the consequences of the colonization of First Nations in Canada and Quebec. Marginalization precedes migration to an urban setting. From childhood, the lives of the Aboriginal women in our sample are conditioned by circumstances, actors, events, and problems that are sufficiently characteristic to be considered a defining path: poverty, non-integration into the conventional job market, involvement in gainful activities that are socially frowned upon, unacceptable or even criminal, violence, alcohol, drugs, homelessness, reliance on food banks and shelters, minimal informal social network and strong institutional social network. As a general rule, the factors that play the greatest role in restricting the women to this path are undoubtedly the relationships they form along the way with other people (partners, spouses, and friends) in similar circumstances.

As a major urban centre, Montréal affects the lives of Aboriginal women in numerous ways. The city isolates the women and, in certain cases, precipitates the deterioration of their living conditions, but it also clearly offers opportunities for survival and protection (clandestine work, assistance and housing resources,[16] health care, anonymity). That being said, Montréal does not appear to offer, at least in the case of our respondents, an opportunity for the sustained improvement of living conditions.

When viewed as a whole, processes of marginalization are not linear and develop in a dynamic fashion. The trajectories followed by the women are punctuated by events that sometimes reinforce, perpetuate or offset the marginalization processes. The accumulation, disappearance, and substitution of the problems the Aboriginal women face makes it difficult to chart the overall direction of their marginalization. It is easier to track the impact of marginalization in particular areas of their lives (e.g., work, health, accommodations) by identifying chains of events and definite ruptures. These ruptures lead to changes that signal the beginning of "ascending" and "descending" cycles whose impact does not extend beyond the limits of the path the women typically follow. Living conditions change on a daily basis, making the city an unpredictable place where chance can make anything happen, with tragic or salutary results.

Notes

1   Partenariat Mikimon is a partnership between Quebec Native Women Inc. and the Institut national de recherche scientifique-Culture et Société (INRS). Mikimon published a study led by Carole Lévesque entitled *Aboriginal Women and Jobs: Challenges and Issues for Employability Programs in Quebec* (Canada, Status of Women Canada, May 2001).

2   See in particular: Nagler, M. (1970) *Indians in the City: A Study of the Urbanization of Indians in Toronto*, Ottawa: Saint-Paul College, University of Ottawa; McCaskill, D. (1970) *A Study of Needs and Resources Related to Offenders of Native Origin in Manitoba*, Ottawa: Correctional Planning Branch, Ministry of the Solicitor General; Brody, H. (1971) *Les Indiens dans le quartier interlope*, Ottawa: Northern Science Research Group, Department of Indian Affairs and Northern Development; Denton, T. (1972) "Migration from a Canadian Reserve," *Journal of Canadian Studies*, 7(2); Dosman, E.J. (1972) *Indians: the Urban Dilemma*, Toronto: McClelland and Stewart Publishing; Gurstein, M. (nd) *Les Amérindiens et l'urbanisation : une étude documentaire analytique*, Ottawa: Direction de la recherche, Politiques, recherche et évaluation, Collectivité(s) Canada, Programme des affaires indiennes et inuit; McCaskill, D. (1981) "The Urbanization of Indians in Winnipeg, Toronto, Edmonton and Vancouver: A Comparative Analysis," Culture, 1(1) pp. 82-89; Krotz, L. (1972) *Urban Indians: The Strangers in Canada's Cities*, Edmonton: Hurtig Publishers Ltd; Yewbury, J.C. (1980) "British Columbia Native Nations in Transition: The Urbanization Process," *Urban Anthropology*, 9, pp. 319-339.

3   See, for example, Maidman, F. (1981) *Native People in Urban Settings: Problems, Needs, and Services, A Report of the Ontario Task Force on Native People in the Urban Setting*, Toronto; Peters, E. (1992) *Native Women's Adaptive Strategies in Urban Milieux*, Kingston: Queen's University; RCAP (Royal Commission on Aboriginal Peoples) (1993) *Aboriginal Peoples in Urban Centres. Report of the National Round Table on Aboriginal Urban Issues*, Ottawa: Royal Commission on Aboriginal Peoples.

4   See Zambrowsky-Cross, S. (1987) *Évaluation des besoins chez les femmes autochtones ayant ou risquant d'avoir des démêlés avec la justice dans la région de Montréal*; Laplante M. and M. Potvin (1991) *Les autochtones de Val d'Or : étude sur les autochtones vivant en milieu urbain Val d'Or*, Centre d'amitié autochtone de Val d'Or; La Prairie (1995) *Visibles mais sans voix: les autochtones dans la ville*, Ottawa, Department of Justice; Gill, L. (1995) *De la réserve à la ville: Les Amérindiennes en milieu urbain au Québec*, Ottawa, Conseil du Statut de la femme.

5   Montpetit, C. (1989) "Trajectoires de vie de migrants autochtones à Val d'Or," paper presented to the Faculty of Graduate Studies at Université de Montréal.

6   INAC (2000) *Comparison of Social Conditions, 1991 and 1996*, Ottawa: Minister of Public Works and Government Services Canada; Silverman, R.A. and M.O. Nielsen (1992) *Aboriginal Peoples and Canadian Criminal Justice*, Toronto and Vancouver: Butterworth; Statistics Canada (1993) *Aboriginal Data: Language, Tradition, Health, Lifestyle and Social Issues*, Catalogue 89-533, Ottawa: Minister of Public Works and Government Services Canada; Statistics Canada (1993) *Schooling, Work and Related Activities, Income, Expenses and Mobility*, Catalogue 89-534, Ottawa: Minister of Public Works and Government Services Canada; Statistics Canada (1993) *Disability and Housing*, Catalogue 89-535, Ottawa: Minister of Public Works and Government Services Canada.

7   Symbolic marginalization leads to a loss of self-esteem, loss of identity, and a sense of worthlessness experienced by an individual whose social usefulness is put into question.

8   This study was conducted in collaboration with Christopher McAll (Director of the Programme de recherche sur le racisme et la discrimination, Centre d'études ethniques, Université de Montréal) and in partnership with the Native Friendship Centre of Montréal, the Native Women's Shelter of Montréal and the Native Women's Association of Quebec. It received financial support from the Social Sciences and Humanities Research Council of Canada as part of its strategic research grants for the study of women and social change.

9   It is important to emphasize that these 10 trajectories are specific to a highly marginalized population and, of course, do not reflect the situation of Aboriginal peoples as a whole.

10 We are aware that Inuit women are underrepresented in our sample and that this underrepresentation diminishes the contrast in trajectories based on origin.

11 It is important to emphasize that these 10 trajectories are specific to a highly marginalized population and, of course, do not reflect the situation of Aboriginal peoples as a whole.

12 The number of women living in women's shelters must be put into context: shelters were a prime location for selecting our respondents.

13 In effect, the respondents are largely unable to identify the variables that situate the socio-economic conditions of their social milieu (occupation, training, schooling, standard of living).

14 If we exclude the case of the 41-year-old respondent.

15 See note 1.

16 It is important to point out that the Native Women's Shelter of Montréal and the Native Friendship Centre of Montréal are two very popular resources. The Friendship Centre plays a key role as a landing point for Aboriginal women and in offsetting the marginalization in living conditions of our respondents.

Prospects for a New Middle Class Among Urban Aboriginal People

Terry Wotherspoon
Department of Sociology
University of Saskatchewan

Aboriginal populations[1] are characterized by increasing diversity, particularly as they integrate into changing rural and urban social environments and new enterprises within Aboriginal and non-Aboriginal business, government, and community sectors. One of the least explored, though potentially contentious, aspects of these processes of differentiation concerns the issue of social class relations. What is the nature and impact of class relations among Canada's Aboriginal people? In particular, how have these class dynamics changed as the Aboriginal population becomes increasingly concentrated in urban settings, and to what extent can it be claimed that a new middle class has emerged within this context? Given the limited attention that these issues have received from researchers and policy-makers, the intent of the paper is not to provide an exhaustive account of statistical trends and analytical details, but rather to outline a number of significant factors that warrant further consideration.

The notion of a new middle class has attracted considerable attention both from those who celebrate the blurring or loss of strict boundaries between social classes, and those who are concerned to maintain the relevance of class and class politics in the contemporary world.[2] At the same time, notions of middle classes and new middle classes, themselves, have a somewhat fluid and enigmatic status within class analysis. They stand out, not so much as class entities, but rather for their intermediate and potentially strategic role between classes, whether understood in terms of their economic functions, their place in political hierarchies and social divisions of labour, or their cultural significance. The shifting and uncertain nature of new middle classes as a whole is intriguing insofar as it has some parallels with the changing dynamics of social relations experienced by Aboriginal people, particularly those living in urban areas.

The discussion that follows is not concerned with reconstructing the terms of debates over social class, or in exploring the often intricate details that enter into the definition and measurement of class relations. Instead, as will be stressed below, the concept of new middle classes is employed in a relatively loose way in order to highlight some of its implications for the social interactions, economic possibilities, and political alignments that are affecting Aboriginal people and their relations both with one another and within Canadian society more generally.

Does Class Matter?

There has been relatively little analysis of social class relations for Aboriginal people in Canada. Discussions about the Aboriginal population have tended to present an image of a relatively undifferentiated group, or else one in which diversity is primarily a consequence of cultural, legal, or regional factors. Class (understood with reference to people's ability to own or control assets that contribute to the production of wealth) sometimes enters the analysis under the guise of depicting Aboriginal people, in general, as occupying part of a distinct "underclass" or colonized group at the margins of Canadian society. Nonetheless, there is also growing awareness that multiple forces and cleavages are pulling Aboriginal populations in diverse directions. The accomplishment of self-government and devolution of government services has been accompanied by increasing scrutiny over social distinctions and political divisions within First Nations and other Aboriginal communities, focusing especially on competing factions or contention between elected chiefs and band councils and the general community membership. These issues, in turn, reveal the importance of factors like gender, age, legal status, identity, and community attachment for contributing to diverse experiences and interests. There is also growing sensitivity to the claim that many conventional western conceptions, including class, have no direct relevance for Aboriginal societies. Some Aboriginal leaders and agencies have advanced this position by arguing that processes like collective bargaining, derived from Eurocentric forms of industrial relations rooted in capitalist class relations, are not valid in a First Nations context unless they can be grounded in an approach to industrial relations derived from indigenous knowledge and practice.

There is often a sense, then, that class does not matter in Aboriginal communities. At one extreme, class is viewed as irrelevant, divisive and contrary to indigenous aspirations for healing, wholeness, and nationhood. On an opposing pole, Aboriginal communities are understood as being further torn apart by multiple forms of social differentiation and diversity, parallel to new types of fragmentation and political realignment taking shape through post-industrial, postmodern societies more generally.

It is critically important to acknowledge both that there are several bases of differentiation within Aboriginal populations and that there are some shared elements of culture, history, and experience that transcend class distinctions. Nonetheless, there are compelling reasons why the analysis of class remains relevant. Class indicators point to the degrees of inequality that mark life conditions and chances both among groups (such as Aboriginal people relative to non-Aboriginal people) and within groups. These inequalities and relationships tend to be further affected by, and have an impact on, how people view themselves in relation to others, their communities, their regions, and their national societies. Class factors enter into broader social problems like social cohesion, integration, inclusion or exclusion, political commitment, ideological dispositions, and political behaviour. Class relations permeate many dimensions of life, both within Aboriginal communities and through the broader social relations that Aboriginal people enter into, in the material conditions they experience, the ways in which they make sense of those circumstances, and the actions that they pursue in making choices and selecting possible future courses of collective action.

With respect to employment, wage labour has long been prevalent within some indigenous economies. More recent patterns of economic development and the emergence of new models of Aboriginal governance have contributed to periodic tension among conflicting class interests (as well as other sources of division) around issues like resource management, relations with large corporations, the direction taken by self-government agreements and associated compensation packages, and access to privileged positions in government bureaucracies and business enterprises. Employees in several First Nations governments, businesses, and other Aboriginal organizations have begun to pursue vigorously trade union certification in order to secure wage increases, improved working conditions, job security, and protection against other forms of vulnerability. Changing patterns of social and economic activity in the home, workplace, and political spheres contribute to further class and gender-based inequalities.[3] In a summary of the growing body of literature in Canada and the United States that demonstrates that Aboriginal people's relations to class and paid employment are much more complex and historically rooted than commonly supposed, Patricia Albers stresses "the unacceptability of perpetuating false dichotomies that represent Native North American economic activity as components of some legendary distanced culture and that as a result divorce them from the economic system at large, especially from various kinds of wage labour that have contributed to the accumulation of capital by Europeans and their descendants in North America."[4]

At the same time, the focus of most analysis of class relations among Aboriginal people has highlighted communities and reserves located in rural areas, reflecting the location of many strategic land bases, structures of governance, local development initiatives, and targeted state programs.

Class dynamics experienced by Aboriginal people within Canada's cities have received only limited attention even though a substantial body of evidence points to the extreme inequalities in socio-economic conditions that prevail within urban contexts. Urban centres are usually better equipped to attract, educate, house, and employ the most qualified persons, those with the strongest labour market positions, and those who possess or seek important social and cultural assets. For Aboriginal people in Canadian cities, these factors coexist with substantial barriers to advancement and higher than average rates of unemployment, poverty, homelessness, victimization, and displacement. Consequently, urban Aboriginal populations reveal profound disparities in incomes, education levels, and living conditions.[5]

It is important to recognize, in these regards, that social classes do not exist simply in the form of statistical comparisons or groupings. Rather, they are social relations that are created, sustained, and experienced through our relative ability to secure our own welfare, to subordinate others, or to rely on other sources to earn an income. One of the more interesting, and controversial, dimensions of class analysis has highlighted the nature and roles of persons who occupy intermediate or contradictory class positions, often referred to as the "new" middle classes. Consideration of the prospects for a new middle class of urban Aboriginal people offers a useful case study by which to gauge the possibilities for eventual alleviation or intensification of the observed disparities.

What About the New Middle Class?

The concept of the new middle classes gained currency in the latter half of the 20th century to draw attention to the proliferation of workers who do not appear to fit neatly into the conventional class categories associated with capitalist social relations. More specifically, the term refers especially to employees of public or private sector agencies whose primary duties are related to relations with other people (in a supervisory or discretionary capacity) or who are engaged in the production and application of high level knowledge or technical information. Such positions typically include middle to upper level managers, administrators, and supervisors; professionals and professional service workers such as doctors, lawyers, teachers, and nurses; and scientists, technicians, and engineers. More recent interest in the dimensions and dynamics associated with the growth of what is variously termed the "new economy" or knowledge-based society, and parallel trends showing a rise in non-standard employment relationships in other sectors, have also considered entrepreneurs, knowledge sector workers, and people who work in the development and application of new technologies as part of the new middle classes. The new middle classes, within these broad definitions, have constituted as much as 40 to 50 percent of the employed workforce in advanced industrial nations since the early 1980s.[6]

Several factors have aroused interest in the new middle classes for both analytical and political reasons. As noted earlier, the relative importance of class, and the positioning and alignment among various class forces, are central to debates concerning the future of capitalism or its displacement by a new post-industrial or postmodern era. Consequently, there is widespread disagreement over whether the middle classes are disappearing, expanding, or simply changing form. The proliferation of a significant segment of new middle classes is seen by some as a sign that class division or polarization between the privileged and dispossessed is more mythical than real.[7] The blurring of class lines makes it difficult to envision any kind of collective action or even co-ordinated policy-making as people's material interests and loyalties dissipate or lose focus. Workers whose jobs reflect their advanced qualifications, specialized knowledge, and personal capabilities, for instance, may be less concerned about collective bargaining and union protection than other forms of benefits, employment factors, and lifestyle choices. Family interests may be focused on the pursuit of self-interest and the transfer of advantages and privileges to their children rather than with the broader social good.[8] On the other hand, new forms of controls, divisions of labour, surveillance, and accountability procedures may in fact limit workers' autonomy, discretionary ability, and other advantages. Processes of proletarianization may coexist with, or even be dimensions of, a shift toward new professional, entrepreneurial, and knowledge-based work, as evident in at least three interrelated trends – pressures for the self-employed and small business or farm operators to enter into paid employment, the restructuring of jobs in such a way that workers' discretion and knowledge are limited or circumscribed by management or technical systems of control, and the displacement of high level workers and jobs by lower level counterparts. Accounts of the new middle classes, then, contain both optimistic and pessimistic assessments of the future of work and prospects for workers.

Dimensions of Urban Aboriginal Middle Class Formation

Issues of class formation have special significance for Aboriginal people who seek equitable access to improved job opportunities in concert with educational and occupational advancement and related benefits. The expansion of middle class positions offers potential for them to gain direct and indirect influence through representation in key decision-making roles and institutional sites. The presence of Aboriginal people in such positions offers role models and advocates who may foster improved options for subsequent generations of Aboriginal children and youth. Growth in the number of Aboriginal people in small business, professional, and managerial positions enhances the pool of personal, fiscal, and community resources that may be mobilized to advance further development of Aboriginal enterprises and communities. These considerations take on special importance when it is recognized that there tends to be a much greater than average degree of polarization between the best-off and worst-off segments of the Aboriginal population with respect to wages, income, and other major indicators.[9] Persons who are in intermediate class situations by virtue of relatively favourable educational, occupational, and income circumstance, are likely to be shielded from the worst problems, such as poor health, inadequate housing and transportation, trouble with legal authorities, and poverty, that confront large proportions of the urban Aboriginal population. The creation of more intermediate positions, whether understood in terms of class, occupation, or earnings, may help to alleviate some of these concerns and promote upward social and economic advancement among the Aboriginal population as a whole.

Conversely, it is possible that movement of greater proportions of Aboriginal persons into new middle class positions may not carry any significant social advantages. Wage and employment parity, for instance, can result from an overall downward shift in wages or greater "levelling out" of the class and occupational structure as well as from upward mobility. It is also possible that persons who pursue better class and occupational opportunities will reorient their interests and loyalties. Changing occupational demands, lifestyle choices, consumption patterns, and other class-related cultural factors may override Aboriginal identity and commitment to the collective interests held by indigenous communities. In the same way that middle classes are not strictly class entities, in these regards, Aboriginal people who occupy such intermediate, often changing, social and economic positions may become subject to what appear to be relatively individualized and fragmented life choices and orientations.

There has been gradual growth, within the Aboriginal population generally, and more specifically among those who live in urban areas, in various jobs and categories associated with middle class positions and identities. There are at least three major components of this expansion – the promotion of entrepreneurship (associated with the conventional middle class or "old" petit bourgeoisie) and professional and managerial employment (considered the "new" middle classes), which is strongly linked in turn to the continuing importance of public sector employment for Aboriginal people.

There is a strong impetus, through both government and non-governmental programs, to promote entrepreneurship and its accompanying ethos as a solution to the need for Aboriginal people to become more fully integrated into economic activity. Recent initiatives and programs, such as the federal Aboriginal Business Development Initiative, the National Aboriginal Economic Development Board, and the Native Investment and Trade Association, have highlighted the importance of business and enterprise among indigenous communities, while showcasing successful Aboriginal programs nationally and internationally.

The evidence on the success of such initiatives is mixed. Industry Canada data show that Aboriginal people remain half as likely as other Canadians (about 3.9 percent compared to 7.9 percent of the respective adult populations) to own a business. However, self-employment and ownership of small businesses has increased dramatically among persons with Aboriginal origins, rising by 170 percent (compared to a national rate of 65 percent) between 1981 and 1996. Among the 20,195 self-employed Aboriginal people reported in the 1996 Census, just over half (51 percent) lived in urban areas, and 36 percent were women. These businesses tend to be relatively small, not highly profitable, prone to failure, and concentrated in resource, tourism, primary industries, and other sectors associated with locations in rural and reserve settings. However, poles of growth have also occurred in urban centres, expressing some diversity and potential for further expansion, both in traditional areas and those associated with knowledge, finance, and innovation.[10] The confluence of several factors, including the traditional nature of many Aboriginal businesses, their location and provision of service and/or employment in or close to Aboriginal communities, and the formation of Aboriginal business organizations, suggests that both class and cultural considerations, as well as more individualized concerns, enter into the emergence of an Aboriginal business sector. However, prospects for any kind of cohesion or solidarity as an entrepreneurial class are undercut by tensions associated with problems that contribute to high rates of business failure and limitations, such as access to credit and capital, or preoccupation with expansion in the case of more successful enterprises.

Aboriginal people, overall, have maintained relatively stable representation in occupational categories that are normally considered to constitute the new middle classes. Between the census periods of 1986 and 1996, among persons aged 15 years and older in the experienced workforce, the proportion of those reporting Aboriginal ancestry and employed in managerial and professional occupations grew from 21.4 to 21.5 percent, slightly below the levels of growth from 26.9 to 28.5 percent of the general population.[11] It is important to keep in mind that these figures should be interpreted with caution, as definitions related to occupational categories and to Aboriginal people are very broad and susceptible to fluctuation over time, encompassing a considerable range of diversity within each category.

Given the importance of advanced education to work associated with the new middle classes, the data in Figure 1 offer a slightly more refined look at the general patterns. Among persons with some post-secondary education (including those who are still attending school, those who have graduated, and those who did not complete their degree, diploma, or certificate program), one third of non-Aboriginal workers were employed in managerial and professional occupations, compared to one in four Registered Indians and one in five other persons reporting Aboriginal identity. However, there are important variations within the general comparisons. The gap between Aboriginal and non-Aboriginal representation in these occupations is lower for women, particularly among Registered Indians, than for men. At the same time, reflecting the high concentrations of women in fields like education and health care, both Aboriginal and non-Aboriginal women are much more likely than men to be engaged in professional work, while they are less likely to occupy managerial positions. In the case of Aboriginal people, and especially Registered Indians living on-reserve, the band economy and structures of governance and economic development foster opportunities for both managerial and professional work, albeit in a manner that reproduces prevalent gender divisions of labour.[12]

Figure 1: Workers in Managerial and Professional Occupations as Proportion of Experienced Work Force with at least some Post-Secondary Education, 1996 Census

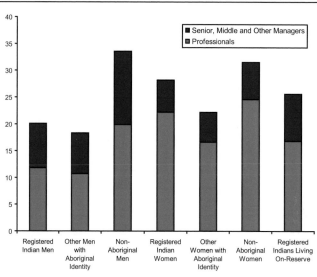

Source: Based on data from Hull (2000), pp. 77-79.

The growing concentration of Aboriginal people in urban centres is also having an impact on prospects for employment in professional fields and, to a lesser extent, managerial occupations. Many public and private sector agencies in both Aboriginal and non-Aboriginal sectors have created initiatives, programs, and hiring policies to attract highly qualified Aboriginal candidates. The concentration and proximity of larger cohorts of professional and managerial colleagues of Aboriginal ancestry within an urban context creates possibilities for interaction and network-building that are less likely to exist in smaller communities in which schools, hospitals, law offices, and business firms are more scattered and have fewer employees. However, even within single institutions, such as large universities and workplaces, Aboriginal students and senior personnel often express a strong sense of isolation, discrimination, and lack of support.

The observed professional and managerial occupational distributions signify, in part, the continuing importance of the state sector in the lives of many Aboriginal people. In addition to its regulatory role, the state is a major employer of, and provider of services and income transfers to, Aboriginal people. New middle class positions are associated with government employment in both of these regards insofar as the rise of the new middle classes historically has accompanied the expansion of state functions to train and maintain a healthy population, manage the marginalized segments of the population, and administer public services. These trends are especially apparent in urban areas which, as observed earlier, simultaneously include high concentrations of the most qualified and highly employed as well as the least qualified, most government-dependent Aboriginal people.

Figures 2A and 2B offer some evidence of the relative importance of these various government functions in the seven census metropolitan areas (CMAs) in which Canadian Aboriginal people are most highly concentrated. In centres that have had relatively vibrant economies and relatively greater integration of Aboriginal people into the general labour

Figure 2A: Employment in Government, Education, Health, and Social Services
(Percentage of Total Experienced Labour Force 15 Years and Over, 1996 Census)

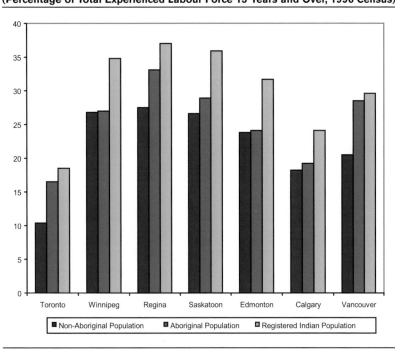

Source: Based on data from 1996 census, Statistics Canada Cat. 94-F009XDB 96001.

force (notably Toronto and, to a lesser extent, Calgary and Vancouver), Aboriginal people are less likely to be employed in key government sectors and less dependent on government transfer income than those in other centres (particularly in the mid-sized Prairie cities), with relatively smaller disparities between Aboriginal and non-Aboriginal populations with respect to both indicators. Substantial differences also prevail within Aboriginal populations, overall and across regions, most evident in the high levels of both employment and income transfers by government among Registered Indians. These figures indicate that the conditions required, at least in part, to develop and sustain a new middle class among Aboriginal as well as non-Aboriginal populations are present even in major cities that do not have the same levels of self-government and band infrastructure present in smaller centres and reserve communities.

Figure 2B: Government Transfer Payments as Percentage of Total Income

(Population 15 years and Over, 1996 Census)

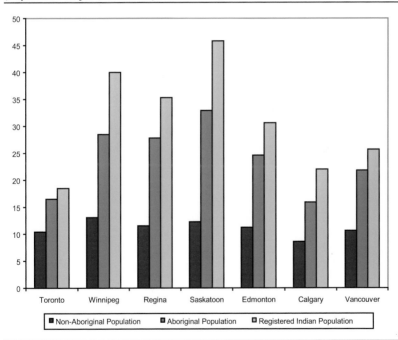

Source: Based on data from 1996 census, Statistics Canada Cat. 94-F009XDB 96001.

Figure 2C: Aboriginal and Non-Aboriginal Populations with Incomes $40,000 and over
(Percentages of Population Fifteen Years and Over Reporting Income in 1996 Census)

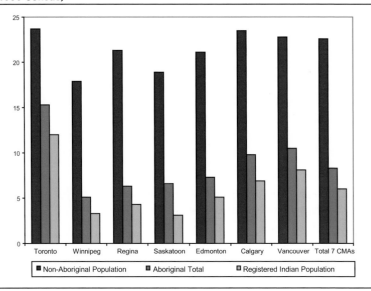

Source: Based on data from 1996 census, Statistics Canada Cat. 94-F009XDB 96001.

Another indication of the potential distribution of persons in new middle class positions can be derived from income figures. It is widely assumed that new middle class employment, in contrast to working class wage labour and persons who derive earnings from self-owned enterprises or investments, tends to be relatively well paid in order to acknowledge educational credentials and employment status. Figure 2C compares the proportion of Aboriginal and non-Aboriginal earners who reported incomes of at least $40,000 (about twice the median income in each centre) in the 1996 Census. Each city contains a segment of five to fifteen percent of the Aboriginal population in this income category (though ranging only between three and six percent among Registered Indians). This suggests, in common with the occupational trends cited earlier, that there is a core of urban Aboriginal workers who are much more favourably situated than the vast majority of the Aboriginal population, although as with occupational distributions, they are also highly underrepresented relative to the non-Aboriginal population. As an indication of relative wealth from investments, the proportion of total income received from sources other than wages and government transfer payments ranged in these cities between 3.1 percent in Winnipeg and 5.3 percent in Toronto for Aboriginal people, compared to a low of 10.1 percent in Toronto and a high of 12.2 percent in Saskatoon and Winnipeg for non-Aboriginal people.

Taking into account these various indicators of occupational status and income, it is clear that there is a relatively small, but distinct, segment of the urban Aboriginal population who occupy positions associated with the new middle classes. Further, many key conditions required for their maintenance and growth, such as the creation of a favourable investment climate, presence of both an Aboriginal and non-Aboriginal clientele for services, sufficient opportunities to develop professional and business networks, and integration into the community, appear to be strongly established.

Prospects for educational improvement offer a further mechanism for potential access to new middle class positions, given the centrality of advanced training and credentials within an economic context that places substantial emphasis on the production of knowledge and capacity for innovation. Education is critical for access to professional and many senior managerial positions, but also serves as a screening mechanism that blocks or selects people out from higher level positions. An aging population, declining birth rates, and relatively stable immigration patterns have forced both government and private sector human resource development officials to pay attention to the longstanding emphasis by First Nations and other indigenous groups on the urgent need to improve educational conditions and outcomes for Aboriginal people. Several factors, including the establishment of First Nations jurisdiction in education, creation of more receptive educational climates and programs for Aboriginal learners in provincial and territorial school systems, promotion of educational advancement among Aboriginal communities, and general educational upgrading among the population as a whole, have contributed to rising levels of educational retention, completion, and credentials within the Aboriginal population.[13]

Improvement in basic education levels, signified both by greater numbers of children and youth attending, staying in school longer, and completing high school and advanced certification, and by adults returning to school later in life, expands the pool of Aboriginal people eligible for positions that require higher educational credentials. However, some of these potential gains may be offset by the increased levels of educational attainment and achievement in the population as a whole. Educational improvement is evident in the increased proportion of Aboriginal people who have completed post-secondary programs and university degrees in all age cohorts.[14]

However, as Figure 3 illustrates, the latter factor remains a concern with regard to the continuing large gap in educational achievement between the non-Aboriginal and Aboriginal populations. Among Aboriginal people, those living in urban areas, especially in the largest cities, are most likely

Figure 3. Selected Education Indicators
by Population Type and Place of Residence
(Percent of Total Populations Aged 15 Years and Over, 1996 Census)

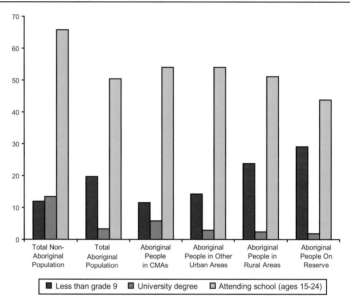

Source: Based on data from Statistics Canada, Canadian Centre for Justice Statistics, Aboriginal People in Canada – Profile Series, June, 2001, Cat. 85-F0033M1E, pp. 12-14.

to be engaged in formal schooling in their early adult years and to have university degrees, reflecting the combined impact of population characteristics and educational and occupational opportunities.

Aboriginal people who pursue and complete post-secondary studies are relatively well-situated for employment in positions associated with the new middle classes, taking into account substantial variation in the programs in which they are concentrated and the credentials they receive. Over three out of five Aboriginal persons with university certificates and degrees, regardless of gender and status, are concentrated in fields related to education, recreation and counselling, social sciences, commerce, management, and administration. Many programs in these areas, as well as in the humanities, engineering, and health care fields which also have high concentrations of Aboriginal graduates, are not strictly oriented to any single career path and do not necessarily culminate in occupational success. Nonetheless, the returns from education remain mixed for Aboriginal graduates. Even large proportions of those who did not enter professional or career-specific programs have had considerable success in securing employment or subsequent entry into programs that offer them professional certification or qualifications for entry into managerial and supervisory positions. However, Aboriginal people with a university degree were about twice as likely to fall into the lowest as opposed to the highest income quintile, and faced additional difficulties, in comparison to other Canadians, that prevented them from achieving the full occupational and economic success to which their education might be expected to contribute.[15]

Some institutional practices have helped to alleviate these problems. The Royal Commission on Aboriginal Peoples, for instance, has drawn attention to the positive results produced by professional development and special access programs that were introduced to alleviate the shortage of qualified Aboriginal persons in a variety of professional and technical fields, including legal studies, social work, teacher training, health care, science and engineering, and business and public administration. These programs, significantly, tend to foster professional communities and support networks that can be crucial to optimize prospects for degree completion and establishment of a career. Compatible orientations also seem to be prevalent among school age Aboriginal children and youth in urban locales. Their remarkably high educational aspirations signify a desire to employ education as a vehicle for upward social mobility, particularly in the professions and other occupations that require advanced credentials or training. The students link these goals, at the same time, to a strong desire to provide service that will benefit their communities and enable them to remain connected with Aboriginal heritage and cultures.[16] The optimism, however, is tempered by serious concerns that arise through their encounters with numerous barriers in their school, community, and personal lives that increase the likelihood that their aspirations may remain unfulfilled.

Implications

In many respects, an increasing segment of urban Aboriginal populations appears to be moving, or becoming positioned for entry, into positions associated with new middle classes. Labour market changes, educational advancement, and emerging business and employment opportunities have increased the numbers and proportions of individuals who are engaged or aspiring to careers in professional and managerial work. Entrepreneurial work is also producing new options for self-sufficiency and managerial and professional expertise. These changes are further fuelled by the expansion of populations, markets, and service needs that contribute to employment options for the growing numbers of urban Aboriginal people who have advanced qualifications, training, and skills. Aboriginal people are gradually becoming more integrated into key professional and administrative roles in diverse sectors. The concentration of highly qualified and experienced Aboriginal people in urban centres has opened doors to develop new networks, contacts, and spheres of influence that are likely to maintain themselves and foster opportunities for further growth and development in these regards. The climate is gradually changing to acknowledge the positive contributions these emergent capacities can offer to promote the interests of Aboriginal people and enhance their ties with organizations that previously have had limited engagement with the Aboriginal population. Commenting on the recent appointment by the Saskatoon Chamber of Commerce of its first Aboriginal president, newspaper columnist Doug Cuthand observes: "We now have second- and third-generation urban Indians who see a place for themselves in society that their parents couldn't see. Traditionally, our people have migrated to the cities and remained on the fringes. The only community involvement for most would revolve around the school or minor sports, mainly activities that involved their children. Today's urban aboriginal people are an important part of the social and economic fabric."[17]

These developments, of course, do not in themselves signify the creation of a distinct urban Aboriginal new middle class. Some consciousness of common interests and concerns is evident in business and professional associations, formal and informal lobby groups, and other networks that provide mutual support, voice, and options to develop professional and business connections. The establishment of professional associations, and related publications and journals like the *Canadian Native Law Bulletin, Aboriginal Nurse,* and *Native Social Work Journal,* represent efforts to foster a collective identity and body of knowledge that arise around the concerns of Aboriginal people in specific occupational roles. Many of these linkages are reflected further in lifestyle choices and consumption patterns that contribute to the cultivation of common social, economic, or political orientations. Further implications that arise from these trends could be explored by considering the extent to which class dynamics are related with important factors, such as spatial arrangements constituted by the location of residential and business establishments, the presence of reserves and treaty lands within urban centres, tax policies, and community infrastructures.

There remain numerous contradictions and dimensions associated with Aboriginal people's class locations, particularly in the intermediate positions explored here. Professional, managerial, and entrepreneurial work tends to be highly individualistic and fragmentary, often producing isolation or tensions to balance personal, family, cultural, and community obligations with career demands. Aboriginal people in these positions frequently strive to maintain a powerful sense of commitment to indigenous communities. The privileged positions that they occupy, relative to many of their urban counterparts, can also produce pressures to reconcile personal success with concerns for social justice and effective action to ensure that Aboriginal people as a whole can gain meaningful opportunities within Canadian society. At the same time, even the successes that they have accomplished can be incomplete or precarious, particularly in the face of continuing racial discrimination and related concerns. Recent analysis of housing data in Toronto, for example, shows that only 53 percent of Aboriginal people in professional and managerial positions, compared with 81 percent of white managers and professionals, were homeowners.[18] Practices that operate as barriers to promotion and career advancement for highly placed, as well as lower level, workers continue to be embedded within many occupational cultures, institutional procedures, and life circumstances. For Aboriginal as well as non-Aboriginal people, the precarious nature of middle-class status is reinforced by evidence pointing to the high degree of entrepreneurial failure, the reality that most professional and managerial workers have limited discretion as paid employees subordinated within larger organizations or decision-making hierarchies, and the limited cohesion among persons in intermediate class positions.

The question as to how effective social and economic advancement can be accomplished for more than limited segments of the population remains a powerful consideration for Aboriginal and non-Aboriginal populations alike. As the urban environment produces growing numbers of success stories as well as tales of despair, it is critical to acknowledge not only the diversity of characteristics and conditions among the Aboriginal population, but also the mechanisms that produce differentiation. Strategic institutional initiatives and policy interventions can be beneficial for individual and community capacity-building when they are employed to guide life transitions from educational and occupational aspirations to economic and social successes. Integration of programs and services in concert with a clear understanding of community needs and strengths is particularly important, as demonstrated by numerous initiatives that have produced positive results, including community schooling and university access programs, professional development and leadership training mentorship, and economic development plans that combine training with meaningful job creation. Further consideration is required to ensure that Aboriginal people have access to sufficient opportunities to employ their credentials and capacities in relevant employment and institutional situations.

Increasing numbers of educated and skilled Aboriginal people are making inroads into key labour market and decision-making positions, their profile enhanced by prominent professional, political, and business leaders. The more difficult transformation entails the creation of environments that will enable considerably larger proportions of the population to have similar options and advantages.

Notes

1   The term Aboriginal people refers in this paper to all indigenous groups, including First Nations, Métis, Inuit, or any other category of First Peoples in Canada based on ancestry and/or identity. Data are drawn from primary and secondary sources collected by Statistics Canada. Unless otherwise specified, data with regard to Aboriginal refers to those persons who reported identifying on the 1996 Census with at least one Aboriginal group and/or who reported being a Treaty Indian or Registered Indian as defined by the *Indian Act* and/or who reported they were members of an Indian band or First Nation.

2   Fukuyama, F. (1992) *The End of History and the Last Man*, New York: The Free Press; Bell, D. (1973) *The Coming of Post-Industrial Society: A Venture in Social Forecasting*, New York: Basic Books, present influential accounts that herald the transcendence of conventional class and ideological divisions by fundamentally new or less clearly defined characteristics. By contrast, the work of E.O. Wright, see, for example, *Classes* (London: Verso, 1987), and Western, M. and E.O. Wright (1994) "The Permeability of Class Boundaries to Intergenerational Mobility Among Men in the United States, Canada, Norway and Sweden," *American Sociological Review*, 59 (August); 606-629, offers perhaps the most widely used applications of class relations in late capitalism.

3   Daniels, D. (1987) "Dreams and Realities of Dene Government," *The Canadian Journal of Native Studies*, 7(1): 95-110; Haddad, T. and M. Spivey (1992) "All or Nothing: Modernization, Dependency and Wage Labour on a Reserve in Canada," *The Canadian Journal of Native Studies*, 12(2): 203-228; Brown, R. (1996) "The Exploitation of the Oil and Gas Frontier: Its Impact on Lubicon Lake Cree Women," in *Women of the First Nations: Power, Wisdom, and Strength*, C. Miller and P. Chuchryk, (eds.), Winnipeg: The University of Manitoba Press, pp. 151-165; Elias, P.D. (1990) "Wage Labour, Aboriginal Rights and the Cree of the Churchill River Basin, Saskatchewan," *Native Studies Review*, 6(2), pp. 43-64; Satzewich, V. and T. Wotherspoon (2000) *First Nations: Race, Class, and Gender Relations*, Regina: Canadian Plains Research Center.

4   Albers, Patricia C. (1996) "From Legend to Land to Labour: Changing Perspectives on North American Work," in *Native Americans and Wage Labour: Ethnohistorical Perspectives*, Alice Littlefield and Martha C. Knack, (eds.), Norman, OK: University of Oklahoma Press, 1996, p. 264.

5   RCAP (Royal Commission on Aboriginal Peoples) (1996) *Report of the Royal Commission on Aboriginal Peoples*, Volume 2: *Restructuring the Relationship*, Ottawa: Minister of Supply and Services Canada, pp. 814-815 and Volume 4: *Perspectives and Realities*, Ottawa: Minister of Supply and Services Canada, pp. 520ff.; La Prairie, C. (1995) *Seen But Not Heard: Aboriginal People in the City*, Ottawa: Minister of Justice Canada; Hull, J. (2000) "Aboriginal Post-Secondary Education and Labour Market Outcomes, Canada, 1996," Report prepared for Indian and Northern Affairs Canada, Winnipeg, October, pp. 77-79; INAC (Indian and Northern Affairs Canada) (2001) *Aboriginal Labour Force Characteristics from the 1996 Census*, Ottawa: Minister of Public Works and Government Services Canada, March, p. 108.

6 Wright, E.O. (1997) *Class Counts: Comparative Studies in Class Analysis*, Cambridge: Cambridge University Press; Livingstone, D.W. (1999) *The Education-Jobs Gap: Underemployment or Economic Democracy*, Toronto: Garamond Press, pp. 154-159; Nakhaie M.R. and J. Curtis (1998) "Effects of Class Positions of Parents on Educational Attainment of Daughters and Sons," *Canadian Review of Sociology and Anthropology*, 35(4) (November): 489-491.

7 See, e.g., Wolfson, M.C. (1997) *Divergent Inequalities – Theory and Empirical Results*, Ottawa: Statistics Canada, Analytical Studies Branch Research Paper Series, No. 66 revised, Cat. no. 11-F0019MPE No. 66.

8 The work of P. Bourdieu has drawn attention to the importance of class factors in strategic positioning for socially valued positions, especially among the new middle classes. See Bourdieu, P. (1984) *Distinction: A Social Critique of the Judgement of Taste*, Cambridge, MA: Harvard University Press; Crompton, R. (1998) *Class and Stratification: An Introduction to Current Debates*, second edition, Cambridge, UK: Polity Press.

9 See, e.g., Bernier, R. (1997) *The Dimensions of Wage Inequality among Aboriginal People*, Ottawa: Statistics Canada Analytical Studies Branch Research Series Paper No. 109, December, p. 8.

10 Industry Canada (1998) *Aboriginal Entrepreneurs in Canada: Progress and Prospects*, Ottawa: Industry Canada, pp. 3, 10-12; see also Chiste, K.B. (ed.) (1996) *Aboriginal Small Business and Entrepreneurship in Canada*, North York, ON: Captus Press.

11 Statistics Canada (1989) *Dimensions: Profile of Ethnic Groups, 1986 Census*, Ottawa: Minister of Supply and Services Canada, Cat. no. 93-154; Statistics Canada (2000) *Dimensions: Portrait of Aboriginal Population in Canada, 1996 Census*, Ottawa: Minister of Public Works and Government Services Canada, Cat. no. 94F0009XDB96001.

12 CCSD (Canadian Council on Social Development) (2000) *Unequal Access: A Canadian Profile of Racial Differences in Education, Employment and Income*, Ottawa: A Report Prepared for the Canadian Race Relations Council, pp. 20-21; Hull, "Aboriginal Post-Secondary Education," p. 4; Satzewich, V. and T. Wotherspoon (2000) *First Nations: Race, Class, and Gender Relations*, Regina: Canadian Plains Research Center, pp. 68-69.

13 See Schissel, B. and T. Wotherspoon (2002) *The Legacy of School for Aboriginal People: Education, Oppression, and Emancipation*, Toronto: Oxford University Press, 2002; chapters assembled in Castellano, M.B., L. Davis, and L. Lahache (2000) *Aboriginal Education: Fulfilling the Promise*, Vancouver: UBC Press.

14 CCSD, *Unequal Access*, pp. 16-17.

15 Hull, "Aboriginal Post-Secondary Education," pp. 34-37; Statistics Canada, 2000, pp. 9-12; CCSD, ibid., pp. 18-22.

16 Schissel and Wotherspoon, *The Legacy of School*.

17 Cuthand, D. (2002) "Natives Taking Increasing Leadership in City," *Saskatoon Star-Phoenix*, May 10, p. A15.

18 Darder, J.T. and S.M. Kamel (2001) "Difference in Homeownership Rates Between Aboriginal People and White Canadians in the Toronto Census Metropolitan Area: Does Race Matter?" *Native Studies Review*, 14(1): 64.

Ensuring the Urban Dream: Shared Responsibility and Effective Urban Aboriginal Voices

Calvin Hanselmann[1]
Senior Policy Analyst
Canada West Foundation

Introduction

Like the population as a whole, Canada's Aboriginal people are increasingly chasing the urban dream – the opportunities and quality of life that cities can offer. Whereas seven percent of Aboriginal people lived in cities in 1951, a mere 50 years have resulted in over one half of the enumerated Aboriginal identity population living in urban areas.[2] The urbanization of Aboriginal people is especially obvious in western Canada, where the 2001 Census showed Aboriginal people can comprise as much as 10 percent of the population of a major city.[3]

This shift in the Aboriginal population, from living primarily in reserve and rural areas to living in urban areas, has not been matched by public policy successes. Federal and provincial governments continue to deny responsibility for this area. At the same time, urban Aboriginal people are rarely represented by effective political and policy voices. These two conditions have inhibited comprehensive, consistent policy and programming responses. To improve urban Aboriginal policy and programming, and therefore make the urban dream a reality, will require that federal and provincial governments set aside their jurisdictional issues while urban Aboriginal people develop voices that can represent their interests.

This paper is based on recent research conducted in six major western Canadian cities. Although the research was limited to selected cities, the findings are relevant to every city in Canada with significant Aboriginal populations. The paper is neither an academic treatise nor a literature review; rather, it provides a brief overview of the contemporary policy and programming landscapes in those six cities, and reviews two factors – jurisdictional wrangling and insufficient involvement by urban Aboriginal people – that have contributed to the state of those landscapes.[4] The paper concludes with suggestions for improving urban Aboriginal policy and programming.

Contemporary Policy and Programming Landscapes

Recent research sought to identify to what extent, if any, federal, provincial, and municipal governments had created differentiated policy and program environments with respect to urban Aboriginal people in six major western Canadian cities: Calgary, Edmonton, Regina, Saskatoon, Vancouver, and Winnipeg.

The research first examined the policy landscapes in the six cities by focusing on urban Aboriginal-specific policies, defined as "an explicit public expression of a governmental or departmental approach to addressing issues confronting urban Aboriginal people."[5] A comparison of socio-economic conditions among urban Aboriginal people with those of non-Aboriginal urban residents drew attention to the particular importance of 17 policy fields.[6]

The research found that governments have implemented urban Aboriginal-specific policies in some, but far from all, important fields. Urban Aboriginal-specific policies were identified in the fields of education, training, employment, income support, economic development, health, homelessness, housing, justice, human rights, urban transition, and cultural support. However, no urban Aboriginal-specific policies were located in the fields of family violence, child care, addictions, or suicide, and there were large gaps in the urban Aboriginal-specific policy landscape with respect to human rights, income support, housing, and urban transition. By contrast, multiple layers of urban Aboriginal-specific policies were found in many cases. The fields in which multiple layers of policy most often occurred were employment, training, and justice; among orders of government, federal and provincial policies were most frequently layered in the same fields in the same cities.

The programming landscapes in the same six cities were also reviewed to identify the "enhanced" programming available for urban Aboriginal people. Enhanced programs are defined as "those that provide designated populations with programmatic consideration at a level beyond that available to the general population."[7] In addition to the policy fields examined earlier, the fields of family, youth, and corrections were investigated.

Similar to the policy findings, the research found that federal, provincial, and municipal governments have created enhanced urban Aboriginal programming in several, but not all, important fields. While the research found literally hundreds of examples of enhanced urban Aboriginal programs, no enhanced programming was found in income support or suicide, and almost none in human rights. The other 17 fields all had programming in each of the cities. The research also found that much of the enhanced urban Aboriginal programming, while funded by federal, provincial, and/or municipal governments, was actually delivered by Aboriginal or non-profit organizations.

The first observation from the research is that – at least to some extent – federal, provincial, and municipal governments have created differentiated policy and programming environments for urban Aboriginal people in six large western Canadian cities. The second – and vital – observation is that governments are not active in every important field. Given that, on average, urban Aboriginal people have significantly lower incomes, are more likely to experience domestic violence, have greater child-care needs, show higher incidences of substance abuse and suicide, and face more acute human rights challenges than do most non-Aboriginal people, the urban Aboriginal policy and programming gaps are noteworthy. The third observation, suggested by the identification of layers of government activity, is that federal, provincial, and municipal governments are not approaching urban Aboriginal issues in a co-ordinated way.

In short, the research identified inconsistencies in urban Aboriginal policy and programming. These inconsistencies may be rooted in the near absence of the kind of comprehensive, systematic approaches that would be expected in an important policy area. The research identified the Government of Canada, Province of Alberta, Province of Saskatchewan, City of Saskatoon, and City of Winnipeg as having "government-wide" urban Aboriginal-specific policies.[8] Setting aside the two municipal governments – municipalities have neither the responsibility nor capacity to systematically or comprehensively address social policy issues – leaves three government-wide urban Aboriginal-specific policies. A close examination of these policies shows little in the way of systematic, comprehensive approaches to urban Aboriginal policy.

First, the Government of Canada's Urban Aboriginal Strategy (UAS) was categorized as a government-wide policy. Although the UAS was first rolled out in 1998, even as late as the spring of 2003 no publicly available document specifies the actual "strategy."[9] Despite this, the federal government has expressed, in numerous presentations and other forms of communications, its intentions: the UAS is the means by which the Government of Canada will address urban Aboriginal issues "through greater internal coordination of federal activities and through partnerships with provinces, municipalities and Aboriginal stakeholders."[10] The Federal Interlocutor for Métis and Non-Status Indians is charged with implementing the UAS. However, the Interlocutor has "no department of government and no significant budget to work with ... [and] no legal authority."[11] Indeed, not all departments of the Government of Canada participate in the UAS; rather, it focuses on involving those departments that have been identified as being key to the initiative. Clearly, the Urban Aboriginal Strategy is not a systematic, comprehensive approach to urban Aboriginal policy.

Second, the Province of Alberta's Strengthening Relationships was also identified as a government-wide urban Aboriginal-specific policy document.[12] Strengthening Relationships is the Government of Alberta's Aboriginal policy framework. It calls for all ministries and agencies to address Aboriginal issues in their business plans and to report on progress in their annual reports. Although urban Aboriginal issues are included in Strengthening Relationships, it is a co-ordinating framework rather than a comprehensive and systematic approach to urban Aboriginal policy.

The third policy, the Province of Saskatchewan's Framework for Co-operation, is that government's approach to issues affecting Métis and off-reserve First Nations people. The Government commits to working in partnership with others on key goals. However, although the document "speaks to working with municipal governments," this is not exactly a commitment to systematically and comprehensively addressing urban Aboriginal issues.[13]

In summary, there is very little in the way of systematic, comprehensive urban Aboriginal policy in major western Canadian cities. So what is the reader to make of this? The dearth of systematic and comprehensive approaches to – and the resultant inconsistencies in – urban Aboriginal policy and programming can largely be attributed to two long-standing issues: a refusal on the part of governments to accept primary responsibility for urban Aboriginal policy and a near absence of effective urban Aboriginal political and policy voices.

Historical Intergovernmental Disagreements

One of the most significant factors contributing to both the challenging circumstances facing many urban Aboriginal people and the contemporary policy and programming environment is disagreement between the Government of Canada and provincial governments over the question of responsibility for urban Aboriginal policy.[14] Although this is an old story, it is one that bears repeating: federal and provincial governments have avoided accepting responsibility for urban Aboriginal policy and "many urban Aboriginal policy challenges are largely the result of a jurisdictional issue that has been transplanted to the urban setting."[15]

The Government of Canada historically took the position – flowing from a narrow interpretation of section 91(24) of the Constitution – that its responsibilities were limited exclusively to status Indians living on-reserve (the Supreme Court expanded federal responsibility to include the Inuit) while all other Aboriginal people, including urban Aboriginal people, were the exclusive responsibility of provincial governments. This posture has softened recently as the Government of Canada has suggested that the division of responsibilities is not exclusive; rather, that the federal government has primary responsibility with respect to First Nations people on-reserve while provincial governments are primarily (but not exclusively) responsible for serving all other Aboriginal people.[16] For their part, provincial governments contend that *all* Aboriginal people are the primary responsibility of the federal government.[17] In short, each order of government continues to deny that *it* holds responsibility for urban Aboriginal policy.

This disagreement over responsibility has hindered effective policy and programming for decades, leading to "inconclusive activity" and a "policy vacuum," in which "[i]naction, indecision and uncooperative behaviour become a substitute for action."[18] The contemporary policy and programming landscape, which lacks systematic, comprehensive approaches and features instead inconsistencies, is rooted to a large part in federal–provincial disagreement and failure to accept responsibility.

Lack of Political and Policy Voices

Another root cause of the difficult policy and programming environment is the near absence of effective urban Aboriginal political and policy voices. This is to a great extent understandable, since urban Aboriginal people are far from homogeneous groups. Aboriginal people in any major city in Canada are drawn from any number of Aboriginal nations and identities. Some urban Aboriginal people have treaty rights, some are Status Indians, some are members of specific Aboriginal nations, and some see themselves as part of an urban Aboriginal identity. Since so many cultures and identities are represented in urban settings, it is not surprising when representation is contested or absent. Nonetheless, the absence of effective urban Aboriginal political and policy voices in many settings has contributed to policy and programming challenges.

In the design and implementation of policies and programs, federal, provincial, and municipal governments rarely meet consistent, unified urban Aboriginal political and policy voices. In some cases, national Aboriginal organizations make contradictory and conflicting claims to represent urban Aboriginal people. This is the case when, for example, the Assembly of First Nations claims to represent all First Nations people (including those living off-reserve), the Métis National Council purports to speak for all Métis people (including those living in urban centres), and the Inuit Kanatami asserts that it is the voice of the Inuit (regardless of residential location) – all at the same time that the Congress of Aboriginal Peoples claims to represent the interests of all off-reserve Aboriginal people and the National Association of Friendship Centres begins to stake its claim as a representative organization. In some urban centres, local, regional, and provincial Aboriginal organizations advancing similar declarations join this cacophony of competing claims. To add to the confusion are recent judicial interpretations, such as *Corbière*, which require First Nation governments to take some account of their off-reserve members.[19] Finally, some proximate First Nations claim to represent their members while others disavow any connection with urban Aboriginal people.

The absence of effective political and policy voices for urban Aboriginal people means that federal, provincial, and municipal governments are confronted by a setting of a sort to which they are unaccustomed. Typically, governments operate in an environment in which they can depend on organized interests to represent the stakeholders in an issue. Urban Aboriginal people do not have that organized voice and, as a result, governments are having difficulty operating in this environment.

Moving Forward

To improve urban Aboriginal policy and programming will therefore require at least two major changes. Decades of squabbling over responsibility have seen inconsistent policies, programs of questionable effectiveness, wasted tax dollars, and lost human lives as the urban dream has been closer to a nightmare for some Aboriginal people. Therefore, the first major change is that federal and provincial governments have to set aside their jurisdictional issues and work together on urban Aboriginal policy.[20] To be truly effective, the federal and provincial governments should agree on shared responsibility for urban Aboriginal policy. The agreement should be formally established and institutionalized so that there is no question but that policies and programs of both the federal and provincial governments will address urban Aboriginal issues. Each order of government should then ensure that appropriate resources are committed to urban Aboriginal issues.

The second major change is that urban Aboriginal people need effective political and policy voices to speak on their behalf.[21] This means that urban Aboriginal people have to set aside their own version of long-standing disagreements. In this case, the disagreement is with respect to representation. Rather than conflicting claims of representation, urban Aboriginal people need to be represented by consistent, unified political organizations. Because each urban Aboriginal "community" is unique, each city will see its own organization – and sometimes more than one organization – develop. To be seen to be legitimate, these organizations must be chosen by urban Aboriginal people, and must be effective at speaking on behalf of their constituencies – constituencies that must be real. In turn, other Aboriginal political leaders need to respect that decision and allow effective urban Aboriginal political and policy voices to develop.

Beyond the two major changes noted above – shared federal-provincial policy responsibility and effective urban Aboriginal political and policy voices – one more condition must be met to ensure successful, effective urban Aboriginal policy and programming in the future. The knowledge base upon which policy decisions are made must be broadened through additional research.[22] Without research findings, it is difficult to persuade decision makers of the importance of urban Aboriginal issues, the necessity to act, or the appropriate course. Therefore, while much has been learned, more research needs to be completed.

First, horizontal or holistic approaches to urban Aboriginal policy and programming have been identified as appropriate means by which to address urban Aboriginal issues.[23] However, these approaches will not become commonplace unless and until accountability frameworks that can facilitate non-traditional approaches, while respecting the requirements of responsible government, are developed. Although the Government of Canada has made some progress in this area, other governments must also be involved. Therefore, research should be conducted into effective accountability and responsibility frameworks that can serve as alternatives to the status quo.

Second, public servants must be encouraged to innovate, while remaining accountable for their actions. The message from above must be that making a mistake will not endanger the career of an innovator. If the current cultures of risk aversion in public services are not overcome, urban Aboriginal policies and programs will continue to be much more static, and much less effective, than should be the case. For this reason, research needs to occur into ways in which public servants can be rewarded, rather than punished, for program innovation.

Third, the need for capacity building among Aboriginal organizations – both service delivery and political – is not going to diminish; rather, it will increase as urban Aboriginal populations grow in absolute and relative terms. The need for financial resources will also increase as urban Aboriginal organizations become more involved with federal, provincial, and municipal governments. Therefore, research into alternative funding mechanisms for urban Aboriginal organizations should be conducted. This research should consider, among the options identified, an examination of own-source revenues for urban Aboriginal political organizations.

Finally, urban Aboriginal issues are under-resourced, particularly in the area of transition programming, and in comparison to reserve-based First Nation communities.[24] Part of the reason for current insufficient resources for urban Aboriginal policies and programming may be the difficulty in making a business case for putting money into urban Aboriginal issues. Therefore, the costs and returns to urban Aboriginal people, government, and society associated with the current levels of support should be calculated and compared to the costs and returns expected from significantly enhanced investments.

Conclusion

The contemporary policy and programming landscapes show that federal, provincial, and municipal governments are somewhat active in urban Aboriginal policy. However, although the findings show that some progress is being made, the inconsistencies mean that more needs to be done. Federal and provincial agreement on shared responsibility is required, and consistent, effective urban Aboriginal political and policy voices must emerge.

In this regard, all is not bleak. There are encouraging examples of intergovernmental co-operation, emerging urban Aboriginal political and policy voices, and recent signs, such as the 2003 federal budget, that some governments are committed to improving urban Aboriginal policy and programming. When effective political and policy voices for urban Aboriginal people emerge, it will be easier for federal, provincial, and municipal governments to work with urban Aboriginal people to improve urban Aboriginal policies and programming. Getting there will require the participation of Canadians, Aboriginal and non-Aboriginal. Urban Aboriginal leaders and Canadian governments – federal, provincial, and municipal – must work together with interested Canadians to ensure that the urban dream is available to everyone.

Notes

1   The opinions expressed in this paper are those of the author and not necessarily of the Canada West Foundation's donors, subscribers, or Board. The author thanks Evelyn Peters for helpful comments.

2   Drost, Helmar (1995) "The Aboriginal-White Unemployment Gap in Canada's Urban Labor Markets," in *Market Solutions for Native Poverty: Social Policy for the Third Solitude*, H. Drost, B.L. Crowley, and R. Schwindt, (eds.), Toronto: C.D. Howe Institute; Hanselmann, Calvin (2003) *Shared Responsibility: Final Report and Recommendations of the Urban Aboriginal Initiative*, Calgary: Canada West Foundation.

3   Statistics Canada 2003) *Aboriginal Peoples of Canada:* Aboriginal origin (10), age groups (11B), sex (3) and area of residence (7) for population, for Canada, provinces and territories, 2001 Census, 20 percent sample data, Catalogue no 97F0011XIE2001003. On-line <www.statcan.ca> accessed March 11, 2003. The major city with the highest proportion of people reporting either Aboriginal origins or Aboriginal identity is Saskatoon. See Hanselmann, *Shared Responsibility*.

4   Readers seeking either academic treatments or literature reviews of urban Aboriginal issues may wish to start with: Peters, Evelyn J. (2002) "Geographies of Urban Aboriginal People in Canada," paper presented to Reconfiguring Aboriginal-State Relations in Canada: State of the Federation 2003, Institute of Intergovernmental Relations, Queen's University, November 2002; or Graham, Katherine and Evelyn Peters (2002) "Aboriginal Communities and Urban Sustainability," in *The Federal Role in Canada's Cities: Four Policy Perspectives*, F. Leslie Seidle, (ed.), CPRN Discussion Paper No. F|27 (Ottawa: Canadian Policy Research Networks or, other papers in this volume.

5   Hanselmann, Calvin (2001) *Urban Aboriginal People in Western Canada: Realities and Policies*, Calgary: Canada West Foundation, p. 11.

6   The policy fields researched were education, training, employment, income support, economic development, family violence, child care, health, addictions, suicide, homelessness, housing, justice, human rights, urban transition, and cultural support. A category named "other" was created to ensure that the research could capture all important policy initiatives. See Hanselmann, ibid.

7   Hanselmann, Calvin (2002) *Enhanced Urban Aboriginal Programming in Western Canada*, Calgary: Canada West Foundation, p. 2.

8   Hanselmann, *Urban Aboriginal People in Western Canada*, p. 12.

9   Privy Council Office official, telephone interview, March 20, 2003.

10 Goodale, Hon. Ralph (2002) "Urban Aboriginal Strategy: Presentation to the Prime Minister's Caucus Task Force on Urban Issues," February 25, 2002.

11 Ibid.

12 Hanselmann, *Urban Aboriginal People in Western Canada*, p. 14.

13 Ibid., p. 14.

14 This overview is necessarily brief. Readers seeking more expansive reviews may wish to consult, for example, Wherrett, Jill and Douglas Brown (1994) *Models for Aboriginal Government in Urban Areas*, Ottawa: Indian and Northern Affairs Canada; RCAP (Royal Commission on Aboriginal Peoples) (1996) *Report of the Royal Commission on Aboriginal Peoples*, Vol. 4: *Perspectives and Realities*, Ottawa: Minister of Supply and Services; Hanselmann, Calvin and Roger Gibbins (2002) "Another Voice Is Needed: Intergovernmentalism in the Urban Aboriginal Context," a paper presented to Reconfiguring Aboriginal-State Relations in Canada: State of the Federation 2003, Institute of Intergovernmental Relations, Queen's University, November 2002; or Graham and Peters, "Aboriginal Communities and Urban Sustainability."

15 Hanselmann, *Shared Responsibility*, p. 7.

16 Goodale, "Urban Aboriginal Strategy," [emphasis in original].

17 RCAP, Vol. 4: *Perspectives and Realities*.

18 Breton, Raymond and Gail Grant, (eds.) (1984) *The Dynamics of Government Programs for Urban Indians in the Prairie Provinces*, Montréal: Institute for Research on Public Policy, p. xxx; RCAP, Vol. 4: *Perspectives and Realities*, p. 542; Hanselmann and Gibbins, "Another Voice is Needed," p. 4.

19 *Corbière v. Canada (Minister of Indian and Northern Affairs)* [1999] 2 S.C.R. 203.

20 Hanselmann, *Shared Responsibility*, pp. 7-9.

21 Hanselmann and Gibbins, "Another Voice Is Needed."

22 The section that follows is excerpted, with permission of the author and publisher, from Hanselmann, *Shared Responsibility*, pp. 16-18.

23 Institute on Governance (2001) "UAS National Case Study," Ottawa: Institute on Governance, December; Hanselmann, Calvin (2002) *Uncommon Sense: Promising Practices in Urban Aboriginal Policy-Making and Programming*, Calgary: Canada West Foundation; Hanselmann, *Shared Responsibility*. The Government of Canada has produced several reports and documents that speak to the importance of horizontal or holistic approaches. A good starting point is: Hopkins, Mark, Chantal Couture, and Elizabeth Moore (2001) *Moving From the Heroic to the Everyday: Lessons Learned From Leading Horizontal Projects*, Ottawa: Canadian Centre for Management Development. Beyond that, interested readers should refer to the Treasury Board of Canada Secretariat Web site.

24 Hanselmann, *Shared Responsibility*.

Exile on Main Street: Some Thoughts on Aboriginal Over-Representation in the Criminal Justice System

Carol La Prairie
Policy, Programs and Integration
Justice Canada

Philip Stenning
Centre of Criminology
University of Toronto

Introduction

The last two decades in Canada have been marked by controversy and public anxiety over the "over-representation"[1] of Aboriginal people[2] in the criminal justice system, especially in its prisons ("over-incarceration"), and what measures may be appropriate to respond to this situation. A host of public inquiries, committee hearings and academic writings have been devoted to analyses of this problem,[3] and it has been commonly asserted that the mere fact of Aboriginal over-representation in the criminal justice system indicates that the system has "failed" Aboriginal people, and has led to Aboriginal people having no confidence in it.

Not surprisingly, such conclusions have led to proposals for radical reform, including advocacy of an entirely separate justice system for Aboriginal people, with its own distinctive Aboriginal police, court (or other dispute resolution fora), and correctional institutions. Such reform proposals, voiced primarily by Aboriginal leaders and non-Aboriginal academics, have been endorsed in the reports of some of the official inquiries set up to examine these issues (notably the self-styled "Aboriginal Justice Inquiry" in Manitoba (Manitoba, 1991), and the subsequent Royal Commission on Aboriginal Peoples (RCAP), which issued a report on this topic in 1996.

Even official government policies in response to the problem of Aboriginal over-representation in the criminal justice system, which typically have not adopted the more radical reform proposals, have nevertheless been based on similar assumptions and conclusions about the nature of this problem. Specifically, official criminal justice policies with respect to

Aboriginal people appear to have been based on the assumption that the over-representation of Aboriginal people in the criminal justice system has been due to a combination of "culturally insensitive" and discriminatory policing ("over-policing"[4] as well as "under-policing"[5]) and criminal justice processing (e.g., sentencing), and a high rate of offending (and victimization) in "Aboriginal communities," which itself is the result of historical colonization, exploitation, and consequent social, economic, and cultural deterioration of such communities.

Not surprisingly, these underlying assumptions have led to the view that the problem of Aboriginal over-involvement can best be addressed by replacing mainstream policing of Aboriginal communities with policing by more "culturally sensitive" autonomous Aboriginal police services, more directly sensitive and accountable to these communities; the establishment of separate "Aboriginal justice" institutions which will better reflect the cultural traditions and current social needs of Aboriginal people; and/or special provisions in mainstream criminal justice processing (such as *Criminal Code* s. 718.2(e), *R. v. Gladue*[6] and *R. Wells*[7]), whereby cases involving Aboriginal offenders will be treated differently from those involving non-Aboriginal offenders. Implicit in most, if not all, of these proposals are assumptions that the problem of Aboriginal over-involvement in the criminal justice system arises from circumstances which are unique to Aboriginal people, and "Aboriginal communities" are identifiable as discrete social entities, in which separate Aboriginal criminal justice institutions can be established and operated more or less independently of the mainstream criminal justice institutions which function in non-Aboriginal communities.

These responses reflect an understanding of Aboriginal over-involvement in the criminal justice system as being attributable mainly, if not exclusively, to cultural differences between Aboriginal and non-Aboriginal people, and the particularly damaging effects of the historical "Aboriginal experience" in Canada. The problem of Aboriginal over-involvement with the criminal justice system is thus viewed as directly linked to Aboriginality itself, and the conclusion is that the "white" criminal justice system is, and will always be, inherently incapable of responding appropriately, effectively, and acceptably to these Aboriginal realities. The circumstances of Aboriginal offenders and victims are thus regarded, by the Supreme Court of Canada and others, as "unique."[8]

However, recent research on the characteristics of Aboriginal offending and victimization, and on the particulars of Aboriginal over-incarceration, as well as on Aboriginal perceptions of the criminal justice system, raise serious questions about the validity of many of these assumptions and the appropriateness of this conceptual framework for understanding and responding to the problem. We address each assumption in turn, beginning with some recent data on Aboriginal perceptions of the criminal justice system, then turning our attention to data on the characteristics of prison populations, the demographics of the Aboriginal population in Canada and, finally, looking at some of the characteristics of Aboriginal crime and victimization, particularly in the urban context.

Aboriginal Perceptions of the Criminal Justice System

A recent publication of the Canadian Center for Justice Statistics (CCJS) titled *Aboriginal Peoples in Canada* (2001a) provided some new and interesting data[9] on perceptions of Aboriginal people[10] about the criminal justice system. Of particular interest in this respect are the somewhat conflicting opinions held by Aboriginal people about different components of the criminal justice system.

When asked: "What kind of a job are your local police doing?" Aboriginal respondents were somewhat less satisfied with the way police are doing their jobs than were non-Aboriginal Canadians. However, when assessing courts and their ability to ensure the guilt or innocence of accused and ensure fair trials, there were no differences between the Aboriginal and non-Aboriginal respondents. Aboriginal respondents were slightly more likely than non-Aboriginal respondents to assess courts as doing a good job in providing justice quickly and helping victims (CCJS, 2001a: 8).

These findings are important because they suggest that there is not a general Aboriginal dissatisfaction with the criminal justice system, but mainly with police. This may have something to do with the fact that, as a group, Aboriginal people have considerably more contact with police. The fact that those who have more frequent contact with police (whether Aboriginal or not) tend to have less favourable views about them is well documented in the research literature (Hagan and McCarthy, 1998). As we shall discuss further below, there is now ample research that indicates that Aboriginal people in Canada are more likely to come to the attention of police both because they are more likely to be victims of a violent offence and because they commit a disproportionate number of violent and public order offences.

Even Aboriginal perceptions of the police are by no means uniform, however. They vary regionally and between urban and rural communities. In a 1994 study of Aboriginal people[11] living in four major urban centres in Canada (two in the Prairies and two in eastern Canada) important regional and city vs. reserve or home community differences were found. In cities, courts were viewed most favourably and police worse in respondent's perceptions of fairness of treatment. In home communities or reserves, police fared much better, and respondents viewed treatment by police, courts, and the criminal justice system generally more favourably than did respondents in cities. Furthermore, perceptions of fairness of treatment by police were also more favourable among Aboriginal people in the eastern than in the Prairie cities (La Prairie, 1994).

Recent inquiries and accusations in Prairie urban areas involving city police and Aboriginal people have no doubt contributed to these negative perceptions and strained relations. In Saskatoon, two officers were found guilty of transporting an Aboriginal man to the outskirts of the city and dropping him off in freezing weather. In Winnipeg, the police department has been accused of racism in its slow response to urgent calls that resulted in the stabbing deaths of two Aboriginal women.

The important bottom line that emerges from these data, however, is that Aboriginal people have apparently not, by any means, generally lost confidence in the criminal justice system, although many of them clearly have serious concerns about the police.

Demographics and Involvement in the Criminal Justice System

While discrimination or "cultural insensitivity" by agents of the criminal justice system may be a plausible explanation for some Aboriginal over-representation in the system, there is growing evidence that the factors that give rise to Aboriginal people's involvement in the criminal justice system are largely the same as those that give rise to non-Aboriginal involvement in it. If class and socio-economic disparity and the disadvantage in people's lives are significant predictors of involvement in the criminal justice system, it is important to examine the implications of this for both Aboriginal and non-Aboriginal populations and offenders.

As Table 1 shows, when gender, age, employment, and education characteristics are examined for *all* inmates in adult correctional institutions in Canada, one finds that in 1996 the following groups were significantly over-represented in adult prison populations:

- males (they comprised 98 percent of the adult prison population but only 49 percent of the general population);
- young people (the mean age of adult inmates is 33, but the mean age of the general population is 41);

▸ the unemployed (49 percent of adult inmates were unemployed at admission to correctional institutions as compared with an unemployment level of 10 percent in the general population); and

▸ the less well educated (34 percent of adult prison inmates had less than a Grade 9 education, compared to 19 percent of adults in Canada).

It should be remembered that the great majority (83 percent) of correctional institution inmates in Canada are non-Aboriginal.[12]

Table 1: Selected demographics, general Canadian, general Aboriginal, general adult inmate and Aboriginal adult inmate populations, 1996

Demographic	Canadian Population %	Aboriginal Population %	General adult inmate population[1] %	Aboriginal adult inmate population[1] %
Gender: Male	49	49	98	91
Mean Age	41	34	33	30
Aged 24 and under	34	53		
Aged 15-24	13	18		
Aged 45+	34	16		
Female single parents[2]	8	19		
Children living with Single parent	15	32		
Unemployed	10	24	49[3]	70[3]
1995 income below $10,000[4]	27	46		
University degree	13	3		
Completed high school	66	46		
Aged 15-19 and still in school	83	68		
Less than grade 9	12	20	37	52

1 Inmate populations refer to inmates in federal, provincial and territorial institutions.
2 Percent of women aged 15-44 who are single parents.
3 At time of admission.
4 Does not include those with no income in 1995.

Sources: CCJS, 2001a and Finn et al., 1999.

Critical to understanding the over-representation of Aboriginal people in inmate populations is understanding how the Aboriginal population differs from the non-Aboriginal one. If the factors that characterize prison populations are to be found more commonly in the general Aboriginal population than in the general non-Aboriginal one, we should not be surprised by Aboriginal over-representation in the correctional system. We therefore turn next to consider the demographics of the Aboriginal and non-Aboriginal populations in Canada.

Current Aboriginal and Non-Aboriginal Population Demographics

As can be seen from Table 1, there are major demographic differences between the Aboriginal and non-Aboriginal populations in Canada. It is clear that in important respects general Aboriginal demographics more closely resemble the demographics of the prison population than do those of the general Canadian population.

Most important in this respect is the significantly higher proportion of Aboriginal people who are in the 15 to 24 age group, compared to the non-Aboriginal population. It is by now well known that those in this age group (especially males) are at highest risk of involvement in the criminal justice system. In that regard, the non-Aboriginal population is very different from the Aboriginal one: there is a proportionately larger "pool" of Aboriginal people in the high-risk (15 to 24) age group (US, 2001; Hagan and McCarthy, 1998). Demographic and criminal justice data reveal younger Aboriginal populations (particularly in the Prairie provinces) and a younger age of initial involvement in the youth justice system (La Prairie, 2002).

People aged 24 and under constitute 53.1 percent of the Aboriginal population in Canada compared to 33.4 percent of the non-Aboriginal population. There are substantial regional variations in these Aboriginal demographics, however. For example, the under-24 group constitutes 51 percent of the Aboriginal population in the Atlantic provinces, 48 percent in Quebec, and 49 percent in Ontario and in British Columbia, but 56 percent in Manitoba, 60 percent in Saskatchewan, and 55 percent in Alberta. These are very significant Aboriginal/ non-Aboriginal and regional Aboriginal differences, which are related to other demographics that are relevant to understanding Aboriginal over-representation.

Table 1 shows that generally, prison inmates are disadvantaged in significant ways compared to the general population, and that, to a lesser extent, these disadvantages are shared by the general Aboriginal population. Aboriginal inmates are the most disadvantaged in these respects. Most importantly for understanding Aboriginal over-representation in the criminal justice system, there are significant regional variations in the disadvantages faced by Aboriginal people. For instance, the concentrations, demographic compositions, and socio-economic circumstances of Aboriginal populations in the Prairie cities are very different from those in other large Canadian cities. The cities with the largest proportions of Aboriginal people living in extremely poor neighbourhoods are Winnipeg (41.2 percent), Saskatoon (30.2 percent), and Regina (26.9 percent). The cities with the smallest are Toronto (15.8 percent), Vancouver (17.1 percent), and Edmonton (19.4 percent). In the eastern cities, similar proportions of Aboriginal and non-Aboriginal people live in poor neighbourhoods, but in Prairie cities the proportion of Aboriginal people living in these circumstances is three or four times that of non-Aboriginal people. In Vancouver and Edmonton, it is twice as high.

In a recent paper exploring variation in Aboriginal disadvantage factors (low income, unemployment, poor education, high mobility, and lone parenting), and subsequent vulnerability to involvement in the criminal justice system in nine major cities across Canada, La Prairie (2002) found these factors to be differentially distributed, with regional distributions paralleling those for over-representation. While the Aboriginal populations in all of the nine cities are generally disadvantaged in relation to the non-Aboriginal populations, there is wide variation in degree of disadvantage, with eastern cities showing the least difference between the two populations and the prairie cities the most. There is much less non-Aboriginal population variation in disadvantage and vulnerability across the nine cities than within the Aboriginal population.

The Relationship Between Disadvantage and Involvement in the Criminal Justice System

As Table 1 clearly suggests, the relationship between socio-economic disadvantage, youth, and involvement in the criminal justice system is certainly not confined to Aboriginal people. For Aboriginal and non-Aboriginal people alike, the most disadvantaged are disproportionately concentrated in urban centres, more particularly in the inner cores of metropolitan areas, which generate both the highest crime rates and the highest over-representation of the disadvantaged (Aboriginal and non-Aboriginal) in the criminal justice system (Edmonton, 1992; La Prairie, 2002). From available research it would appear that even Aboriginal communities which are close to, or on the periphery of, urban centres do not generate as much Aboriginal crime as these inner city areas (La Prairie, 1994).

The research on the involvement of inner-core, urban Aboriginal people in the criminal justice system has been largely restricted to Edmonton, Regina, Saskatoon, and Winnipeg. One of the reasons for this attention is because the Prairie provinces exhibit such high levels of Aboriginal over-representation in correctional institutions (Trevethan, 1991; CCJS, 2000a; La Prairie, 1994). They are also the cities with the highest percentages and concentrations of Aboriginal people living in their inner core areas (La Prairie, 2002). However, the Downtown Eastside (DTES) in Vancouver, which has gained notoriety because of its high drug use and crime problems but has a population which is not predominately Aboriginal, exhibits similar crime and disorder problems to those in inner city areas with high Aboriginal population concentrations.

Data from the 1996 Census suggest that Aboriginal people comprise approximately 31 percent of the DTES. But two important facts stand out about the DTES that have as much to do with the remaining 69 percent of the DTES population. The first is that the DTES is the most socio-economically deprived area of the city. The proportion of the 1996 population below the Low-Income Cut-Off at 51.8 percent is higher than that for Vancouver (31.0 percent), and BC (19.6 percent). The DTES also ranks lowest in the city in levels of education acquired; 53 percent of its population live in single room occupancy dwellings (SROs), and 39 percent in subsidized housing. Most homeless people also gravitate to the DTES because of the availability of services and acceptance (Healy, 2000: 15). Alcohol abuse is "rampant in the DTES" (Healy, 2000: 21). One in four drug-induced deaths in all of BC occurs among Vancouver DTES residents, and the area has the highest proportion of alcohol-related deaths. The DTES also experiences more years lost before age 75 as a result of accidents, injuries, suicides, and homicides (McLean, 2000).

The second fact that is critical for the argument put forward here is that the DTES has the highest reported crime rates in the city of Vancouver (McLean, 2000). Although the DTES contains only three percent of the population of the city of Vancouver, in 1997 the area accounted for 19.6 percent of all reported violent crime, 81.3 percent of all drug arrests and nearly 16 percent of all calls for police service. One quarter of all murders in Vancouver occur in the DTES, and the homicide rate for males in 1990 was nine times higher than for the rest of the city. There is also a serious property crime problem in the DTES because of the number of pawnshops and illegal businesses (Healy, 2000: 33-34). Although the drug use levels are the highest in the city, Aboriginal people constitute only 28.5 percent of injection drug users but, interestingly, the proportion for Aboriginal females is twice that for males (McLean, 2000). This may account for what is generally considered to be a disproportionate number of Aboriginal women in the sex trade in the DTES. In her report on the DTES, Healy found that of the 600 women working in the sex trade, 70 percent were Aboriginal, and many of the problems facing prostitutes in the DTES were tied to drug use, primarily alcohol and heroin (Healy, 2000: 39-41).

What these data strongly suggest is that over-representation (whether of Aboriginal people or others) in the criminal justice system may well have more to do with certain demographic and socio-economic characteristics of the areas from which it arises than with what is generally accepted as the main cause (i.e., racial discrimination or "cultural insensitivity" on the part of police and other criminal justice officials). To put it another way, police and other criminal justice officials are called upon to respond to patterns of crime and victimization in certain neighbourhoods (notably poor inner-city neighbourhoods), which make it understandable, if not inevitable, that the most disadvantaged people in those neighbourhoods (be they Aboriginal or non-Aboriginal people) will more frequently come to the attention of the police and, consequently, be statistically over-represented in the criminal justice system.

The "Particular Circumstances" of Aboriginal People

There is no question that the particular demographics of the Aboriginal population of Canada (a higher proportion of people in the "high risk" 15 to 24 age group, lower education levels, higher unemployment, higher rates of substance abuse and addiction, etc.) lead to their over-representation in these vulnerable neighbourhoods, and hence to their overall over-representation in the criminal justice system. There can equally be little doubt any more that these "particular circumstances" of many Aboriginal people are reflected in Aboriginal involvement in both crime and the criminal justice system, both as offenders and victims. It is now well established that Aboriginal crime is quantitatively disproportionate to the amount of crime in the non-Aboriginal population (CCJS, 2000; La Prairie, 1996; Trevethan, 1991; Roberts and Doob, 1994). This means that the rates of Aboriginal crime (i.e., crimes committed by offenders identified as Aboriginal per 100,000 members of the Aboriginal population) are considerably higher than rates of non-Aboriginal crime.

Research also indicates that Aboriginal crime is predominately intra-racial (i.e., most victims of Aboriginal crimes are Aboriginal) (Silverman and Kennedy, 1993; Trevethan, 1991; Roberts and Doob, 1994; Griffiths et al., 1995), and research in the Prairie provinces shows that Aboriginal victims are much more likely to be assaulted by someone they know than are non-Aboriginal victims (Trevethan, 1991).[13]

In 1997, in the three major urban areas of Saskatchewan, the proportion of Aboriginal accused was anywhere from three to seven times higher than their proportion of the population. The Aboriginal crime rate per 10,000 population was 10 times higher than expected. In Regina, the rate of offences of violence committed by Aboriginal offenders was 15 times higher than the rate for non-Aboriginal offenders, and the other *Criminal Code* offences (administration of justice, weapons, impaired driving) in all three centres were 14 times higher. In the same study, 42 percent of all victims were Aboriginal although they comprised only two percent of the city population (CCJS, 2000). These findings are similar for inner-city Aboriginal women, especially in Prairie cities.

Recent findings from the General Social Survey corroborate the extreme over-representation of Aboriginal people as victims. In that survey, the rate of victimization among Aboriginal people was 206 per 1,000 population (over 15 years of age) as compared to 81 for Canada, and 39 for immigrants. The relative rates for spousal violence are similar. Aboriginal women were three times and Aboriginal men two times as likely to be victims as non-Aboriginal women and men (CCJS, 2001b: 11).

It must be remembered, however, that none of these data are broken down by city environment (i.e., inner vs. outer city) or by socio-economic level. The evidence from Vancouver's Downtown Eastside, discussed above, suggests that if more in-depth analyses were conducted along these lines, Aboriginal and non-Aboriginal crime and victimization in these areas might look much more similar.

Right Problem, Wrong Solutions?

A major part of the problems that lie at the root of this disproportionate Aboriginal crime and over-representation in the criminal justice system cannot be satisfactorily or appropriately addressed through adjustments to the exercise of discretion by police or other criminal justice officials on the basis of race, or by attempts to make such officials more "culturally sensitive," or by changing the racial composition of the criminal justice workforce. This is particularly true in the case of Aboriginal offending, since so much of it is intra-racial; "cultural sensitivity" toward such offending may too easily involve insensitivity to Aboriginal victimization. Furthermore, many of the proposals for alternative Aboriginal justice institutions are put forward on the assumption that the problem of Aboriginal over-representation in the criminal justice system arises from the failure of the mainstream criminal justice system to meet the needs of "Aboriginal communities." The reality, however, is that much of this Aboriginal over-representation derives from communities (inner-city neighbourhoods) that are not exclusively or distinctively Aboriginal. Yet these are the standard criminal justice policy responses to the problem of Aboriginal over-representation in the criminal justice system.

The Need for a Different Approach

The lessons to be learned from what we know about Aboriginal offending and over-representation in the criminal justice system are unlikely to be very palatable to those who persist in attributing these problems to racial discrimination or cultural insensitivity on the part of the criminal justice system and its workforce. The oft-repeated mantra that "the criminal justice system has failed Aboriginal people" can be fairly regarded as no more than a specific reference to the more general truth that the criminal justice system is able to make a very limited contribution toward the reduction (let alone elimination) of problems of crime and victimization more generally in our society, no matter who is involved in them as offenders and victims. We can only term it a "failure" in this respect if we have unrealistic expectations of its potential to generate solutions to these problems in the first place. In fact, as many criminologists have argued for a long time, much of what is done in the name of criminal justice may actually exacerbate rather than alleviate such problems (MacNaughton-Smith, 1970). This is just as likely to be true for Aboriginal as for non-Aboriginal communities.

An honest answer to the question: "What can the criminal justice system do to reduce Aboriginal crime and victimization, and hence Aboriginal over-representation in the criminal justice system?" is, regrettably and probably, "not much," since the underlying conditions that give rise to these problems are so far beyond the capacity (or qualifications) of the police and other criminal justice officials to respond to them. But this is just as true for non-Aboriginal as for Aboriginal crime and victimization.

A good start would be a candid recognition that the circumstances and conditions that give rise to Aboriginal over-representation in the criminal justice system are not in any significant sense unique to Aboriginal people. Although Aboriginal people disproportionately experience these circumstances and conditions, they are not qualitatively different from the circumstances and conditions experienced by others (notably young, single, poorly educated, lower-class males with substance abuse problems, of almost any ethnicity) who are also seriously over-represented in the criminal justice system. Consequently, they are not circumstances or conditions that one needs to be either Aboriginal or particularly "culturally sensitive" to Aboriginal people to address. Not surprisingly, there is little evidence that "culturally based" criminal justice policy responses in this area have alone had any significant impact in reducing Aboriginal involvement in crime and victimization or over-representation in the criminal justice system, despite the program emphasis that has been placed on them over the last 30 years or so.

Of course, our argument that separate Aboriginal justice institutions, and provisions for differential treatment of Aboriginal offenders within the mainstream criminal justice system, are, by themselves, unlikely to provide effective solutions to the problem of Aboriginal over-involvement in the criminal justice system will be received as heresy by those who see the promotion of such institutions as a key plank in the campaign for Aboriginal self-government. An ideological commitment to Aboriginal self-government, however, cannot be accepted as a reason to disregard the overwhelming evidence about the genesis of Aboriginal involvement in crime and the criminal justice system which has accumulated in recent years. Those who believe that self-government could be a panacea for such problems would do well to reflect that this has so far not proved to be the case in non-Aboriginal society. Despite the capacity to govern their own affairs, there remain certain clearly identifiable non-Aboriginal groups which are still substantially "over-represented" in crime and the criminal justice system in much the same way that members of the Aboriginal population are. These groups are too often the non-Aboriginal poor and disadvantaged.

Notes

1   We use the term "over-representation" to refer simply to the situation in which the proportion of Aboriginal people involved in the criminal justice system, as offenders or victims, is greater than the proportion of Aboriginal people in the general population (i.e., a purely statistical over-representation). Use of the term in this sense does not involve any judgment as to whether such disproportionate representation may or may not be justified (or justifiable) (e.g., by disproportionate offending and/or victimization).

2   The *Constitution Act*, 1982 recognizes that Aboriginal peoples include North American Indians, Métis, and Inuit. More specifically, Registered or Status Indians refers to those peoples who qualify for registration under the *Indian Act* of 1985.

3   For a recent review of these see Roberts and Stenning, 2001.

4   "Over-policing" refers to the proposition that police discriminately target Aboriginal suspects, leading to over-representation of Aboriginal people in arrest and charge statistics.

5   "Under-policing" refers to the proposition that Aboriginal crime victims do not receive equal attention from police as that received by non-Aboriginal victims, with the result that crimes committed against them are not processed through the criminal justice system.

6   [1999] 1 S.C.R. 688.

7   [2000] 1 S.C.R. 207.

8   *R. v. Gladue* [1999] 1 S.C.R. 688, paras. 37 and 77.

9   The data come from the 1999 Statistics Canada General Social Survey.

10 The data are from the 1999 Statistics Canada General Social Survey Aboriginal sample and include people who identify themselves as Aboriginal.

11 Aboriginal people living in inner city areas were contacted on the street, in social agencies and drop-in centres in each of the four cities. Another Aboriginal person, who was a part of the research and lived in and was familiar with the Aboriginal population in the particular inner city area, made the contacts.

12 Overall, people who self-identified as Aboriginal accounted for 17 percent of admissions to federal and provincial/territorial custody in 1998-99. This proportion varied greatly by jurisdiction, however, from a high of 76 percent in Saskatchewan to a low of two percent in Quebec. See CCJS (2001a: p. 10 and Table 1).

13 Offences are disproportionately against the person, and spouses, ex-spouses, and partners are often victims. Aboriginal victims also tend to be younger than non-Aboriginal victims and are more likely than non-Aboriginal victims to receive some kind of physical injury (CCJS, 2000).

References

CCJS (Canadian Centre for Justice Statistics) (2000a) *Police-Reported Aboriginal Crime in Saskatchewan*, Ottawa: Statistics Canada.

—— (2001a) *Aboriginal Peoples in Canada*, Ottawa: Statistics Canada, Cat. No. 85F0033MIE.

—— (2001b) *A Profile of Criminal Victimization: Results of the 1999 General Social Survey*, Ottawa: Statistics Canada, Cat. No. 85-553-XIE.

Doob, Anthony N., Michelle G. Grossman, and Raymond P. Auger (1994) "Aboriginal Homicides in Ontario," *Canadian Journal of Criminology*, 99 (January): 29-62.

Edmonton, Inner City Violent Crime Task Force and the Edmonton Aboriginal Representative Committee (1992) *Edmonton Inner City Improvement for the Aboriginal Community in Edmonton*, Edmonton, Alberta.

Finn, A., S. Trevethan, G. Carriere, and M. Kowalski (1999) "Female Inmates, Aboriginal Inmates, and Inmates Serving Life Sentences: A One Day Snapshot," *Juristat* 19(5) Ottawa: Statistics Canada, Canadian Centre for Justice Statistics.

Griffiths, C.T., E. Zellerer, D.S. Wood, and G. Saville (1995) *Crime, Law and Justice Among the Inuit in the Baffin Region, N.W.T. Canada*, Simon Fraser University, Criminology Research Center.

Hagan, John and Bill McCarthy (1998) *Mean Streets: Youth Crime and Homelessness*, Cambridge: Cambridge University Press.

Healy, S. (2000) *The Downtown Eastside: A Community in Crisis*, Human Resources Development Canada.

La Prairie, C. (1991) *Justice For the Cree: Communities, Crime and Order*, Cree Regional Authority, Nemaska, Quebec.

—— (1994) *Seen But Not Heard: Native People in the Inner City*, Ottawa: Department of Justice.

—— (1996) *Examining Aboriginal Corrections in Canada*, Aboriginal Corrections Policy Unit. Ottawa: Ministry of the Solicitor General.

—— (2002) "Aboriginal Over-Representation in the Criminal Justice System: A Tale of Nine Cities" *Canadian Journal of Criminology*, 44(2): 209-232.

MacNaughton-Smith, Peter (1970) "What Is Crime and Why Do We Fight It?" Unpublished public lecture, University of Toronto, Centre of Criminology, Toronto, January 1970 (copy available from the authors).

Manitoba, Public Inquiry into the Administration of Justice and Aboriginal People (1991) *The Justice System and Aboriginal People*, Volume 1, Winnipeg, Queen's Printer.

McLean, M. (2000) *Vancouver Drug Epidemiology and Drug Crime Statistics 2000*, Vancouver: Canadian Community Epidemiology Network on Drug Use (CCENDU).

Moyer, S. (1992) *Race, Gender and Homicide: Comparisons Between Aboriginals and Other Canadians*, Ottawa: Ministry of the Solicitor General.

RCAP (Royal Commission on Aboriginal Peoples) (1996) *Bridging the Cultural Divide: A Report on Aboriginal People and Criminal Justice in Canada*, Ottawa: Minister of Supply and Services Canada.

Roberts, J.V. and A.N. Doob (1994) "Race, Ethnicity and Criminal Justice," in *Crime and Ethnicity, Crime and Justice*, M. Tonry, (ed.) Annual Vol. 21, Chicago: Chicago University Press.

Roberts, J.V. and P. Stenning (2001) "Empty Promises: Parliament, the Supreme Court and the Sentencing of Aboriginal Offenders," *Saskatchewan Law Review*, 64(1): 137-168.

Silverman, Robert and Leslie Kennedy (1993) "Canadian Indian Involvement in Murder," in Deadly Deeds: Murder in Canada, R. Silverman and L. Kennedy, (eds.), Nelson, Canada.

Trevethan, S. (1991) *Police-Reported Aboriginal Crime in Calgary, Regina and Saskatoon*, Ottawa: Canadian Centre for Justice Statistics.

—— (2000) *The Over-Representation of Aboriginal People in the Justice System*, Prepared for Department of Justice, Evaluation Unit, Ottawa: Statistics Canada, Canadian Centre for Justice Statistics.

United States, Surgeon General (2001) *Youth Violence: Report of the Surgeon General*, Washington: Public Health Service.

Is There a Need for Aboriginal-Specific Programming for Aboriginal Offenders?

Shelley Trevethan
Director of Community Research
Correctional Service of Canada

Over-Representation of Aboriginal People in the Criminal Justice System

Various inquiries and reports have noted that Aboriginal people are over-represented in virtually all aspects of the criminal justice system (e.g., CSC, 2000; Henderson, 1999; RCAP, 1996; Solicitor General, 1988). As reported by the Royal Commission on Aboriginal Peoples (RCAP) (1996) "Reports and inquiries…have not only confirmed the fact of over-representation [of Aboriginal offenders in the criminal justice system] but, most alarmingly, have demonstrated that the problem is getting worse, not better." According to the 1996 Census, Aboriginal people represent approximately two percent of the adult population in Canada (Statistics Canada, 1996). The data illustrate that their proportions are increasing. In 1991, Aboriginal people represented 11 percent of the federal inmate population (CSC, 1991). A little more than a decade later, this has increased to 18 percent (CSC, 2002). Therefore, Aboriginal people are incarcerated at about nine times their proportion in the Canadian population.

The January 2001 Speech from the Throne illustrates the priority of addressing issues facing Aboriginal people (Government of Canada, 2001). It says: "…it is a tragic reality that too many Aboriginal people are finding themselves in conflict with the law. Canada must take the measures needed to significantly reduce the percentage of Aboriginal people entering the criminal justice system, so that within a generation it is no higher than the Canadian average".

La Prairie (1997) discusses four possible causes of Aboriginal over-representation in the criminal justice system. These include differential criminal justice system processing as a result of cultural conflict and racial discrimination, higher Aboriginal offending rates, the commission of offences that are more likely to result in custodial sentences by Aboriginal people, and criminal justice policies and practices that have a differential impact on Aboriginal offenders due to their socio-economic conditions. Although some reports discuss differential treatment of Aboriginal persons by criminal justice personnel, Tonry (1994) suggests that differences in criminal characteristics, not racial animus, are the primary cause of justice system disparities.

The profile of Aboriginal offenders differs from non-Aboriginal offenders in a number of important areas. Aboriginal offenders tend to be young, single, have low education and high unemployment, which is most likely a reflection of the Canadian Aboriginal community at large. While this profile is also characteristic of non-Aboriginal offenders, the issues of education and employment appear to be more problematic among Aboriginal offenders (CSC, 2002). A substantial number of reports have noted a link between socio-economic risk factors (i.e., poverty, unemployment) and the proportion of Aboriginal persons in the criminal justice system (e.g., INAC, 1990; La Prairie, 1997; RCAP, 1996). Moreover, these reports have also identified a larger proportion of Aboriginal than non-Aboriginal people living under strained conditions. Apart from socio-demographic differences, Aboriginal offenders are generally incarcerated for more violent offences, have fewer current convictions and receive shorter sentences than non-Aboriginal offenders. In addition, Aboriginal offenders have more extensive youth and adult criminal histories. Aboriginal offenders have higher failure rates at various stages in the correctional system. They are rated at higher security and higher risk, and have different needs than non-Aboriginal offenders. The most prominent of these needs appears to be in the substance abuse and personal/emotional domains. Finally, with few exceptions, the situation for Aboriginal offenders appears to be quite similar at the provincial/territorial level (Trevethan et al., 2000). The different profiles not only provide a partial explanation for the over-representation of Aboriginal offenders in the criminal justice system, but also emphasize the need for different treatment approaches.

Aboriginal Programming

A number of studies have found that many Aboriginal offenders were raised without Aboriginal language, culture, teachings, or ceremonies (Ellerby and MacPherson, 2002; Heckbert and Turkington, 2001; Johnston, 1997; Trevethan et al., 2001). However, these core aspects of Aboriginal identity appear critical to the healing process. It is important to provide Aboriginal offenders with the opportunity to participate in programs that introduce Aboriginal culture and spirituality or allow them to continue to develop their understanding. Further, the ability of a program to aid Aboriginal offenders acquire the skills to manage their risk to re-offend may be heightened by a cultural approach. According to Heckbert and Turkington (2001), Aboriginal spirituality and cultural activities are major factors in successful reintegration.

Further, a few studies indicate that programs may be more effective if run by Aboriginal facilitators. For instance, Johnston (1997) found that Aboriginal offenders said they are more trusting and comfortable with Aboriginal facilitators, especially spiritual leaders and Elders. Similarly, Mals et al. (1999) found that to enhance the effectiveness of correctional programs and treatment in Australia, it is important to have Aboriginal facilitators in place. These findings suggest that the treatment effect of programs may be substantially reduced if Aboriginal facilitators are not in place.

The Correctional Service of Canada is moving toward the use of Aboriginal-specific programs. For instance, the development of a national healing program for Aboriginal offenders in federal facilities is in process. Furthermore, healing lodges under Section 81 of the *Corrections and Conditional Release Act* have been implemented in a number of provinces. Section 81 of the Act allows Aboriginal communities to provide correctional services. Healing lodges are meant to aid Aboriginal offenders in their successful reintegration by using traditional healing methods, specifically, holistic and culturally appropriate programming.

In 1999, 13 Aboriginal-specific programs were identified for federal offenders (Epprecht, 2000). These programs address a wide range of issues, including substance abuse, sex offender programming, and anger management. Since that time, other Aboriginal-specific programs have been developed. For instance, Fenbrook Institution is currently delivering an Inuit-specific sex offender program. The Tupiq program follows universally accepted relapse prevention theory; however, it integrates Inuit culture by using Inuit delivery staff, healing therapy, and cultural references. Similarly, the Native Clan Organization of Manitoba delivers a blended traditional healing/contemporary treatment program for Aboriginal sexual offenders. A number of institutions are currently providing the In Search of Your Warrior program, which focuses on helping Aboriginal offenders break their cycle of violence. The foundation for this program is the culture, teachings, and ceremonies of Aboriginal people.

A few studies have found that Aboriginal-specific programming is more effective for Aboriginal offenders. For instance, Weekes and Millson (1994) found that an Aboriginal pre-treatment substance abuse program produces significant improvement in knowledge and attitudes regarding substance abuse, general problem solving, and recognition of Aboriginal cultural factors. Ellerby and MacPherson (2002) found that, prior to the introduction of a blended traditional healing/contemporary treatment program for Aboriginal sexual offenders, treatment completion rates were lower for Aboriginal than non-Aboriginal offenders. However, once culturally relevant and appropriate programming became available, this difference disappeared. Sioui and Thibault (2001) found that certain programs are more effective in reducing recidivism if they are Aboriginal-specific. For instance, participation in programs focusing on employment and education reduced recidivism, but only if they were Aboriginal-specific. However, participation focusing on social relationships, community needs, and emotional needs reduced recidivism regardless of whether the programs were specifically for Aboriginals or not.

Both Johnston (1997) and Sioui and Thibault (2001) conclude that there is little access to Aboriginal-specific programs. However, Sioui and Thibault argue that Aboriginal-specific programs provide positive results.

Conclusion

Although both Aboriginal and non-Aboriginal offenders may have similar reasons for being incarcerated, it is clear that Aboriginal offenders have more risk factors and different needs. Therefore, the way to address these needs may be different. From the little research that is currently available, it appears that Aboriginal-specific programs may better prepare Aboriginal offenders for reintegration into society.

References

Canada, CSC (Correctional Service of Canada) (1991) *Basic Facts About Corrections in Canada*, Ottawa: Supply and Services Canada.

—— (2000) *National Overview of Programs, Services and Issues Related to Aboriginal Offenders*, Report prepared by the Aboriginal Issues Sub-Committee to the Heads of Corrections.

—— (2002) *One-Day Snapshot of Aboriginal Offenders – March 2002*, Research Branch, Ottawa.

Canada, INAC (Indian and Northern Affairs Canada) (1990) *Indian Policing Policy Review*, Task force report, Government of Canada.

Canada, Solicitor General of Canada (1988) *Correctional Issues Affecting Native Peoples*, Correctional Law Review Working Paper No. 7.

Canada, Statistics Canada (1996) *Census of Population*.

Ellerby, L.A. and P. MacPherson (2002) *Exploring the Profiles of Aboriginal Sex Offenders: Contrasting Aboriginal and Non-Aboriginal Sexual Offenders to Determine Unique Client Characteristics and Potential Implications for Sex Offender Assessment and Treatment Strategies*, Research Report R-122, Correctional Service of Canada.

Epprecht, N. (2000) "Programs for Aboriginal Offenders: A National Survey, *Forum on Corrections Research*, 12(1): 45-47.

Government of Canada, *Speech From The Throne*, 2001.

Heckbert, D. and D. Turkington (2001) *Turning Points: A Study of the Factors Related to the Successful Reintegration of Aboriginal Offenders*, Research Report R-112, Correctional Service of Canada.

Henderson, J.Y. (1999) *Changing Punishment for Aboriginal Peoples of Canada*, Presented at the Canadian Institute for the Administration of Justice, Saskatoon, Saskatchewan.

Johnston, J.C. (1997) *Aboriginal Offender Survey: Case Files and Interview Sample*, Prepared for Correctional Service Canada, Research Branch, Research Report R-61.

La Prairie, C. (1997) "Reconstructing Theory: Explaining Aboriginal Over-Representation in the Criminal Justice System in Canada," *Australian and New Zealand Journal of Criminology*, 30(1): 39-54.

Mals, P., K. Howell, A. Day, and G. Hall (1999) "Adapting Violence Rehabilitation Programs for the Australian Aboriginal Offender," *Journal of Offender Rehabilitation*, 30(1,2): 121-135.

RCAP (Royal Commission on Aboriginal Peoples) (1996) *Bridging the Cultural Divide: A Report on Aboriginal People and Criminal Justice and Canada*, Ministry of Supply and Services Canada.

Sioui, R. and J. Thibault (2001) *The Relevance of a Cultural Adaptation for Aboriginals of the Reintegration Potential Reassessment Scale (RPRS)*, Research Report R-109, Correctional Service of Canada.

Tonry, M. (1994) "Editorial: Racial Disparities in Courts and Prisons," *Criminal Behaviour and Mental Health*, 4: 158-162.

Trevethan, S., S. Tremblay, and J. Carter (2000) *The Over-Representation of Aboriginal People in the Justice System*, Canadian Centre for Justice Statistics, Statistics Canada.

Trevethan, S., S. Auger, J.P. Moore, M. MacDonald, and J. Sinclair (2001) *The Effect of Family Disruption on Aboriginal and Non-Aboriginal Inmates*, Research Report R-113, Correctional Service of Canada.

Weekes, J.R. and W.A. Millson (1994) *The Native Offender Substance Abuse Pre-Treatment Program: Intermediate Measures of Program Effectiveness*, Correctional Service Canada, R-35, Ottawa.

Educational Outcomes of Aboriginal Students in British Columbia: The Impact of "Good Schools" on Test Scores

John Richards[1]
Faculty of Business
Simon Fraser University

Aidan Vining
Faculty of Business Administration
Simon Fraser University

Introduction

Aboriginal people in Canada have lower educational levels than do other Canadians. The amount of education matters: North American evidence suggests that average returns to education level (quantity) have consistently risen during the latter part of the 20th century (Katz and Murphy, 1992; Juhn et al., 1993; Buchinsky, 1994; Bratsberg and Terrell, 2002). This educational premium appears to apply to historically disadvantaged groups, including North American Aboriginal people, as much. (or indeed more) as to others in the labour force (Antecol and Bedard, 2002; Bradbury, 2002; Drolet, 2002; Pendakur and Pendakur, 2002).

There is also evidence that, for a variety of reasons, most Aboriginal people attend schools of lower than average quality. Quality also matters for earnings: "There is mounting evidence that quality [of schools] – generally measured by test scores – is positively related to individual earnings, productivity and economic growth" (Hanushek, 2002: 6; see also, for example, Murmane et al., 1995, 2000; Strayer, 2002).

The combination of lower levels of education and lower quality of education obviously places Aboriginal people in a disadvantageous position from an earnings perspective. Given the strong relationship between education levels and incomes, it is safe to assert that in contemporary industrial societies, no community or group can collectively avoid poverty unless a majority of adults have completed high school, and a plurality have higher education levels. While achieving this educational goal is not easy, there is considerable evidence that this can, and is, being achieved. Improving the quality of Aboriginal education appears to be more difficult. Although quality schools matter, deciding what this means in terms of Aboriginal educational policy is problematic, because knowing the output of good schools as reflected in test scores and its subsequent impact on earnings (valuable though it is for some purposes) does not directly help policy-makers *design* good schools. For this purpose, policy-makers need to better understand the relationship between school inputs and school outputs.

Unfortunately, the relationship between various input measures and quality of education is murkier than the broader link between educational levels and incomes. This reflects the fact that the links between schools' characteristics, the socio-economic characteristics of students, their parents and neighbourhoods, and student performance and quality are themselves unclear. Empirical studies that use conventional input proxies for quality, such as student-teacher ratios, have produced conflicting empirical findings on the link between these inputs and output measures of school quality and between these inputs and subsequent earnings. For example, Betts (1995, 1996) and Grogger (1996) find that student-teacher ratios have little or no impact on earnings. Other studies find a substantial effect (Card and Krueger, 1992; Altonji and Dunn, 1996; Angrist and Lavy, 1999; Kreuger, 1999; Bratsberg and Terrell, 2002). Similarly, the evidence on the relationship between school expenditures and educational outcomes has produced conflicting findings. Some studies find a positive relationship between expenditures and educational outcomes (Sander, 1993; Hedges et al., 1994; Ferguson and Ladd, 1996; Hedges and Greenwald, 1996; Bratsberg and Terrell, 2002; Wilson, 2002). But many other studies surveyed by Hanushek (1989, 1996, 1997) find no such relationship.

This paper examines these issues in the context of Aboriginal students attending provincial schools in British Columbia. British Columbia is the first Canadian province to conduct province-wide annual tests of all students in three grades in the core subjects of reading, writing, and numeracy. These results are available by school, and within schools by a number of student characteristics, including whether the students are Aboriginal (these data are unique). This allows us to assess, by school, some of the factors determining Aboriginal performance.

Although for most schools median Aboriginal results are below those for non-Aboriginal students in the same school, this is not true for all.

Additionally, Aboriginal test results are better in those schools where non-Aboriginal results are better. Using simple OLS regressions, we find that the most significant variable to explain Aboriginal results in a school is the performance of non-Aboriginal students in the same school.

The paper proceeds as follows. First, it reviews briefly the link between Aboriginal education levels and incomes across Canada. Second, it describes and analyzes British Columbia's school test results for the latest year available, 2000-01. The final section discusses policy options.

Aboriginal Educational Levels and Income in Canada

In Canada, the link between educational achievement and income improvement holds as much for Aboriginal peoples as for others. Figure 1 summarizes 1995 median incomes for Aboriginal and non-Aboriginal respondents, disaggregated at eight educational levels. The data on which the following statistics are calculated are drawn from a special run on the master file of the 1996 Canadian Census. (For a detailed discussion see Drost and Richards, 2003.) The Aboriginal population is further divided into those living on- and off-reserve.[2] As Aboriginal education levels rise, so do their median incomes.

Figure 1: Medians of Aboriginal and Non-Aboriginal Income Recipients by Education, 1995

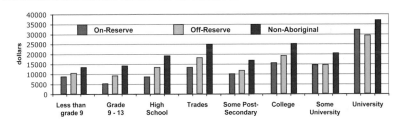

Figure 2 presents the relationship between education and income in another way. At each education level, the non-Aboriginal median income is set to 100, and Aboriginal incomes are adjusted accordingly. Presenting the data this way allows us to consider, at various education levels, how large is the relative Aboriginal/non-Aboriginal income gap.

Figure 2: Normalized Medians of Income Recipients by Education Level, 1995
(Non-Aboriginal medians equal 100, all education levels)

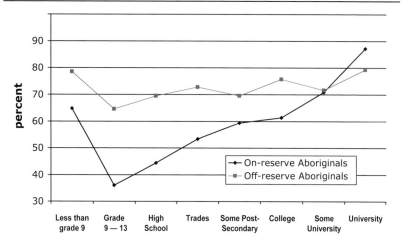

There is only one exception to the conclusion that more education leads to higher incomes. The lowest Aboriginal medians and largest relative gaps occur, not at the lowest education level, but at the level of incomplete high school. At very low education levels, much of people's income derives not from earnings but from social transfers, such as welfare payments. Hence, some of the explanation for the absolute and relative decline between the first and second education level may be the loss of such transfers as Aboriginal recipients earn more. Thereafter, as education levels rise, not only do Aboriginal median incomes rise, they also rise relative to those of non-Aboriginal recipients with similar levels of education.

Aboriginal Students and Schools

The recently released 2001 Census shows that only 31 percent of all Aboriginal people now live on-reserve (down from 33 percent in 1996); 20 percent live in rural off-reserve areas (unchanged from 1996), and 49 percent live in urban areas (up from 47 percent in 1996). Furthermore, among the Indian (identity) population, over half now live off-reserve, and almost a quarter live in cities (Canada, 2003).

One reason for Indians who could live on-reserve instead of choosing to move off-reserve is likely that they perceive schools for their children to be superior. Certainly, those living off-reserve achieve higher average education levels. Figure 3 shows the cumulative education profile, at the time of the 1996 Census, among Aboriginal (both off- and on-reserve) and non-Aboriginal individuals. At all education levels, the profile for off-reserve Aboriginal people dominates that for those on-reserve. While better off- than on-reserve, education levels among off-reserve Aboriginal people are still well below those of other Canadians.

Figure 3: Education profiles among Aboriginals and Non-Aboriginals, 1996

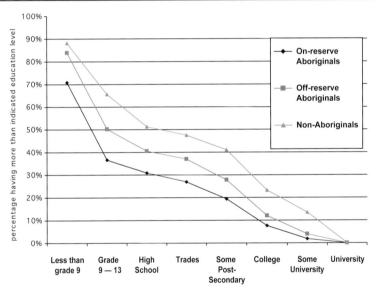

The Auditor General of Canada (Canada, 2000:4-5) has conducted one of the more forceful recent reviews of on-reserve Aboriginal education. The summary conclusion is that:

> ... the Department [of Indian Affairs] needs to resolve several major issues. These include the need to articulate its role in education, to develop and use appropriate performance measures and to improve operational performance.

The performance of Aboriginal students in off-reserve provincially run schools has been much less studied. British Columbia affords some unique data to this end.

Aboriginal Students in British Columbia Off-Reserve Schools

Approximately 35,000 Aboriginal students attend off-reserve schools in British Columbia; 12,000 attend school on-reserve.[3] Since 1999, the provincial education ministry has organized annual province-wide exams in writing, reading, and numeracy, in three grades: 4, 7, and 10. With some exceptions, all provincial students in these three grades sit the relevant Foundation Skills Assessment (FSA) exams, on which they receive one of three scores: not meeting expectations, meeting expectations, and exceeding expectations. To preserve confidentiality, results are not publicly available by student, but they are available by school, and within schools by a number of student characteristics. As mentioned one such characteristic is whether the students are Aboriginal (see Appendix 1 for further details).

The most widely used statistic from FSA exams is the percentage of student scores, by school, that meet or exceed expectations.[4] For the 2000-01 school year, 149 schools reported at least some results for both Aboriginal and non-Aboriginal students.[5] Within each of these schools, we calculate a "meet/exceed" statistic for both Aboriginal and for non-Aboriginal students. For our purposes, we construct this statistic by averaging over all grades and all subjects in the school. Among these 149 schools, the median meet/exceed statistic for non-Aboriginal students is 76.5 percent. The interquartile range is 71.2 to 81.4 percent. The median meet/exceed school statistic for Aboriginal students is 61.5 percent, 15.0 percentage points lower. The Aboriginal interquartile range is 51.6 to 73.3 percent. While most schools report an Aboriginal meet/exceed statistic below that for non-Aboriginal students, in 23 schools the reverse is true.

If we define "doing well" to mean an average meet/exceed statistic for the school above the median for non-Aboriginal students, one half of all schools are, by definition, doing well by their non-Aboriginal students. In only 27 schools among these 149 is the Aboriginal meet/exceed statistic above 76.5 percent. Hence, by this measure only about one British Columbia school in five is doing well by its Aboriginal students.

Regression Analysis: Explaining Aboriginal Student Outcomes

To understand better what is going on within schools, we undertake regression analysis of Aboriginal test scores.[6] We start for Regression 1 with a simple hypothesis that outcomes depend on average income among families (Aboriginal and non-Aboriginal) in the neighbourhood surrounding the school. Regression 2 adds a variable to capture the effect of a school being in what is defined as a "very poor" neighbourhood. Regression 3 also adds the meet/exceed statistic among non-Aboriginal students in a school, as an indicator of whether the school "does well" by its Aboriginal students. Table 1 summarizes the results of these three regressions.

Table 1: Regression models to explain Foundation Skills Assessment (FSA) outcomes among Aboriginal students in British Columbia, 2000-01 school year

	Regression 1	Regression 2	Regression 3
Intercept	33.33[d] (3.46)	39.19[c] (3.35)	-0.16 (-0.01)
Average family income in school neighbourhood (thousands of dollars)	0.58[c] (2.96)	0.47[b] (2.01)	0.12 (0.57)
"Poor neighbourhood" (1: neighbourhood family poverty rate exceeds 32.6 percent, twice 1996 national average; 0: elsewhere)		-5.14 (-0.89)	-6.15[a] (-1.20)
Proportion of school non-Aboriginal student scores which meet or exceed expectations (percent)			0.75[d] (6.47)
R-square	0.056	0.061	0.271

Notes: Dependent variable is percentage of Aboriginal student scores, by school, which meet or exceed expectations. Figures in parentheses are t-test statistics. Level of significance is indicated by the following legend:

a   0.15 significance (one-tail t-test)
b   0.025 significance (one-tail t-test)
c   0.005 significance (one-tail t-test)
d   0.0005 significance (one-tail t-test)

Regression 1 shows that higher neighbourhood income implies higher school scores among Aboriginal students: the average family income variable has a positive statistically significant coefficient. Family income does not, however, explain much of the variance (R-square is only 0.056).

Many studies of urban poverty attach particular importance to negative dynamics operating within "very poor" neighbourhoods.[7] Regression 2 adds a variable to capture this effect. The variable is set to one in the event of a school's being in a neighbourhood in which the family poverty rate is more than twice the national average; zero otherwise. The poor neighbourhood effect lowers the meet/exceed statistic by about five percentage points, but the variable coefficient is not significantly different from zero.

Underlying Regression 3 is the question: "Do schools that do well by their non-Aboriginal students also do well by their Aboriginal students?" Figure 4 plots actual (and predicted) Aboriginal FSA results against non-Aboriginal FSA results, by school. Clearly, there exists a positive correlation. The regression suggests that a one percentage point rise in the non-Aboriginal meet/exceed statistic leads to a 0.75 percentage point rise among Aboriginal students in the same school. Whatever the activities within certain schools generating good (or bad) results among non-Aboriginal children, they appear to affect Aboriginal children to nearly the same extent. According to this specification, the very poor neighbourhood effect persists and is of similar magnitude as in the previous regression. The coefficient for this variable is now (weakly) significant.

Figure 4: Foundation Skills Assessment (FSA)Results among British Columbia Schools with both Aboriginal and non-Aboriginal Students, 2000-2001

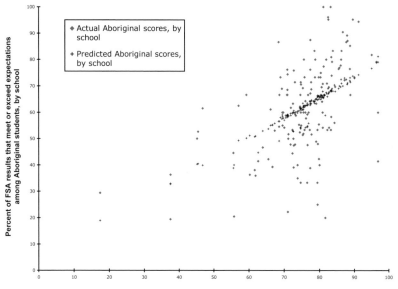

Percent of FSA results that meet or exceed expectations among non-Aboriginal students, by school

Once non-Aboriginal scores within a school are introduced, the incremental effect of income – beyond the very poor neighbourhood effect – disappears. Family characteristics, including family income, may well matter, but the non-Aboriginal school score statistic is capturing the effect. Many North American studies discuss the importance of family income and other family dynamics (e.g., Haveman and Wolfe, 1995; Jaggia and Kelly-Hawke, 1999). These studies assess many plausible links between family dynamics and school outcomes. Children from middle class families may generate a school more conducive to learning among all students than do children from poor families. Middle class parents may take a more active interest in school activities.

Recall that in regressions 1 and 2 average family income and the very poor neighbourhood effect do not by themselves explain much about Aboriginal school performance. While income matters in determining school outcomes, what schools do is also important. In Regression 3, the coefficient for test scores among non-Aboriginal students is highly significant and increases the R-square to 0.271. This suggests the importance of school-specific practices in explaining student outcomes.

A final caveat. Even Regression 3 leaves a lot unexplained. For many schools, the gap between actual and explained Aboriginal scores remains large.

Some Thoughts on Structural Change to Urban School Systems

Over the last half century, American schools have striven to improve black education outcomes. In many ways, this challenge is analogous to that faced by Canadian schools with rising Aboriginal student enrolments. On tests of core curriculum performance – tests similar to the FSA – over the last three decades, American schools have achieved considerable convergence between black and white test scores. In a recent analysis of this convergence, Cook and Evans (2000: 749) conclude "that nearly 75% of the convergence is due to changes within schools, that is, to a narrowing in the gap in test scores between white and black students with the same level of parental education and who attend the same school."

From our regression analysis, a similar result emerges. Schools that do well (badly) by their non-Aboriginal students also tend to do well (badly) by their Aboriginal students. One policy implication is to learn from good schools and, as in the United States, attempt to reduce within-school differences in student outcomes.

Cook and Evans note a potentially important problem. They find some evidence to suggest that black students are increasingly to be found in schools of lower quality. To the extent this is so, the explanation appears to be some combination of residential segregation by race and income, and abandonment of the public school system by many middle class urban parents.

The analogue in Canada is the growth of Aboriginals living disproportionately in very poor urban neighbourhoods and attending schools whose academic outcomes are, in general, below those in non-poor neighbourhoods. Let us assume that those schools in which the overall meet/exceed statistic is below the relevant bottom quartile, are relatively weak. Only 15.6 percent of the scores of non-Aboriginal students are from these schools, against 28.8 percent of the scores of Aboriginal students. (Recall that we are considering here only those schools reporting both Aboriginal and non-Aboriginal test scores.) Given this concentration in relatively weak schools, some have concluded that expanding best practices within the public school system is not enough. They want, in addition, schools that engage Aboriginal families more intimately, and that make more extensive use of Aboriginal culture within the school curriculum. The rationale for such structural innovation is to replicate in an urban environment what former Premier Allan Blakeney has termed the "cultural comfort" of the reserve.

> I see it as next to impossible for us to be able to create reserves which provide an appropriate economic base for all or most of the growing population of Aboriginal people. We know that some will wish to remain [on-reserve]... We know that some will move to the cities and integrate with the economic mainstream. We know that some will move back and forth – a transitional group...[Aboriginals] leave the reserve because there is no economic opportunity for them and particularly for their children. It seems to me that they return to the reserve because on the reserve they experience a sense of place... and also because on the reserve they have a level of cultural comfort. (Blakeney, quoted in Richards, 2001:24-25).

We do not have evidence directly applicable to Aboriginal education outcomes. There is however evidence to suggest that "separate" schools controlled by cultural minorities do increase educational attainment among their children (Evans and Schwab, 1995; Neal, 1997). Inspired by the precedent of distinct public school systems in many provinces based on language and religion, Blakeney has proposed an Aboriginal-based system in cities having large Aboriginal communities. A more modest option is to give particular schools within a public system the mandate to emphasize Aboriginal culture. Such schools become "charter" or "magnet" schools.

An example of a charter or magnet school is the recently established Amiskwaciy Academy (2003) within the Edmonton public school system. It is open to any Edmonton family with school-age children. Unlike a typical neighbourhood school, it has given itself a specialized mandate: to honour Aboriginal traditions.

Either option, school board or magnet/charter school, has the potential to increase Aboriginal parental engagement in the school system, which may in turn improve student outcomes. But "separate schools" are not a panacea: they may subtract from a shared sense of community, and they may not maintain academic standards.

If school boards are to undertake this innovation, it becomes important to impose clear guidelines in order to minimize potential problems. The following conditions seem important to us.

> Parents, both Aboriginal and non-Aboriginal, should have freedom over choice of either an Aboriginal or conventional school for their children.

> In the case of an Aboriginal school authority, it should be democratically elected by the parents of all children in the system, including non-Aboriginal parents who choose to place their children in a school falling under its jurisdiction.

> To maintain standards, all schools should be required to teach the provincially mandated core curriculum, and all students should sit province-wide exams in core subjects.

> The school administration must be shielded from political pressures that may arise to lower standards.

Mutatis mutandis, the first three conditions have been important for the successful co-existence of Catholic and non-denominational public school systems in Canada. The fourth point emphasizes that any urban Aboriginal school authority must address outcomes. Certainly, pressure to avoid outcome measurement would not be unique to this model of Aboriginal-run schools. But the need to resist such pressure and establish educational legitimacy would be greater for such schools, particularly in the short term.

Conclusion

The recently released 2001 Census Aboriginal data illustrate, once again, the significance of the urban Aboriginal population. While this community is becoming increasingly numerous, federal Aboriginal policy remains oriented toward on-reserve matters, and the provinces remain too passive in their programming.

In Manitoba and Saskatchewan, a quarter of all children are now Aboriginal. If Aboriginal education outcomes do not substantially improve over the next generation, both Aboriginal and non-Aboriginal residents of these two provinces face some serious education problems. A similar fate may befall regions of the other provinces and poor urban neighbourhoods with large Aboriginal populations. To address these problems will not be easy. The first step is acknowledgment that only a minority of Aboriginal people are choosing to live on-reserve or in rural areas. The second step is a concerted effort by provincial governments to implement policies that enable better Aboriginal student outcomes.

Appendix
Description of the Foundation Skills Assessment (FSA) Program

Below is a description of the FSA program on the Web site of the British Columbia Department of Education (2003). The Web site includes online access to a file containing the 2000-01 results.

> The Foundation Skills Assessment is an annual province-wide assessment of British Columbia students' academic skills, and provides a snapshot of how well BC students are learning foundation skills in Reading Comprehension, Writing, and Numeracy.

> The assessment is administered every spring to Grade 4, 7 and 10 students in public and provincially funded independent schools. The most recent assessment took place in May 2002, when approximately 150,000 students wrote.

> FSA is designed and developed by British Columbia educators. The skills tested are linked to the provincial curriculum and provincial *performance standards.*

> The main purpose of the assessment is to help the province, school districts, schools and school planning councils evaluate how well students are achieving basic skills, and make plans to improve student achievement.

> FSA is an integral part of government's commitment to ensuring quality education for all students.

> FSA results, together with other information collected by teachers, provide important information for district accountability contracts and for school growth plans developed by school planning councils.

> FSA results are produced for the province, district, school and individual students.

> FSA results are returned to districts and schools each fall to help develop school plans for improving student learning, and to share with individual students and parents.

For several reasons, the FSA results for Aboriginal students are incomplete. First, student identification as Aboriginal when sitting the FSA exams is voluntary. To preserve confidentiality, the Department does not reveal data for Aboriginal students when the aggregate number of scores in a school is below five. Based on anecdote, it also appears some schools intentionally withhold Aboriginal student results; the motivation for doing so is not clear. For all these reasons, FSA scores by individual schools for their Aboriginal students must be treated with caution. Despite these shortcomings, the FSA exam results provide valuable insight into off-reserve Aboriginal student performance.

Notes

1   The authors thank Susan Anzolin and Evelyn Peters for helpful comments on an earlier draft. The usual caveat applies: the authors alone are responsible for the conclusions and any errors that remain.

2   These data rely on the Aboriginal identity, as opposed to the ethnic origin, definition. The data include all Aboriginal people, whether they identify as North American Indian, Métis, or Inuit. The on- and off-reserve distinction relies on the census determination, not that of Indian and Northern Affairs Canada (INAC). Off-reserve includes both Aboriginal people living in cities and in rural non-reserve communities. The education data summarized in Figure 3 refer to people 15 years and older, who are not currently in school. These data do not control for age beyond that.

3   The British Columbia education ministry relies on voluntary self-identification to code whether a student is Aboriginal.

4   See Hertzman et al. (2002). The authors map numerous characteristics among Vancouver children, by neighbourhood. They plot the percentage of Grade 4 students failing to meet FSA expectations (i.e., one minus the proportion that meet or exceed expectations).

5   One school with Aboriginal outcomes reported no non-Aboriginal students. As our regressions make use of the non-Aboriginal student scores as a regressor, this school was excluded from consideration.

6   The regressions reported here use OLS techniques to explain the meet/exceed statistic among Aboriginal students, by school. These provide useful results. However, there is potential bias. The preferable procedure is to fit a logistic curve, using a simultaneous equation estimation technique.

7   Richards (2001) provides a brief survey of literature on urban poverty, including theories of negative dynamics in very poor neighbourhoods. Several studies of poor neighbourhoods in Canada have used the criterion of census tracts having more than twice the national average family Low-Income Cut-Off (LICO) rate.

References

Altonji, J. and T.A. Dunn (1996) "Using Siblings to Estimate the Effect of School Quality on Wages," *Review of Economics and Statistics*, 78(4): 665-71.

Amiskwaciy Academy (2003) <http://amiskwaciy.epsb.net>.

Angrist, J.D. and V. Lavy (1999) "Using Maimonides' Rule to Estimate the Effect of Class Size on Scholastic Achievement," *Quarterly Journal of Economics*, 114(2): 533-75.

Antecol, H. and K. Bedard (2002) "The Relative Earnings of Young Mexican, Black, and White Women," *Industrial and Labor Relations Review*, 56(1): 122-35.

Betts, J.R. (1995) "Does School Quality Matter? Evidence from the National Longitudinal Survey of Youth," *Review of Economics and Statistics*, 77(3): 231-50.

—— (1996) "Do School Resources Matter Only for Older Workers?" *Review of Economics and Statistics*, 78 (4): 638-52.

Bradbury, K.L. (2002) "Education and Wages in the 1980s and 1990s: Are All Groups Moving Up Together? *New England Economic Review*, First Quarter: 19-46.

Bratsberg, B. and D. Terrell (2002) "School Quality and Returns to Education of U.S. Immigrants," *Economic Inquiry*, 40(2): 177-98.

British Columbia (2003) *Foundation Skills Assessment (FSA)*, Description and data available at <www.bced.gov.bc.ca/assessment/fsa>.

Buchinsky, M. (1994) "Changes in the U.S. Wage Structure 1963-1987: Application of Quartile Regression," *Econometrica*, 62(2): 405-58.

Canada (2000) "Indian and Northern Affairs Canada: Elementary and Secondary Education," *Report of the Auditor General of Canada*, Chapter 4, available at <www.oag-bvg.gc.ca>.

—— (2003) *Aboriginal Peoples of Canada: A Demographic Profile*, No. 96F0030XIE2001007. Available at <http://www.statcan.ca/cgi-bin/downpub/freepub.cgi>. Ottawa: Statistics Canada.

Card, D. and A.B. Krueger (1992) "Does School Quality Matter? Returns to Education and the Characteristics of Schools in the United States," *Journal of Political Economy*, 107(1): 152-200.

Cook, M. and W. Evans (2000) "Families or Schools? Explaining the Convergence in White and Black Academic Performance," *Journal of Labor Economics*, 18(4): 729-754.

Denmert W. (2001) *Improving Academic Performance among Native American Students: A Review of the Research Literature*, U.S. Department of Education. Available at <www.ael.org/eric/denmert>.

Drolet, M. (2002) "New Evidence on Gender Pay Differentials: Does Measurement Matter?" *Canadian Public Policy*, 28(1): 1-16.

Drost, H. and J. Richards (2003) "Income On- and Off-Reserve: How Aboriginals Are Faring," *Commentary*, 175. Toronto: C.D. Howe Institute.

Evans, W. and R. Schwab (1995) "Finish High School and Starting College: Do Catholic Schools Make a Difference?" *Quarterly Journal of Economics*, 110(4): 947-974.

Ferguson, R. and H. Ladd (1996) "How and Why Money Matters: An Analysis of Alabama Schools," in *Holding Schools Accountable*, H. Ladd, (ed.), Washington, D.C: Brookings Institution, pp. 265-298.

Grogger, J. (1996) "Does School Quality Explain the Recent Black/White Wage Trend," *Journal of Labor Economics*, 14(2): 231-53.

Hanushek, E.A. (1989) "The Impact of Differential Expenditures on School Performance," *Educational Researcher*, 18(4): 45-51.

—— (1996) "School Resources and Student Performance," in *Does Money Matter? The Link Between Schools, Student Achievement, and Adult Success*, G. Burtless, (ed.), Washington, D.C: Brookings Institution, pp. 43-73.

—— (1997) "Assessing the Effects of School Resources on Student Performance: An Update," *Educational Evaluation and Policy Analysis*, 19(2): 141-164.

—— (2002) "The Long Run Importance of School Quality," Working paper 9071, Cambridge, MA: National Bureau of Economic Research.

Haveman, R. and B. Wolfe (1995) "The Determinants of Children's Attainments: A Review of Methods and Findings," *Journal of Economic Literature*, 33(4): 1829-1878.

Hedges, L. and R. Greenwald (1996) "Have Times Changed? The Relationship Between School Resources and Student Performance," in *Does Money Matter? The Link Between Schools, Student Achievement, and Adult Success*, G. Burtless (ed.), Washington, D.C: Brookings Institution, pp. 74-92.

Hedges, L. R.D. Laine, and R. Greenwald (1994) "Does Money Matter? A Meta-Analysis of Studies of the Effects of Differential School Inputs on Student Outcomes," *Educational Researcher*, 23(3): 5-14.

Hertzman, C., S. McLean, D. Kohen, J. Dunn, and T. Evans (2002) *Early Development in Vancouver: Report of the Community Asset Mapping Project*, Available at <www.earlylearning.ubc.ca/vancouverreport.pdf>.

Jaggia, S. and A. Kelly-Hawke (1999) "An Analysis of the Factors that Influence Student Performance: A Fresh Approach to an Old Debate," *Contemporary Economic Policy*, 17(2): 189-198.

Juhn, C., K.M. Murphy, and B. Pierce (1993) "Wage Inequality and the Rise in the Returns to Skill," *Journal of Political Economy*, 101(3): 410-42.

Katz, L.F. and K.M. Murphy 1992 "Changes in Relative Wages, 1963-87: Supply and Demand Factors," *Quarterly Journal of Economics*, 107(1): 35-78.

Kreuger, A.B. (1999) "Experimental Estimates of Education Production Functions," *Quarterly Journal of Economics*, 114(2): 497-532.

Murmane, R., J.B. Willett, Y. Duhaldeborde, and J.B. Taylor (2000) "How Important Are the Cognitive Skills of Teenagers in Predicting Subsequent Earnings?" *Journal of Policy Analysis and Management*, 19(4): 547-568.

Murmane, R., J.B. Willett, and F. Levy (1995) "The Growing Importance of Cognitive Skills in Wage Determination," *Review of Economics and Statistics*, 77(2): 251-266.

Neal, D. (1997) "The Effects of Catholic Secondary Schooling on Educational Achievement," *Journal of Labor Economics*, 15(1): 98-123.

Pendakur, K. and R. Pendakur (2002) "Colour My World: Have Earnings Gaps for Canadian-Born Ethnic Minorities Changed Over Time?" *Canadian Public Policy*, 28(4): 489-512.

Richards, J. (2001) "Neighbors Matter: Poor Neighborhoods and Urban Aboriginal Policy." *Commmentary*, no.156, Toronto: C.D. Howe Institute.

—— (2003) "A New Agenda for Strengthening Canada's Aboriginal Population: Individual Treaty Benefits, Reduced Transfers to Bands and Own-Source Taxation," *Backgrounder*, 66, Toronto: C.D. Howe Institute.

Sander. W. (1993) "Expenditures and Student Achievement in Illinois," *Journal of Public Economics*, 52(3): 403-16.

Strayer, W. (2002) "The Returns to School Quality: College Choice and Earnings," *Journal of Labor Economics*, 20(3): 475-503.

Wilson, K. (2002) "The Effects of School Quality on Income," *Economics of Education Review*, 21(6):

Urban Aboriginal Economic Development

John Loxley
Department of Economics
University of Manitoba

Fred Wien
Maritime School of Social Work
Dalhousie University

Introduction

While it is still the case that most discussions about programs to support Aboriginal economic development focus on First Nation reserves usually located in rural areas, the situation is changing rapidly. This is, of course, in part due to the fact that urban Aboriginal populations continue to grow and are now estimated to be close to 50 percent.[1] In addition, urban Aboriginal populations are becoming better organized and are pressing their claims for consideration to municipal, provincial, and federal governments.

The field of urban Aboriginal economic development is also becoming more complicated and dynamic. Up until about a decade ago, it seemed quite adequate to discuss the subject under two headings: the economic development activities of longstanding urban reserves, and the efforts of more dispersed urban Aboriginal populations without a land base and with less well developed governing structures to secure a more stable and rewarding economic base.

The new element that has been added to the mix has been First Nations and Métis, usually based in rural locations, adding an urban component to their economic development strategies. This can take many forms, from the simple addition of an urban office location, to the development of an investment and business strategy that includes taking advantage of opportunities in urban areas, to the formal creation of urban reserves with explicit economic development objectives.

This more recent development underlines the point that urban Aboriginal economic development should not be regarded as a self-contained process. Increasingly important linkages are being forged between rural and urban locations and with non-Aboriginal economies as well.

In this chapter, we will discuss urban Aboriginal economic development from three vantage points: longstanding urban reserves, the urban economic development strategies of rural First Nation and Métis communities, and the situation of urban Aboriginal populations without a land base. We will argue that, from an economic development standpoint, the most difficult task is faced by the last of these three groupings. Thus we devote the bulk of our paper to the economic development challenges faced by Aboriginal persons who have migrated to or grown up in urban areas, but outside the context of a reserve and its attendant governing structures. Through a case study of Winnipeg, we outline three strategic approaches to urban Aboriginal economic development in this context.

Statistical data typically reveal that, on indices measuring health, education, employment, or income, urban Aboriginal populations fall somewhere in between rural Aboriginal people and urban non-Aboriginal people. That is, they are better off on these measures than their rural counterparts but still a considerable distance behind the non-Aboriginal population living in the same urban area (RCAP, 1996; Hanselmann, 2001). But these are summary statistics based on averages and as such, they hide the variety of circumstances that are found in the urban area. By outlining three different vantage points on the economic development situation faced by urban Aboriginal people, and by providing a more in-depth look at the most disadvantaged segment through a case study format, we hope to bring to light some of the diversity that actually exists.

Longstanding Urban or Near-Urban Reserves

When First Nation reserves were created in the 1800s and early decades of the 1900s, they were typically located in rural areas. As urbanization proceeded in Canada, especially in the 20th century, urban areas began to encroach upon rural reserves with the result that some reserves are now completely encompassed by urban or town boundaries, while others find themselves located adjacent to major urban areas. Sometimes, too, Aboriginal communities have relocated, by choice or not, and ended up closer to urban areas. At present, as much as a quarter of all reserves in Canada are classified by Indian and Northern Affairs Canada (INAC) as being urban (Frood, 1999: xiv).

In comparison with urban Aboriginal populations without a land base, those living on urban reserves have certain advantages relevant to economic development. The land base itself can be a considerable asset for it provides space for businesses to become established and permits both businesses and residents to benefit from tax advantages that come with location on a reserve. First Nations associated with reserves also have more clearly defined governance structures. Even though elected chiefs and band councils may be controversial in some cases, challenged by citizens for lacking accountability and by traditionalists for lacking legitimacy, nevertheless it is clear on reserve what the government is and who speaks on behalf of the community. Reserves also have a more clearly defined membership – everyone is listed on the band list – and the membership tends to be fairly homogeneous, with most persons belonging to the same cultural grouping and having the same historical roots. Finally, First Nations with a land base are recognized by the federal government under the Indian Act, and qualify for a variety of funding programs, ranging from core funding for their governance structures, to education funding for students, to support for the employment of economic development officers and the provision of capital for business development. At least for persons living on the urban reserve, it is fairly clear that the federal government takes responsibility for funding programs and services even if some provincial services are not available for on-reserve residents.

Because of these considerations and because they are located closer to larger markets than is the case for their rural counterparts, urban or near-urban reserves are able to pursue various economic development strategies. While initially they might establish small, service-sector businesses designed to meet the consumption needs of their on-reserve residents, some move beyond this stage of business development to the establishment of businesses that cater to a wider, non-Aboriginal market. This the case for those reserves that have developed gaming facilities, for example, like the St. Mary's reserve in Fredericton, New Brunswick or those that develop tourism facilities, craft enterprises, or shopping complexes geared to a much wider market. Examples include the golf courses that are a prominent feature of economic development at the Kahnawake reserve next to Montréal, or the ambitious commercial development undertaken by the Millbrook reserve which is adjacent to Truro, Nova Scotia and located on a principal highway route in the province.

Location in or near an urban area also offers the prospect to the on-reserve labour force of working off-reserve in (usually) non-Aboriginal employment settings. While discussions of Aboriginal economic development typically focus on business development, obtaining jobs as part of the labour force of a particular area is also an important aspect of economic development, although a difficult one due to discriminatory and other barriers. Apart from the income it provides for Aboriginal families, employment in the non-Aboriginal urban economy also provides valuable work experience, which can be useful for reserve-based economic development in preparing a skilled and trained labour force. Urban or near-urban reserves vary widely in the extent to which their labour force has been successful in finding employment off-reserve, but the Six Nations reserve located adjacent to

Canada's so-called Golden Horseshoe area is remarkable for the extent to which reserve residents have been able to find employment off reserve (Newhouse et. al., 1994).

While urban or near-urban reserves have some advantages in comparison with urban Aboriginal populations without a land base, we do not mean to imply that everything is smooth sailing. Some urban reserves have not been able to make inroads into the urban labour market, nor have they been able to develop businesses that could take advantage of the wider urban market. The Membertou reserve in Sydney, Nova Scotia, for example, is located within the Sydney industrial area but historically has not drawn significant benefit from that fact, although for a time a few Membertou residents were employed in the coal and steel industries. While the situation may be changing somewhat now, Membertou's urban strategy is focused at least as much on Halifax, some 400 kilometres away but a metropolitan area with a larger, more vibrant economy and the location where joint venture and other forms of business partnerships can more readily be negotiated.

Urban or near-urban reserves also have their own development challenges, ranging from sometimes difficult negotiations with the surrounding municipality for service agreements to the especially difficult challenge of developing an economy more in keeping with Aboriginal values. Many of the obstacles that affect rural reserves also apply in the urban area (e.g., the limitations on borrowing funds for on-reserve businesses because of the impediments imposed by the *Indian Act*, the delays in getting INAC approval for development projects, and the leakage effect whereby reserve income quickly drains away to the benefit of off-reserve businesses). Speaking to an audience of Calgary business people about Calgary's wish for a transportation corridor through Tsuu T'ina lands, Chief Roy Whitney of the Tsuu T'ina Nation raises some of the cultural differences and tensions involved in being next to a major urban area:

> Our system of consensus governance or direct democracy will be exercised when the proper time comes. The final agreement [for the transportation corridor], then must be meaningful to our people. We are prepared to listen and to consider what Alberta and Calgary have to say. We ask that Alberta and Calgary do the same for us. We are prepared to consider all reasonable options except one. We will not consider any deal that contemplates giving up our land and our heritage. We have heard calls for the City to buy our land, force a sale and pay us the value of raw land. To all of you here today who think we can be convinced or induced to sell our land, I have only one thing to say, and believe me when I tell you, Tsuu T'ina land is not for sale... not now, not ever (Whitney, 2000: 5, 6).

The Urban Economic Development Strategies of Rural Communities and the Creation of New Urban Reserves

As noted above, the new element in urban Aboriginal economic development is the expansive strategy of rural First Nations, tribal councils, and other Aboriginal organizations that look to urban areas as the site of economic opportunity. This takes a variety of forms, from establishing an urban office base where deals can be negotiated with corporate players to purchasing a hotel in an urban area to accommodate students or to host the countless meetings that for various reasons are best held in an urban location. A tribal council which brings together several rural First Nations may develop an investment strategy that relies heavily on purchasing urban-based businesses, and indeed in Manitoba the Tribal Councils Investment Group (TCIG) is a partnership of several tribal councils that follows such a strategy, although not to the exclusion of rural business opportunities as well (Wuttunee, 2002). The northern Alberta Métis settlements, too, have an urban headquarters in Edmonton and an economic development strategy that underlines the importance of identifying larger economic development projects that go beyond the limits of what one community can manage and that contemplates some urban opportunities (Wien et. al., 2000).

Interesting issues concerning the relationship between the tribal council or central organization and the member communities arise in this context, including how the tribal council handles the distribution of revenues from investments to the member communities, and dealing with opportunities that might also be pursued by a member First Nation. A case in point is the Tribal Councils Investment Group, an organization established in 1990 by the seven tribal councils of Manitoba. TCIG has established the following principles of operation.

- ▸ TCIG does not compete with First Nation communities, economic development groups or tribal councils
- ▸ Our policy is to get involved in projects beyond the capacity of individual groups
- ▸ When projects of a local or regional nature come to our attention, we automatically forward the information to the appropriate group
- ▸ The local group may pursue the interest solo, request us to partner with them, request our advice on the project, or pass on the opportunity
- ▸ TCIG also accommodates independent bands and private investors in its investment activities (Wuttunee, 2002: 10).

What leaves a bigger footprint on the urban area, however, is the trend over the past decade or so to establish new urban reserves. This strategy is particularly evident in Saskatchewan, although examples can be found in most if not all provinces. The impetus comes in part from a 1987 INAC initiative called the Additions to Reserves Policy, and in the west from the Treaty Land Entitlement Process. The latter attempts to come to grips with the fact that treaty obligations in the numbered treaty area have not always been honoured, for example, with respect to the setting aside of a certain number of acres of land based on the population of a band of Indians that is a signatory to the treaty. Treaty land entitlement agreements seek to make restitution, either in the form of cash grants or in the form of land (usually Crown lands) being made available. Either way, an urban reserve can result. Indeed, those who benefit from the treaty land entitlement process are most interested in adding an urban location to their land holdings for economic development purposes. Some examples follow.

> In Saskatchewan, urban reserves are generally the creations not of groups of Indians living within a particular urban centre but of band councils situated on parent reserves in rural areas of the province. Thus, the mandate of urban reserves in Saskatchewan is derived from rural-based bands, whose goal is to have urban reserves serve the overall interests of the band membership.

> Urban reserves are found in several cities, towns and villages in the central and southern regions of the province of Saskatchewan. They include the cities of Prince Albert, Saskatoon and Yorkton, as well as the towns of Fort Qu'Appelle and Meadow Lake, and the villages of Lebret and Duck Lake....

> In North Battleford [for example], Indian bands now own a number of parcels of land within the city limits, some of which will be converted into reserves. Most notable are lands earmarked for reserve status to house the Golden Eagle Casino, pursuant to an agreement signed between the provincial government and the provincial Indian organization, the Federation of Saskatchewan Indians.... In Saskatoon, plans are proceeding for a second and third urban reserve in the downtown business area, as well as two or three others in the northern industrial area of the city. The Yellow Quill Band, located in the Tisdale area, has purchased Canterbury Towers, a nine-storey office building that will house the First Nations Bank of Canada, the first Indian-owned chartered bank in the country; the Battlefords Tribal Council has purchased Avord Towers, an office and retail complex; and the English River

Band, located some three kilometres north of Meadow Lake, has acquired three commercial properties in the industrial belt of the city..." (Barron and Garcea, 1999: 3, 4).

It remains to be seen how these urban developments located on newly created reserves will turn out, but the trend for rural Aboriginal communities and organizations to forge an urban component to their development strategies adds a new, dynamic dimension to the field of urban Aboriginal economic development. It also challenges the insightful observation made by Newhouse and Paul more than a decade ago to the effect that rural Aboriginal economies could be described as "enclave" economies with little connection to urban and non-Aboriginal economies (Newhouse and Paul, 1990). For many rural Aboriginal communities, this is no longer the case.

The Economic Development Strategies of Urban Aboriginal Populations Without a Land Base

A third type of urban Aboriginal economic development is represented by those who have moved to and/or grown up in an urban area of Canada but without a collective land base and outside the context of a reserve. This is a diverse Aboriginal population, in the sense that it brings together people from various First Nations who have come to a particular urban area, and from Métis and Inuit populations as well. They are not as concentrated geographically as would be the case if they resided on an urban or rural reserve, and they are likely to be represented by a host of political, economic, and service organizations, most struggling to make ends meet on the basis of project to project funding. In this context, a fair amount of debate and division takes place about who speaks for the urban Aboriginal population, whether it be discrete Indian, Métis, or Inuit organizations, whether it be "status blind" urban service agencies or organizations, or rural, treaty-based First Nations that claim to speak on behalf of all of their band members, including urban dwellers.

In our view, it is this more dispersed urban Aboriginal population without a land or reserve base that faces the most challenging obstacles to economic development, particularly that portion concentrated in the more low-income portions of the urban area. For this reason, we devote the balance of this paper to a case study of Aboriginal economic development in Winnipeg with a focus on the inner city population. The essential characteristics of this type of urban economic development and the strategies that have been developed over several decades to come to grips with this situation are described below.

Case Study: Aboriginal Economic Development in Winnipeg

Over 60 percent of the 129,000 Aboriginal people in Manitoba live in urban areas, around 55,000 of them in Winnipeg (Hanselmann, 2002, Loxley, 2000: 7) where the Aboriginal population is growing at rates well in excess of the rest of the population.[2] It is estimated that within 20 years, one in every four people entering the labour force will be Aboriginal (Winnipeg, 2001:13). The Aboriginal community is very heterogeneous and has representation in all walks of life including business, the judiciary, entertainment, education, government, and the professions. Thus, for many Aboriginal people, the progression through education to employment is no different from that of non-Aboriginal people. But the community as a whole has much higher levels of poverty on average than the rest of society. Thus, in 1996, while the average rate of poverty among families in Winnipeg was 28.4 percent, itself an unacceptably high rate, that for Aboriginal families was 64.7 percent and for Aboriginal families living in the inner city, a staggering 80.3 percent (Lezubski et al., 2000: 40). There are many reasons for this, including lower labour force participation rates and higher unemployment rates, in turn the result of lower educational levels, greater incidence of single parent families, poor health and living conditions, social instability, and the barriers of institutionalized racism. What is clear, however, is the urgent need to address the problem.

Institutional Capacity

In an effort to improve the lot of the community, Aboriginal people have struggled to build an institutional capacity in Winnipeg, to provide political direction, to lobby governments for resources, to provide services directly to their people, and to build an economic development planning and implementation capability. In the process, these institutions have become an important source of employment and income generation for the community.

To begin with, a number of Aboriginal political organizations are headquartered in Winnipeg. The five principal ones are the Assembly of Manitoba Chiefs (AMC), the Manitoba Métis Federation (MMF), the Southern Chiefs Organization, the Manitoba Keewatinowi Okimakanak (MKO) representing First Nations in Northern Manitoba, and the Aboriginal Council of Winnipeg (ACW). The first two are province-wide bodies headquartered in Winnipeg. The second and third are regional sub-groupings of chiefs, the latter representing the north. The ACW was established in 1990, a product of the amalgamation of the Winnipeg Council of Treaty and Status Indians, which represented Status Indians, and the Urban Indian Association, which represented Status Indians, Non-Status Indians, and Métis.

Of these organizations, only the MMF has developed an institutional capacity for economic planning and development, backed up with financial resources. The Federation established the Manitoba Métis Community Investments Inc. (MMCII) in 1984 to undertake economic development initiatives essentially in rural Métis communities. In January 1991, the MMF established the Louis Riel Capital Corporation (LRCC). It was originally capitalized at $7.6 million but lost over a half of that in the federal budget cuts of 1994-95. It employs five staff. <http://www.mmf.mb.ca/pages/LRCC_info.htm>. To date it has disbursed $7.5 million in a range of economic sectors, from agriculture to retail and has been reimbursed $4.5 million to date. While few of the 272 loans made so far have been advanced in Winnipeg, there are no constraints on its ability to lend there except the viability of borrowers. The LRCC also provides business services and runs the Youth Loan Fund.

The MMF, therefore, has a pool of capital and some economic and financial expertise. It also has some office, storage, and construction capacity. While these resources are minimal and quite inadequate for a frontal assault on Métis and Non-Status economic problems, they constitute a base from which to start. The other political organs have no such base in Winnipeg.

The federal government refuses to make resources available to the AMC or the Southern Chiefs for planning or financing economic initiatives. This suggests the government is not really interested in developing the capacity of the Indian community to shape their own economic development agenda, preferring to involve First Nations' organizations in its economic programs only on its own terms (e.g., as applicants to federal programs). Here the Aboriginal political organizations can serve at best only in a purely advisory capacity.

Once they leave the reserve, Status Indians find themselves in an ambiguous position. Since the federal government does not accept the principle of portability of treaty rights, and since bands have no incentive to transfer funds to urban areas to provide services to migrants, their own funding being hopelessly inadequate, urban Indians find themselves in a nether land. They have no obvious political representation and by and large, the AMC has not directed its attention to their predicament. In Saskatchewan, urban reserves have been established which allow First Nations businesses and workers a tax free shelter within the urban areas; they also clarify the issue of political representation. In 1975 Khan-Tineta-Horn proposed that an urban reserve be located 10 miles outside Winnipeg (Damas and Smith, 1975: 6) but the Neeginan proposal, discussed below, was felt to be a more appropriate alternative. The concept of urban reserves has, however, resurfaced in Manitoba as a result of the provincial government's initiative on Aboriginal casinos. These are required to be located on reserve land or, alternatively, on land being negotiated under treaty land entitlement, in which case proponents would need to demonstrate they had met any concerns of adjacent local municipalities (Manitoba First Nations Casino, 2000: 3).

Two proposals came forward for urban reserves, one in Thompson and one in Brandon. Both of these were rejected in civic referenda widely considered to have been conducted on the basis of misinformation about the nature of the proposals. The Brandon proposal had the support of the majority on Council but was strongly opposed by the Mayor (*Brandon Sun*, June 16, 2002). Sioux Valley, the First Nation involved, agreed that the casino would contribute to the city's revenues as if it were a regular business (i.e., it opted not to exercise its tax free status). The proposal was, nonetheless, voted down in an October 2002 referendum. A third proposal to locate a casino in Headingley, just outside the Winnipeg city boundary, on land owned by the Swan Lake First Nation, was withdrawn after the local residents again vetoed the proposal. A nearby racetrack which wanted to head off the competition to its own gambling business was front and centre in raising fears about Aboriginal people taking up residence in Headingley, and the racist basis of its fear mongering was successful in killing the proposal (Dubois et al., 2002). The rejection of these proposals has thrown the whole Aboriginal casino strategy of the New Democratic Party (NDP) Government into disarray.

Some years ago the AMC made putative attempts to establish a Winnipeg tribal council, but it did not have the will, ability, or resources to succeed. There are, however, some urban Status Indians who believe that the tribal council approach is not the way to further their interests and have tended to throw their support behind the Aboriginal Council.

The Aboriginal Council has the backing of numerous Aboriginal institutions in Winnipeg and of some very prominent urban Aboriginal activists, Status, Non-Status, and Métis alike. Its position is that Aboriginal people should have the right to self-determination regardless of place of residence. ACW believes that "status blind" institutions would best serve the interests of urban Aboriginal people, to deliver services regardless of legal distinctions between Aboriginal people (ACW, 1992), but at the same time is careful to point out that it does not believe in a melting pot approach to urbanization. Rather, it respects the diversity of the different groups and believes in the portability of treaty rights.

The Council also suffers from a lack of resources receiving only limited core funding from the province. It has no in-house economic development capacity, but it does have a huge volunteer base and close ties with numerous inner-city Aboriginal organizations, and it draws on these to lever resources from government agencies for specific development projects.

A number of non-urban tribal councils have their headquarters physically located in Winnipeg (though legally based on reserves for tax reasons). The most significant of these is the Southeast Resource Development Council, Inc., which represents nine bands in southeastern Manitoba. This Council owns two extremely profitable buildings, a parking lot, a junior hockey team in the city, and part ownership of two golf courses. It also provides significant educational supports in Winnipeg for students coming into the city, partially through a residential high school which it owns. It has an economic development capacity through its Economic Development Division, which employs seven staff, four of whom are Aboriginal, and a Community Futures Organization. Both organizations focus entirely on community development on the reserves. Southeast has discussed plans to set up a fast food outlet in the centre of the city and has, in the past, discussed establishing a travel agency and a cheque-cashing facility. The council has a number of economic ventures designed to serve its reserve members, such as a building supply store, an electrical contractor, and an airline, but all of these are based outside of Winnipeg.

The Dakota Ojibway Tribal Council also has a large presence in Winnipeg representing First Nations in southwest Manitoba, though it is also based in Brandon. Its health and housing authorities, Community Futures Development Corporation, investment wing, fire and safety, social development, and child and family services, all have a presence in Winnipeg. Five of the six other tribal councils maintain modest offices in Winnipeg.

While each of the tribal councils and the MMF have financial arms, there is no capital corporation devoted solely to the needs of Aboriginal people living in Winnipeg. There is, however, a small Me-Dian Credit Union, which has struggled in the past, and the Alberta based Peace Hills Trust Company has a branch in the city.

Aboriginal women have felt the need for their own political organizations for some years, and with the emphasis they have been putting in recent years on male violence, their organizations have become very prominent. In Winnipeg, the main women's bodies are the Original Women's Network and the Mother of Red Nations Women's Council of Manitoba Inc. Neither has the resources to develop its own economic decision-making capability, but they work closely with the Aboriginal Council and contain women with considerable experience in building development projects from the ground up. Aboriginal women have been very active in establishing institutions in Winnipeg that provide housing, child care, cultural facilities, shelters for women and children, health care facilities, and training institutions. What is clear is that any efforts to strengthen the institutional capacity for Aboriginal organizations to formulate economic policies and plans and to implement them, must also involve making resources available to women's organizations so their experiences and insights can be given full expression, and their particular problems and needs can be addressed.

Approaches to Economic Development

There are three clearly defined approaches to economic development in Winnipeg advocated by Aboriginal people.

The Incubator Approach

The first approach may be called the incubator approach and it consists of providing a variety of economic functions from a central location, under one roof. The idea is that each venture would benefit from being in proximity to the next, sharing space, reducing overhead costs, having access to services and to clientele. While the building would be under the ownership and control of an Aboriginal organization, the businesses housed there would tend to be privately owned. The origin of this approach can be traced back to Stan Fulham (1981) who envisaged a partnership between Aboriginal organizations and the state "to establish and promote a private business sector for Native people" (Fulham, 1981: 74). Jointly, the Aboriginal and senior levels of government would create a Native economic development and employment council (NEDECO) which would, in turn, establish a native development corporation (NDC). The NDC would operate a number of subsidiary companies, offering them financial and administrative services, and would create a Native industrial centre, a business complex to house companies. The council would negotiate contracts with government, Crown corporations and private business for corporation subsidiaries to supply goods and services employing Aboriginal people. It would concentrate on labour intensive activities, would work with government to set up appropriate training schemes and would maintain an inventory of Aboriginal people, their skills and employment experience to maximize their employment opportunities, both within the corporation and elsewhere.

The industrial centre would house a credit union for staff and businesses, and several other personal service enterprises, such as a café/restaurant, barbershop, hairdresser, shoe-repair shop. By sharing premises, both subsidiaries and other businesses would economize on costs (subsidized where justified), and would have ready access to managerial expertise and a source of finance. Fulham also advocates setting aside government purchasing of supplies and services to benefit specifically Aboriginal businesses. While relying heavily on government resources, for purchasing and for training, and while drawing on community input for the council and the corporation, the underlying objective of this approach is to build an Aboriginal private business sector.

Fulham poses this strategy in opposition to affirmative action, which he views as a negative approach (Fulham, 1981: 75) and, in this respect, his views are quite at odds with those currently held by Aboriginal groups in the city. Also at odds with contemporary thinking in the Aboriginal community is the degree of state supervision of the quite cumbersome institutional structure which Fulham envisages.

Some of Fulham's thinking embraces ideas put forward initially in 1969 by the Indian and Métis Friendship Centre for a native community in Winnipeg. The proposal was fleshed out in some detail between 1972 and 1975 as Neeginan, a Cree expression which can be translated as "Our Place" (Damas and Smith, 1975: 10). This envisaged the creation of an ethnic quarter in Winnipeg for Aboriginal people to serve as a transitional milieu for those moving into the city. It would have its own housing, social service and economic facilities, and would be run by Aboriginal people. A 1975 report went into considerable architectural detail for the community services centre which would be the focal point of the community, housing social service agencies, shops, schools, residential accommodation, and Aboriginal political organizations. The report also examined alternative locations in the inner city.

Though formulated over 20 years ago, Fulham's views, and related proposals such as Neeginan, have had an important impact on contemporary Aboriginal policy and actions. The incubator approach (or franchise as Fulham would have it) was influential in the proposal to establish the Aboriginal Centre of Winnipeg in what used to be the Canadian Pacific Railway Station which is located in the heart of the core area.

The idea behind the Aboriginal Centre was that it would bring under one roof a variety of Aboriginal organizations providing services to the community. Existing organizations would be encouraged to move their offices there. It would house an Aboriginal institute, which would deliver existing and new employment and training related services. Attempts would also be made to bring in public sector agencies providing services to Aboriginal people. A restaurant and child-care facility would be set up to cater to those working or being trained in the building. Finally, there was provision for light industrial activities, such as catering, printing, and publishing, and for conferences in the huge, 146,000 square feet building.

Considerable progress has been made in realizing this plan, which contains many elements of the Neeginan proposal, especially the community service centre component, without the emphasis on building a separate neighbourhood as such. The building was purchased in December 1992, initially by means of the CPR taking back a mortgage, and later by means of loans from the Assiniboine Credit Union. By 1999, the Centre had 25 tenants and was fully occupied. Aboriginal firms which have established there include a security company, a woodworking enterprise, and an auto body shop (none of which are currently operational) a printer, a newspaper, a computer lab, a restaurant (which is in part a training initiative) and an art gallery. Many other tenants provide important services to the community, such as literacy, counselling, employment advice and training, and health and wellness. The Aboriginal Council of Winnipeg, the Original Women's Network and the Manitoba Association of Friendship Centres are also located there as are a number of non-Aboriginal entities which provide services to the community, such as the post office, legal aid, and human resources organizations of government A number of large conferences are also held there. After many years of struggling, the building is now fully occupied and annual rents bring in over $700,000 a year.

This represents a considerable accomplishment for the Aboriginal community of Winnipeg. The Aboriginal Centre will undoubtedly become a focal point for the community and represents the realization of an idea long in the making.

The Centre is not, however, without some potential dangers. The project is highly dependent, both directly and indirectly, on state funding for rental income. This is not, of course, unusual for Aboriginal institutions, but the centrality of that funding to the ongoing commercial viability of the Centre is, perhaps, somewhat unique. Diversifying the tenants helps reduce risk in this regard, as does diversifying the types and sources of state funding. In late 1999, there were 25 tenants drawing funding from the federal, provincial, and city governments, as well as Aboriginal educational authorities, so one could argue that this risk has been recognized and addressed to some degree.

Second, the geographic concentration of Aboriginal organizations in one building limits the extent to which they can be incorporated into holistic, community development, based on balanced growth within neighbourhoods. It could be argued that this is a necessary, structural weakness of the incubator approach.

Third, the incubator concept has been only partially successful with regard to commercial businesses. The ones listed earlier are important initiatives but are not highly integrated, sharing little but a common roof. Some of the services which might have accomplished this and which were originally in the plan, have not materialized (e.g., the credit union, perhaps because of scale problems).

Finally, the large concentration of Aboriginal institutions, each with a different mandate and agenda, calls for a high degree of diplomacy in the handling of problems and disagreements among tenants and between tenants and the Centre. In the past, internal political dissension in the Aboriginal community has led to the loss of a key tenant, and turmoil in the Aboriginal Council has, on occasion, threatened the stability of the whole enterprise. The Aboriginal Business Development Centre, a federally funded tenant which offered counselling to small businesses in an "Aboriginal friendly" environment also imploded for political reasons. The Centre appears, however, to have successfully overcome these challenges.

The biggest success of the Aboriginal Centre may prove to be that of resurrecting the Neeginan concept and pushing it through to implementation. The serious problems of the inner-city became apparent in the late 1990s with extensive Aboriginal gang activity, a rapidly deteriorating housing stock and an outbreak of arson. In 1999, the Pan Am Games were held in Winnipeg, and the politicians decided that Main Street needed a facelift. Proceeding with the Neeginan concept was felt to be a way of meeting several objectives at once; clearing up derelict hotels on Main Street; replacing them with an impressive structure celebrating Aboriginal strength and culture; placating the Aboriginal leadership; and offering financial support (over $6 million) to the community's own solutions to the economic and social problems it faces. Neeginan seemed to offer all of this.

Construction of the Thunder Bird House, Neeginan's home, was completed in early 2000. This strikingly impressive building was designed by Douglas Cardinal who sees it as "a place of rebirth and vitality; a place of healing and sharing." It will have several components; a place for Aboriginal art and culture; a youth complex and a commercial complex/business incubator. The incubator component is exactly the same as that envisaged for the Aboriginal Centre and Douglas Cardinal describes it thus: "In this village, we will provide stores which will offer an assortment of goods and merchandise such as: food, clothing, gardening equipment, leather goods, and other necessities. We will have banks, bookstores, video stores, pool halls, movie theatres, arcades, and restaurants" (Cardinal, undated).

While it is separate from the Aboriginal Centre, both the latter and Neeginan share a common conceptual foundation and both provide for commercial incubators. Neeginan has been a cultural success, but it has not been able to develop the business side at all, and it appears unlikely it will have more success in this regard than the Aboriginal Centre, which is located just across the street.

The Neechi Approach

The second, and contrasting approach to Aboriginal economic development in Winnipeg focuses on community economic development. It was put forward by members of the Neechi Foods Co-op Ltd (a worker owned co-operative community store) in their *Its Up To All Of Us* guide (Winnipeg, 1993). They laid down 10 community development criteria (subsequently expanded to 11) by which to assess proposed or actual community initiatives. The first three of these essentially advocate a convergence approach to economic strategy as they provide for the use of local goods and services, the production of goods and services in the local economy, and the reinvestment of profits locally. The point here is to emphasize the potential of the inner-city market to sustain economic livelihoods. This means that income earned in the inner-city should, as far as possible, be spent there, and preferably on goods and services which are actually produced there. This contrasts with the current situation in which substantial inner-city income leaks away in expenditures elsewhere in the city on goods and services which are not produced in the inner-city. Neechi encourages both Aboriginal residents and non-Aboriginal residents and others earning incomes in the core, to use their purchasing power to benefit the local community. The idea is to spend in such a way that leakages from the inner-city economy are minimized, and economic linkages within it strengthened. This would reduce dependence on outside markets and build greater community self-reliance.

The fourth principle is to create long-term employment for inner-city residents, to reduce dependence on welfare and food banks, enable people to live more socially productive lives, and to build personal and community esteem. In the process, of course, more income would be available for spending in the community. Related to this, the fifth principle calls for the training of local residents in skills appropriate for community development.

The sixth principle or guideline is the encouragement of local decision making through local, co-operative, forms of ownership and control, and grass-roots participation. The aim would be to strengthen community self-determination as people work together to meet community needs.

Principles seven and eight recognize the importance of community development promoting public health and a safe and attractive physical environment. The ninth principle stresses the centrality of achieving greater neighbourhood stability by providing more dependable housing, encouraging long-term residency, and creating a base for long-term community economic development.

The 10th principle is that the whole approach is premised on safeguarding and enhancing human dignity. While there is a personal dimension to this, in the form of promoting self-respect, much of the emphasis is social, recognizing the need to generate community spirit, encourage equality between the sexes, and respect for seniors and children. The Neechi criteria also call for the promotion of social dignity regardless of physical or mental differences, national or ethnic background and colour or creed. Above all, community development should promote Aboriginal pride.

More recent additions to the principles provide for co-operation between community economic development initiatives for mutual benefit, for greater emphasis on income equality, and for provision for dispute resolution in the community.

This is an exhaustive and demanding set of criteria by which to evaluate community development proposals. Underlying it is a definite vision of both the process and the goal of community economic development.

The Neechi approach to economic development is not merely an intellectual one. It is rooted in and shaped by practical experience. The principles evolved during two training programs conducted in the early 1980s for Métis and Indian economic development and finance officers. Sponsored by the MMF and the All-Chief's Budget Committee of the AMC, but run independently, these programs have produced over 50 well trained Aboriginal staff, most of whom are now employed by Aboriginal organizations in the province. Out of these courses, which combined rigorous classroom work with practical on-the-job experience, came a series of community planning meetings in the summer of 1985, run by the trainees. Four projects were identified in these meetings as being high on the list of priority needs in the community in Winnipeg; a food store, a housing co-op, a commercial daycare and a crafts shop, and the trainees proceeded to appraise each, working in conjunction with project working groups. All but the last of these has now been implemented and, in the early years, were loosely "federated" under the umbrella of the Winnipeg Native Family Economic Development (WNFED), a mutual support group.

Neechi Foods Co-op is an Aboriginal workers' co-op operating a grocery store and Aboriginal specialty shop in the inner-city. The objectives of the co-op are to offer Aboriginal people a better selection of food at better prices, to promote community health (which it does in a number of ways (e.g., by not selling cigarettes and by subsidizing sales of fruit to children), to promote Aboriginal pride and employment, to keep money circulating in the community, to foster sharing, co-operation and local control, and to create capital for new projects. The store employs four full-time and five part-time employees, all Aboriginal, and annual sales are now in the region of $0.5 million. A move to open a second, high-end Aboriginal craft store in the fashionable Osborne Village part of downtown was, however, unsuccessful.

The housing operation affiliated with WNFED is the Payuk Inter-Tribal Co-op, which has a 42-unit apartment block and five duplex units. One aim is to provide a safe and supportive environment for Aboriginal women and children (e.g., alcohol is prohibited in the building). Rents are tied to ability to pay. The Nee Gawn Ah Kai Day Care is located in the Payuk building, has space for 30 children and employs six people.

The Ma Mawi Wi Chi Itata Centre, Canada's first major urban Aboriginal child and family support service which now employs 55, largely Aboriginal, staff was also associated with WNFED. This organization was the outcome of efforts by the Winnipeg Coalition on Native Child Welfare, which also worked closely with the Economic Development Training Program, underlining the holistic, integrated approach to economic and social reform subscribed to by an influential section of the community.

A number of collectively owned Aboriginal enterprises have been established in recent years which are quite consistent with the Neechi approach. A security company, mentioned above, was doing quite well and was a viable enterprise until it ran into unexpected problems with management. A group of women have set up a co-operative enterprise making star blankets while another operates a successful catering business.

The Neechi approach has clearly influenced the thinking of the Aboriginal Council in its formulation of an economic development strategy for Aboriginal people in the city. It argues for "a community economic development planning process geared towards developing a convergent, self-reliant local economy based upon community economic development principles: maximising income retention, strengthening and promoting economic linkages, and maximising community employment." (ACW, 1992). It argues for the development of linkages between the urban Aboriginal community and reserves and rural Métis communities, but it would also like to see treaty administration centres established in Winnipeg to meet the needs of off-reserve Indians. The Council puts a major emphasis on the Aboriginalization of the staff and control of the social service delivery system catering to Aboriginal clientele. They see Aboriginalization as an important component of community economic development and extend it to education (with calls for an Aboriginal school board and control over all aspects of urban Aboriginal education), health, services to women, seniors, youths, and ex-inmates; in short, to all sections of Aboriginal society. This "decolonization" would be based on the principle of participation by all sections of Aboriginal society and would be accomplished, ideally, in co-operation with the other political organizations. This strategy has, therefore, some unique features, but at root, as a convergence strategy, it is essentially that proposed by Neechi.

The Neechi/WNFED approach to economic development shares some things in common with the Fulham approach. They both recognize the importance of Aboriginal organizations in the process; they both stress the importance of developing linkages and mutually supporting economic initiatives, both within Winnipeg and between the city community and Aboriginal communities outside; they both recognize the importance of having support services available to Aboriginal businesses, and especially of appropriate training. Both argue the importance of providing decent long-term housing, and both admit the social desirability of non-Aboriginal support for Aboriginal ventures even when more lucrative investment outlets or cheaper purchases could be had elsewhere.

There are, however, crucial differences between these two approaches which need to be highlighted. First of all, the Neechi approach is much more clearly grounded in grass-roots community activism than is the Fulham model and its variants, and envisages a much less significant role for

Aboriginal political organizations in the economic development process. Second, the Neechi model attaches a much greater importance to community ownership and control than does Fulham, who is more wedded to the promotion of private Aboriginal business. Third, the Neechi approach is a much more holistic one, in which economic development is seen as one aspect, albeit a very important one, of healthy communities, in which economic opportunity, health and educational development and social and environmental stability go hand in hand. Fourth, and related, Neechi would attach less importance to the physical aggregation of economic enterprises under one roof, preferring more spatial balance and securing supportive services and economies of scale in other ways. Finally, the Neechi model promotes restoring economic balance and community self-reliance through economic restructuring which in some ways challenges the logic of the market economy. Fulham's approach, on the other hand, accepts the dominant market on its own terms and seeks to break into it with state assistance.

The Employment Equity, Employment Agreement Approach

The Assembly of Manitoba Chiefs has taken an eclectic approach to economic development in Winnipeg. It is supportive of both the incubator concept and of community-based initiatives of the kind advocated by Neechi. But it also promotes a third approach, arguing for aggressive employment equity initiatives in the public sector, and for the opening up of employment opportunities in the private sector. The AMC has been particularly insistent on greater accessibility to mainstream employment opportunities and has developed a close working relationship with some large-scale private employers. It has adopted a carrot and stick approach, pressing its case legally under human rights and employment equity legislation, but accompanying this with partnership agreements with employers under which it helps them achieve a more representative labour force.

In 1990, the AMC filed 51 human rights complaints with the Canadian Human Rights Commission to increase Aboriginal representation in the labour force. By 2000-01 it had become a signatory to 36 employment equity agreements with both the private and public sectors. It entered into agreements with both Air Canada and Canadian Airlines to increase Aboriginal employment among counter service agents, flight attendants, maintenance and ground crews, and administrative and technical support workers. While some progress was made, the turmoil in the industry and the amalgamation of the two companies led to a hiring freeze which has adversely affected the agreements. It has had more success with banks.

The AMC and its forerunners have put particular emphasis on trying to secure a much greater Aboriginal presence in governmental institutions and especially in those dealing directly with Aboriginal people. In recent years, it has signed partnership agreements with Manitoba Hydro (2000), Manitoba Public Insurance (2001), and the Winnipeg Regional Health Authority (2001), each of which is a huge employer, with a total of some 33,000 staff among them, and each of which has hired an Aboriginal person to assist the process. The AMC is party to a joint staff review with Indian and Northern Affairs Canada, which aims to Aboriginalize 50 percent of the staff in Manitoba, mainly located in Winnipeg. By January 2001, 105 out of 218 staff, or 48.2 percent were Aboriginal, a major accomplishment.[3] Data on Aboriginal representation in other departments in Winnipeg are not available, but in the province as a whole, there are 616 Aboriginal employees of the federal government out of a total of 5,974, or 10.3 percent, well above Aboriginal representation in the labour force. Many of these jobs were, however, seasonal or temporary in nature. Aboriginal people are also under represented in executive positions, holding down only two percent of such positions across the country, although hiring data show that attempts are being made to address this problem (all these data from Treasury Board, 2001: Tables 3, 5, 6, and 9).

In the provincial civil service, there were 1,148 Aboriginal employees at March 31, 2001, representing 7.85 percent of the total. This is slightly in excess of the proportion of the provincial labour force which is Aboriginal, 7.5 percent but well below the government's own target of 10 percent. Of the total of 8,248 civil servants employed in Winnipeg, 421 or 5.1 percent were Aboriginal (Manitoba, 2001: 1). Recently the province announced that it will devolve responsibility for Aboriginal child welfare to the Aboriginal community and this, over time, should expand employment opportunities for Aboriginal people in this area which operates at arms length from the government but which is fully funded by it.

In the City of Winnipeg, 4.4 percent of the workforce was Aboriginal in 1999 (Winnipeg, 2001: 29). This represented about 404 employees out of a total of 9,178, a proportion which was slightly less than the Aboriginal participation in the city labour market as a whole, at 4.6 percent. Aboriginal people are, however, much less represented "as one moves upwards in authority and pay" (Winnipeg, 2001: 30).

Even the private sector is beginning to recognize the importance of a more representative labour force. The Winnipeg Chamber of Commerce and the Business Council of Manitoba, in conjunction with Manitoba Education and Training and the Aboriginal Human Resource Development Council of Canada, have launched the Aboriginal Employment Initiative. In February 2002, they organized an Aboriginal job fair at which 40 private sector employees interviewed an expected 300 to 400 Aboriginal students and employees, from which a minimum of 125 new job placements were expected to result (Winnipeg, 2002).

The employment equity and employment approach has, therefore, yielded solid accomplishments and the groundwork has been laid for greater Aboriginal representation in the public and private sector labour force. Given the aging labour force in Winnipeg, the relatively low unemployment rate (less than five percent in early 2002) and the acute shortages of skilled labour in many sectors, the demand for labour is much less of a problem than it has been for years. The opportunities to overcome the "long and well-documented history of institutionalized racism and systemic barriers to full participation" (Winnipeg, 2001: 13) have never looked better for Aboriginal people, but government policy needs to be tailored to meet this challenge.

Conclusion: Government Policy and Urban Aboriginal Economic Development

In this article, we have identified three vantage points from which to view urban Aboriginal economic development – from the point of view of longstanding urban or near-urban reserves, from the perspective of rural First Nation and Métis communities that individually or collectively have developed an economic development strategy with an important urban component, and from the perspective of a more dispersed urban Aboriginal population without a land base.

Our case study of Winnipeg has concentrated on the latter situation in particular, and has described three strategic approaches to achieving a measure of socio-economic development in the urban context. To some extent these three approaches are not incompatible and, in any event, the problems facing the community are so severe that there is room for eclecticism. What the approaches have in common is the need for supportive public sector policies and programs, but this raises at least three issues: co-ordination, instability, and dependence.

With respect to co-ordination, the fact that three different levels of government – four if Aboriginal governments are included – have a stake in urban Aboriginal economic development leads almost inevitably to problems of gaps and overlaps in government policy and programs. We have already mentioned the inequitable access to government programs arising from the fact that INAC typically shies away from any off-reserve and Métis-related funding commitments. Our Winnipeg case study also illustrates that there is no co-ordinated government policy to facilitate greater involvement of Aboriginal people in the Winnipeg economy, no coherent, comprehensive, approach involving all three levels of government, as there was some years ago with the Core Area Initiative and the more recent, though less focused and less generous, Winnipeg Development Agreement. There is talk of developing an Urban Aboriginal Strategy at the provincial level, but so far this has not materialized.[4]

All three levels of government have put financial resources into neighbourhood development corporations for housing initiatives and SEED Winnipeg, a micro bank, has received funding from the federal government and, mainly in recent years, from the provincial government. These programs do benefit, but are not aimed exclusively, at Aboriginal people.

A second major concern is the instability of public funding. In Winnipeg, for example, in spite of recent, welcome, interest and commitments by the province, funding has been vulnerable to a change of government. For that reason, there have been proposals for establishing a community economic development foundation which would be funded as an endowment, thereby guaranteeing stability whatever the government in power. The attraction to practitioners is evident, but for government it entails providing a pool of capital one time, up-front, and this is much more demanding and inflexible, and much less attractive politically than being able to make annual or triennial funding announcements (Loxley, 2003).

This dilemma brings to the fore a central reality of most approaches to Aboriginal economic development in Winnipeg and other urban centres at this time: all of them rely, to one extent or another, on government funding for their success. Even the Neechi approach, which is premised on self-reliance, requires initial funding given the poor capital base of the Aboriginal community. Certainly, the existence of the Assiniboine Credit Union, the most enlightened financial institution in the city, and one which subscribes to the Neechi principles, reduces the severity of this financial gap, but there is a limit to what Assiniboine can do in what is clearly a high risk area of lending.

It is not likely that this dependence on government funding will end anytime soon, but lessons are being learned across the country about how, over time, solid Aboriginal economies can be rebuilt. Keys to the transition include the continuing development of strong Aboriginal institutions to assist the process of economic change in such areas as governance, strategic planning, making financial capital available, and building human resource capacity. Other lessons arise from the aggressive way in which some First Nation, Métis, and Inuit communities have responded to changes in their structure of economic opportunities, whether this has been achieved by treaty land entitlements, recognition of Aboriginal and treaty rights by the courts, the negotiation of comprehensive or specific land claims, or agreements to develop gaming facilities. One of the striking features of urban Aboriginal economic development of the kind that we have discussed in Winnipeg has been the paucity of interventions that would significantly change the opportunity structure for urban Aboriginal populations without a land base, and that would invest in establishing the kind of institutional structures that would permit Aboriginal people to take advantage of new opportunities.

Notes

1   However, the number of Aboriginal persons living in urban areas is often overstated and depends, of course, on how both "Aboriginal" and "urban" are defined. Some estimates are as high as 60 or 70 percent, but the Royal Commission on Aboriginal Peoples after a careful look at not-so-straightforward data concluded with a figure of 44 percent based on 1991 data which include the urban (non-reserve) Aboriginal identity population (RCAP, 1996: 806).

2   Recently released results from the 2001 Census give an Aboriginal population of 55,755 in the City of Winnipeg (Statistics Canada, 2003).

3   <http://www.manitobachiefs.com/corp/corporate.html>.

4   The provincial government is the most active of the three in terms of training, business development, and support for community economic development initiatives, but the level of involvement still leaves much to be desired. The NDP Government has renewed funding cut off by the previous Conservative Government to Aboriginal political organizations, the Indian-Métis Friendship Centre and other organizations. It has established a $3 million Neighbourhoods Alive Program aimed mainly at Aboriginal people, which has a number of components, housing renovation and home ownership, recreational facilities for youth and funding for training of Aboriginal workers in health care and child and family services. The province has the $1 million Aboriginal Economic and Resource Development Fund and puts $5.5 million a year into the Access Program, assisting students, 70 percent of whom are Aboriginal, to overcome barriers to post-secondary education. There are also provincial programs in health, child care, domestic violence, justice, and employment placement. The province estimates that it spends $374 million a year on Aboriginal people in Winnipeg, compared with only about $10 million spent by the federal government, but it is impossible to verify both these numbers (and certainly excludes federal contributions through transfers).

References

ACW (Aboriginal Council of Winnipeg) (1992) *Discussion Paper: Self-Determination for Urban Aboriginal People*, based on a submission to the Royal Commission on Aboriginal Peoples, Edmonton, Alberta, June 21-23, 1992.

Barron, F. Laurie and Joseph Garcea (1999) "Introduction", in *Urban Indian Reserves: Forging the New Relationship in Saskatchewan*, F. Laurie Barron and Joseph Garcea, (eds.), Saskatoon: Purich Publishing, pp. 1-21.

Canada, Statistics Canada (2003) *Aboriginal Peoples of Canada*, <http//www12.statcan.ca/english/census01/products/analytic/companion/abor/canada.cfm>.

Canada, Treasury Board Secretariat (2001) *Employment Equity in the Federal Public Service, 2000-2001*, Government of Canada, Ottawa.

Cardinal, Douglas (nd) *Neeginan: A Vision of Hope and Healing*, for the North Main Task Force, Winnipeg.

Damas and Smith Limited (1975) *Neeginan: A Report on the Feasibility Study*, Prepared for Neeginan (Manitoba) Incorporated, April.

Dubois, Alison, Wanda A. Wuttunee, and John Loxley (2002) "Gambling on Casinos," *Journal Of Aboriginal Economic Development*, 2(2): 56-67.

Frood, Peter (1999) "Foreword" in *Urban Indian Reserves: Forging New Relationships in Saskatchewan*, F. Laurie Barron and Joseph Garcea, (eds.), Saskatoon: Purich Publishing, pp. xiii-xiv.

Fulham, Stanley A. (1981) *In Search of a Future*, Winnipeg: Kinew Publishers.

Hanselmann, Calvin (2001) *Urban Aboriginal People in Western Canada: Realities and Policies*, Calgary: Canada West Foundation.

—— (2002) "Urban Aboriginals Must Choose a Single Voice," *Winnipeg Free Press*, June 20, p. A13.

Lezubski, Darren, Jim Silver, and Errol Black (2000) "High and Rising: The Growth of Poverty in Winnipeg," in *Solutions that Work: Fighting Poverty in Winnipeg*, Jim Silver, (ed.), Halifax and Manitoba: Fernwood and CCPA, pp. 26-51.

Loxley, John (2000) "Aboriginal Economic Development in Winnipeg," in *Solutions that Work: Fighting Poverty in Winnipeg*, Jim Silver, (ed.), Halifax and Manitoba: Fernwood and CCPA, pp. 84-110.

—— (2003) "Financing Community Economic Development in Winnipeg," *Economie et Solidarité*.

Manitoba (2001) *Employment Equity Program, April 1, 2000 – March 31, 2001*, Winnipeg.

Manitoba First Nations Casino Project Selection Committee (2000) *Manitoba First Nations Casino Project: Request for Proposals*, Winnipeg, January 19.

Newhouse, David and Ken Paul (1990) "Indian Reserve Economies as Enclave Economies," Peterborough: Trent University, Dept. of Native Studies.

Newhouse, David, Saud Choudry, Stephen Sliwa, Mark Ahonen, and Andrew Barbour (1994) *The Six Nations Economy: Its Development and Prospects*, Ottawa: Royal Commission on Aboriginal Peoples.

RCAP (Royal Commission on Aboriginal Peoples) (1996) "Economic Development" Chapter 5, Volume 2, Part Two of the *Report of the Royal Commission on Aboriginal Peoples*, Ottawa: Canada Communications Group, pp. 775-1024.

Whitney, Chief Roy (2000) Presentation to the Calgary Chamber of Commerce, Calgary: Tsuu T'ina Nation.

Wien, Fred, Stephen Cornell, John Loxley, and David Newhouse (2000) *Governance for Socio-Economic Development: The Institutions of the Alberta Métis Settlements*, Edmonton: Alberta Métis Settlements General Council.

Winnipeg, Chamber of Commerce (2002) "Let's Get to Work Aboriginal Job Fair," Press release, January 31.

Winnipeg, City of (2001) *Mayor's Task Force on Diversity: Final Report*, Winnipeg, October 30.

Winnipeg, Native Family Economic Development (1993) *Its Up To All Of Us*, February.

Wuttunee, Wanda (2002) "Partnering Among Aboriginal Communities: Tribal Councils Investment Group (TCIG)," *Journal of Aboriginal Economic Development*, 3(1): 9-17.

The Invisible Infrastructure: Urban Aboriginal Institutions and Organizations

David Newhouse
Department of Native Studies
Trent University

Aboriginal peoples have been moving to urban centres and creating communities for themselves for at least 75 years, and especially since the end of World War II. The Royal Commission on Aboriginal Peoples (RCAP, 1993a) report on urban Aboriginal peoples describes this movement.

> Sometime after the Second World War, Aboriginal people began what some people call the "First Wave" into urban centres. This first, large migratory movement of Aboriginal people from reserves and settlements peaked in the mid-1960s. An Aboriginal baby boom in the 1960s combined with several other factors to provoke this migration. The most important were severe economic conditions, poor housing, inadequate resources, limited educational opportunities, and high rates of unemployment and alcohol abuse in their home communities.

> There's also no doubt that many of these Aboriginal migrants were seeking jobs, an education, better housing and adequate social services. Some Aboriginal people continue to move, returning back and forth between urban centres and their home communities. However, many Aboriginal people remain in urban centres. They are far more likely to rent homes, to change addresses more often and to live in poorer neighborhoods than non-Aboriginal people. They are also more likely to migrate between urban centres and other regions of the country than non-Aboriginal Canadians.

This huge movement of people has led to the establishment of Aboriginal organizations. Growing out of the friendship centre movement, a huge network of institutions has emerged within the urban Aboriginal communities. Over the last four decades (1960-2000), urban Aboriginal landscapes have been transformed through the emergence of Aboriginal organizations designed to meet the many needs of a growing urban population. This network of organizations has been neglected in the research literature on Aboriginal peoples which focuses to a large extent on, as Allan Cairns (2000) characterizes it, "maximizing the constitutional space for Aboriginal self-government and has paid negligible attention to the needs of the urban Aboriginal population."

Canadian censuses have consistently reported over the last 40 years a significant presence of Aboriginal peoples residing in urban centres. The two most recent censuses and the Aboriginal Peoples Survey indicate that the urban Aboriginal population ranges somewhere between 40 and 60 percent of the total Aboriginal population, depending upon the method of counting and the definitions used. There is some evidence of long-term urban residency among Aboriginal peoples. These residents are developing a culture that is in some ways distinctly urban while at the same time distinctly Aboriginal.

Aboriginal organizations emerged, first as community clubs and then later as social service agencies for Aboriginal populations. Indian clubs began to appear in Canadian cities in the 1950s: Toronto (North American Indian Club, 1951), Vancouver (Coqualeetza Fellowship Club, 1952), and Winnipeg (Indian and Métis Friendship Centre, 1958). These clubs fostered a sense of community, provided a meeting place, and began to create a visible Aboriginal presence. During the 1960s, Indian and Métis friendship centres began to appear in greater numbers. In 1960, there were three. By 1968, there were 26; by 1972, 43; by 1983, 80; 1996, 113, and by 2002, 117 signifying the presence of cohesive Aboriginal communities and leadership. The early centres assisted Aboriginal individuals to adjust to life in the city. Over the 40 years of their existence, friendship centres have become one of dozens of Aboriginal organizations in most urban locations. In many cases, the centres serve as important community centres, fostering the development of an urban Aboriginal community ethos and spirit. Aboriginal friendship centres have assumed important and significant roles in the development of urban Aboriginal communities. These roles have been recognized through continued federal funding through the Migrating Native Peoples Program and the Aboriginal Friendship Centre Program.

The Report of the Royal Commission on Aboriginal Peoples (RCAP, Vol. 4, p. 52) characterizes the urban environment as not amicable to Aboriginal peoples: "the stress of the unwelcoming city, confusion, the experience of racism and the inability to find employment push some into crime" make the experience of city living unpleasant, difficult and disconnecting. Urban institutions "often conflict with Aboriginal cultural values" and can "easily undermine a positive cultural identity." The Commission reports that the central issue facing urban Aboriginal peoples is one of cultural identity. It argues for measures to enhance the cultural identity of Aboriginal peoples living in urban centres as well as measures to improve the quality of life for urban Aboriginal peoples: employment and educational services, health care, business development, and some form of self-government.

Second, the Commission advocates for the development of a network of Aboriginal service institutions to meet the needs of a growing urban Aboriginal population, forecast to grow to 405,000 people by 2016, double its 1996 size. The Commission (RCAP, 1996: Vol. 4, p. 556) reports: "Many aboriginal agencies already exist. In some cases, they are competing for Aboriginal clients (and for funding based on the number of clients they attract) with non-Aboriginal agencies. Potential users are unaware of their services." The report however does not go on to describe this network, although it does pay special attention to friendship centres and their evolving roles in urban Aboriginal communities.

Peter Drucker, an American management theorist, writing in 1973, said that North American society is becoming a society of organizations. This has become particularly true for Aboriginal peoples living in urban settings. In 1993, in preparation for a small paper for the Royal Commission on Aboriginal Peoples, I attempted to get a sense of this landscape (RCAP, 1993b). At that time, using the Arrowfax Directory, I was able to count approximately 6,000 Aboriginal organizations in Canada. Approximately half of these were small, less than three person, businesses. The other half were not-for-profit organizations that I would classify as non-governmental organizations(NGOs) providing a wide range of services to Aboriginal peoples, regardless of residence or legal status. The vast majority of these were located in urban centres.

In the decade since the initial attempt at counting, the number of Aboriginal organizations, both for-profit and NGOs, has risen: Aboriginal Business Canada (2000) reports that there are now somewhere in the range of 20,000 Aboriginal small businesses. The same appears to have happened in the NGO sector. A quick survey of starting dates of Aboriginal NGOs shows that most were established within the last 20 years with the exception of Aboriginal friendship centres, the key nodes in the web of Aboriginal urban institutions.

The Battleford Indian and Métis Friendship Centre describes the history of friendship centres and the roles they played in urban Aboriginal institutional development.

> Friendship Centres were first created in Winnipeg and Vancouver in 1958 by Aboriginal people to assist those Aboriginal people moving from reserves and rural areas to urban centres. These centres began as drop-in centres where friends and relatives newly arrived would gather to seek advice and assistance from those already established. Initially, new arrivals were directed to the various agencies that could assist them in such areas as shelter, education and employment. Gradually, voluntary groups comprised largely of non-Aboriginal people opened actual drop-in centres to respond to the increased demand. Initially, these centres were financed by private donations, but as the movement grew, it became necessary to secure government funds to ensure continuous operation.
>
> As migration continued, Aboriginal people seeking education, skill training and better employment opportunities made their way to Canada's urban centres. Migrating Aboriginal peoples became one of the country's most disadvantaged minority groups, suffering from social isolation, loss of identity, a low level of participation in community life and a lack of understanding of the basic processes and institutions of urban society. As a result, an increasing number of Friendship Centres were established. Friendship Centres gradually evolved into a community-supported response to alcohol abuse and the related social problems faced by Aboriginal peoples in the city. Consequently, Centres began to provide referral services to mainstream social agencies and services, and later counseling related to housing, employment and the justice system. By the late 1960's, Aboriginal people assumed control of the Friendship Centre movement.[1]

Aboriginal people move to cities as individuals and families, and join communities. While people do not necessarily reside in Aboriginal neighbourhoods, in a manner similar to other ethnic groups, a sense of Aboriginal community does exist in many places. Central to community is a set of institutions established to meet community need and desire, that survive the ever changing agendas and presence of individuals and personalities and, subsequently, continue to exist over time. The idea of an urban Aboriginal community has been little explored in the research literature.

The urban Aboriginal experience for the most part has been examined through the lenses provided by sociology. First, through the lens of the urban-folk continuum, where urbanity is an experience distinct and separate from rural life: one is either urban or rural. Those who move to urban settings from rural Aboriginal communities are seen as becoming acculturated and assimilated. Second, the urban experience is viewed through the lens of disintegration, resulting in social disorganization and cultural breakdown from the clash between a traditional rural way of life and a modern urban life in which the dominant experiences are loneliness, despair, anomie, and racism resulting in alcoholism and poverty. Third, the urban experience is viewed through the lens of culture, in this case, the culture of poverty: Indians are poor, will always be poor because they are born into poverty, are raised in poverty, live their lives in poverty, and develop a culture based upon these lives, and pass this culture on to their children.

Until recently, the idea that Aboriginal peoples who live in cities, either by choice or by policy push and pull, might enjoy it was a hard one for many to grasp. A positive urban Aboriginality is seen by many as an anomaly and is marked by a sense of shame and loss.

There has been little research that has examined and analyzed urban Aboriginal communities with all the attendant structures and processes. Urban Aboriginal research has tended to focus upon the experiences of individuals and their adjustment to urban life, paying only incidental attention to community. Missed in this focus are two key sets of issues.

The first set revolves around community. What are urban Aboriginal communities? Who constitutes them? What is the life experience in urban Aboriginal communities? How do communities develop and change? What is considered a healthy urban Aboriginal community?

The second revolves around institution. What are the institutions of urban Aboriginal life? What functions and roles do they serve? How do they develop and change? Who are the people who work within them? What difference do these institutions make? What problems do the institutions encounter?

One of the few studies to examine urban Aboriginal institutional development in some detail was undertaken in the United States. Weibel-Orlando (1991: 4) reports that since the 1920s the Los Angeles Indian community has seen more than 200 American Indian institutions become established, deliver programs and services and then fade away to be replaced by others or not at all. In the early 1980s, the end of her 20-year study period, she reports: "The Los Angeles Indian community structure is sustained by a network of and intersecting participation in an impressive array of institutionalized political, economic, medical, religious, educational, recreational and informational organizations, all of which are based on pragmatic but fragile constructions of ethnic unity."

These institutions are distinct, "recognized by both members and observers as the social structures that provide a continuing sense of history, community and ethnic identity (traditional and novel) for those Indians who have chosen to 'have a foot in both worlds' and to 'try making it' in the city" (Weibel-Orlando, 1991: 81).

Weibel-Orlando classifies the institutions that she found into eight categories: political, economic, and social services, healing, religious, educational, recreational, communicational, and kinship, marital and familial. She argues that a "holistic description of the social structures that provide a sense of community…must include the institutions of family, kinship and marriage" (p. 83). She concludes:

> In an urban context characterized by residential dispersion and tribal and factional heterogeneity, regular, consistent, predictable, face-to-face interactions in the context of ethnic institutions are the mechanisms by which Indians in Los Angeles approximate traditional community structures and ethos (p. 83).

The Canada West Foundation inventoried organizations in six western Canadian cities: Vancouver, Calgary, Edmonton, Saskatoon, Regina, and Winnipeg as part of three studies on urban Aboriginal peoples. The inventory (Hanselmann, 2002a) uses a different schema than Weibel-Orlando, and consists of over 300 organizations in 14 categories: education, training, employment, economic development, family violence, child care, health, housing, justice, cultural support, family, youth, corrections, and other. The other category consists mostly of religious and political organizations. Missing from both studies is an inventory of the Aboriginal private sector.

The organizational presence that is now common to Aboriginal urban communities becomes a key ingredient to the improvement of the quality of life for urban Aboriginal peoples. These organizations have come to be seen as legitimate both in the eyes of community members and the larger community. The Aboriginal Friendship Centre Program, which provides funding to the network of 117 centres across the country has adopted as one of its program principles this idea: "Aboriginal Friendship Centres are recognized as legitimate urban Aboriginal institutions responding to the needs of Aboriginal peoples."[2]

These institutions are also seen as closer, more responsive to, and accountable to, Aboriginal communities. They are, according to the RCAP report on Aboriginal peoples in urban centres (1993a), seen as operating in a manner that is consistent with traditional Aboriginal understandings of the world.

> The participants said non-Aboriginal agencies have different goals and priorities from Aboriginal social service agencies. Aboriginal agencies, such as friendship centres, view an individual person's problems as "symptoms of deeper problems" that are rooted in "racism, powerlessness and cultural breakdown". The non-Aboriginal agencies, they said, tended to look at conditions as isolated problems and to view the individual as deficient. As a result, the workshop participants said, Aboriginal agencies are trusted more than non-Aboriginal agencies by Aboriginal urban people.

Over the last decade in particular, urban Aboriginal organizations are now assuming key roles in the delivery of services in health, through organizations like the Vancouver Native Health Society walk-in clinic and Poundmakers Lodge in Edmonton, education in programs like the Saskatchewan Urban Native Teacher Education Program in Regina and Saskatoon, and the Joe Duguette High School in Edmonton, in economic and employment development through organizations like the Estey School Aboriginal Employment Program in Saskatoon, Anishinaabe Oway-Ishi (Aboriginal Youth employment preparation and placement program) in Winnipeg, to name a few.

Governments at all levels have also supported the development of this infrastructure through a variety of funding programs, both in terms of ongoing funding for operations and for programs and projects: the Aboriginal Friendship Centre Program, Community Heath Funding Program, Cultural Centre Funding. The Canada Mortgage and Housing Corporation created an urban Native housing program delivered through Aboriginal housing co-operatives and organizations: "Recognizing that Aboriginal housing institutions operated their projects in a distinct way from mainstream not for profit organizations, a distinct Urban Native Housing Program was funded under 56.1 (now 95) of the NHA in 1985.... Today (2002), there are over 100 urban Aboriginal Housing institutions responsible for over 10,000 unilateral federal rental units. These rental units are operated in all major urban centres across Canada. Funding for the continued expansion of urban Aboriginal housing ceased in 1993."[3]

In addition to roles in service delivery, Aboriginal organizations now have key roles in cultural and community development through the network of Indian/Métis friendship centres, cultural education centres, artists co-operatives and organizations like Urban Shaman in Winnipeg, Aboriginal language teaching and development organizations such as Our Elders Speak Wisdom Society in Vancouver, traditional song and dance societies, and the powwow circuit.

Urban Aboriginal people have also developed political institutions to advance their own interests in the city, in the form of Aboriginal councils of local Aboriginal organizations and formal advisory bodies to municipal councils. A cadre of individuals can act as learned and informed representatives of the Aboriginal community in various mainstream fora dealing with Aboriginal issues. The Aboriginal Council of Winnipeg captures this type of political institution.

> The Aboriginal Council of Winnipeg was established in 1990 when the Urban Indian Association and the Winnipeg Council of Treaty and Status Indians joined forces. This union was driven by the belief that the interests of the urban community would be better served by an organization that could address urban issues without regard for the somewhat artificial legal distinctions historically imposed upon indigenous people.[4]

A similar council in Vancouver is a "a voluntary association of (14) 'service provider' organizations and agencies serving the Aboriginal community in Vancouver, British Columbia. It is a working relationship – a collaborative association of peer organizations and agencies."[5]

Urban Aboriginal spiritual organizations have also emerged as part of the mix. Organizations which offer traditional spiritualities sit alongside Christian ones: Kateri Tekak with a Parish, an Aboriginal Catholic Church in Regina, the Father Latour Native Pastoral Centre in Calgary.

Recreation and athletic organizations of all types are also a common feature of urban Aboriginal life: baseball, hockey, lacrosse, rodeo, golf, urban sports camps also have appeared and enjoy much support. Youth organizations such as the Ben Calf Robe Society in Edmonton, and White Buffalo Youth Lodge in Saskatoon provide a diverse range of opportunities for youth recreation and development.

This institutional presence is almost invisible to public policy-makers. Where it is seen, it is viewed primarily as a means for the delivery of programs to a disadvantaged group of people. Few see the vast array of Aboriginal cultural, artistic, heritage, educational, economic, community development, and political institutions that dot the landscape. This invisibility is not surprising as it indicates the presence of urban Aboriginal peoples who are interested in creating and participating in healthy vibrant communities and who see the city as an opportunity and renewal rather than a place of cultural erosion. As long as the urban environment is seen in the terms exemplified by the RCAP final report, urban Aboriginal peoples and their institutions will always be seen through the lens of deficiency and erosion, always struggling to live up to the cultural expectations of their rural compatriots.

The urban Aboriginal issue is broader than "maintenance of cultural traditions, building a strong community off-reserve and meeting the social and economic needs of this growing population" (Statistics Canada, 2002). Fostering and supporting the development of urban Aboriginal institutions indicates the ongoing presence of people in cities and challenges notions of Aboriginal identity and place in Canadian society. To state that one is urban is still, in many cases, to invite both contempt and sympathy.

A rising sense of community, a desire to maintain and emphasize cultural differences as well as the recognition of the inherent right to self-government for Aboriginal peoples has led to increased political aspirations for Aboriginal stewardship of programs and services and some form of self-government. Fostering the development of urban Aboriginal governments poses a difficult challenge for policy-makers in all governments: municipal, provincial, federal, and Aboriginal. This challenge involves further institutional development. Peters (1992: 52) argues that "forms of self government are the various institutional arrangements which can be put into place to enable the Aboriginal peoples to make their own collective decisions."

The experience of urban Aboriginal life is mediated through community institutions. Participation in them gives a sense of community, a sense of history and a sense of shared values. They connect people to each other, both in the cities and in rural/reserve communities. They also give people a sense of influence and control as well as providing opportunities for employment, volunteer work, and leadership. They provide a way in which one can begin to shape the contours of everyday life.

The Canada West Foundation in a report (Hanselmann, 2002b: 7) on urban Aboriginal peoples in western Canada documents the leadership role that Aboriginal institutions play in the development of Aboriginal communities: "Members of urban Aboriginal communities conceived many of the successful projects described (in the report)" and impressed those around them. "[W]hen asked what lesson could be given to colleagues, the response was: 'build on existing Aboriginal organizations and what they are doing.'"

Implications for Public Policy and Research

One of the central notions of indigenous thought is community. Public policy research, which focuses primarily on individuals, will not result in policies that support and enhance the web of institutions that sustain the individual in daily life. It is important to broaden current research efforts to include community and institution as research objects and participants.

It is important to research urban Aboriginal communities in order to gain an understanding of their development and goals and how they might be supported as well as gain some understanding of their composition, structure, and community processes. Who constitutes them? How is life experienced in urban Aboriginal communities? How do communities develop and change? What is considered a healthy urban Aboriginal community? How are decisions made in a community? Who participates?

It is also important to investigate urban Aboriginal institutions. What are the institutions of urban Aboriginal life? What functions, roles do they serve? How do they develop and change? Who are the people who work within them? What difference do these institutions make? What problems do the institutions encounter?

It is also important to investigate emerging models of self-government and to document the particular challenges facing urban Aboriginal governments and the solutions that may be possible.

Notes

1   <http://www3.sk.sympatico.ca/afcsask/north/history.htm>.

2   <www.nomatterware.com/NoMatterWare/Web/Policies>.

3   <http://www.metisnation.ca/MNC/IN_housing.html>.

4   <http://www.abcentre.org/serv6.html>.

5   <http://www.angelfire.com/bc2/vac/about_page.html>.

References

Aboriginal Business Canada (2000) *Aboriginal Entrepreneurs in Canada-Progress and Prospects.*

Cairns, Allan (2000) "Aboriginal Peoples' Two Roads to the Future," *Policy Options,* (January/February).

Canada, Statistics Canada (2002) <www.statcan.ca/english/freepub/92-125-GIE/html/abo.htm>, July 24.

Drucker, Peter (1973) *Management: Tasks, Responsibilities, Practices,* HarperCollins.

Hanselmann, Calvin (2001), *Urban Aboriginal People in Western Canada: Realities and Policies,* Calgary: Canada West Foundation, September.

—— (2002a) *Enhanced Urban Aboriginal Programming in Western Canada,* Calgary: Canada West Foundation, January.

—— (2002b) *Uncommon Sense: Promising Practises in Urban Aboriginal Policy-Making and Programming,* Calgary: Canada West Foundation, August.

Peters, Evelyn (1992) "Self-Government for Aboriginal People in Urban Areas: A Literature Review and Suggestions for Research," *Canadian Journal of Native Studies,* 12(1).

RCAP (Royal Commission on Aboriginal Peoples) (1993a) *Aboriginal Peoples in Urban Centres,* Royal Commission on Aboriginal Peoples.

—— (1993b) *From the Tribal to the Modern: The Development of Modern Aboriginal Society,* November.

—— (1996) *Report of the Royal Commission on Aboriginal Peoples, Royal Commission on Aboriginal Peoples,* Ottawa: Canada Communications Group-Publishing.

Sanderson, Frances and Heather Howard-Bobiwash (1997) *The Meeting Place: Aboriginal Life in Toronto,* Toronto: Native Canadian Centre of Toronto.

Weibel-Orlando, J. (1991) *Indian Country, L.A. Maintaining Ethnic Community in a Complex Society,* Chicago: University of Illinois Press.

Urban Aboriginal Governance: Developments and Issues

Roy Todd
Trinity and All Saints College
University of Leeds

Introduction

The urbanization of Aboriginal people in recent decades has led to debate about appropriate models for governance, negotiations about responsibilities, roles, and structures, and the development of new policy initiatives. Since the Royal Commission on Aboriginal Peoples (RCAP, 1996) made a series of recommendations for urban Aboriginal governance, there have been positive responses from federal, provincial, and municipal tiers of government. At the same time, the pressing needs of Aboriginal people in urban areas have led to urgent demands from Aboriginal people for new frameworks for governance and calls for negotiations about new organizational structures, programs, projects, and policies. The momentum of change has been such that the introduction of new policy initiatives has outpaced some of the more abstract discussions of principle and inherent rights that are located in political theory and legal analysis. In this context of changes in practice, and continuing negotiation and innovation, this paper covers three main aspects of self-government for Aboriginal people in urban areas:

▶ models of urban Aboriginal governance;

▶ programs and organizational forms; and

▶ issues and points of discussion.

The main aim is to provide a snapshot of the current situation while recognizing that there is continuing change in the emerging practices and policies that are outlined.

Models of Urban Aboriginal Governance

Graham (1999: 378) defines governance for urban Aboriginal people as the "institutions, services, and political arrangements dedicated to meeting and representing the needs and interests of the urban Aboriginal population."

Graham includes health care and education institutions within the scope of her definition and acknowledges the dual function of some organizations, combining advocacy and services for Aboriginal people. A more extended listing of urban Aboriginal institutions would include those assisting young people, women, and elders, child and family support services, and groups specifically acting as centres of liaison with state bodies such as police and court services. The functional orientation of Graham's definition leads us to raise questions about participation and process in the emergence of Aboriginal organizations. Who represents Aboriginal people? How are Aboriginal organizations formed, developed, and established? How are urban Aboriginal organizations accountable to the people they serve? While these questions cannot be fully answered here, they do serve as indicators of points of discussion and contention.

Accounts of the urbanization of the Aboriginal population tend to emphasize relatively recent trends in demographic data (e.g. Driedger, 1996; Peters, 1996; Todd, 2001), for the consequences of the shift toward urban areas have included new needs for services, creation of new Aboriginal organizations, and shifting balances of power in Aboriginal governance. The migration of people from reserves into urban areas is undoubtedly significant for understanding current policy needs as well as the related context of recent steps in Aboriginal politics. However, the longer-term historical dimensions of the urban situation are an essential component in understanding the complexity of the emergent structures of governance.

Many of Canada's towns and cities have grown rapidly, on and around land that was already inhabited by Aboriginal people. As the National Association of Friendship Centres (NAFC) and the Law Commission of Canada (LCC) notes (1999: 8): "Almost all cities in Canada are built on the sites of pre-existing Aboriginal settlements". The NAFC and LCC (1999) comment that some urban areas have developed on Aboriginal settlements, thus displacing Aboriginal people (e.g., Edmonton, Calgary, Winnipeg); some urban areas have enclosed Aboriginal settlements (e.g., Fredericton); and some are adjacent to Aboriginal settlements (Montréal and Sault St. Marie). Some cities combine all these forms of overlay of urban boundaries and Aboriginal patterns of life (e.g., Vancouver).

The political consequences of these two strands – the migration of Aboriginal people, and their long-term residency in cities and towns – are inevitably complex. In some cases there have been protracted negotiations and renegotiations to establish organizational frameworks for urban Aboriginal governance that respect and reflect the origins of recent Aboriginal migrants as well as those First Nations with pre-established territorial rights. In some cities there are complex inter-organizational divisions of labour and by now, relatively well established multi-agency systems of working to generate new funding or to confirm roles in the provision of services.

The NAFC and LCC (1999) outline three main models of urban self-government:

- ▶ by Aboriginal nation;
- ▶ by the Aboriginal community as a whole within the urban boundary; and
- ▶ by territoriality (or majority), whether established by nation or not.

Focus groups organized by the NAFC gave mixed responses to governance by Aboriginal nation, offered the lowest support (and opposition) for a model based upon territoriality or majority, and gave broadest support for that based upon the Aboriginal community as a whole.

The complexity of the conditions for the formation of coherent urban Aboriginal governance can be demonstrated by survey data and by case study. Data summarized by the Royal Commission on Aboriginal People (1996) shows a concentration of Aboriginal residents by nation in some cities, with diversity in others. For example, 81 percent of Thunder Bay's Aboriginal residents are Ojibwa, while 63 percent of Edmonton's are Cree. The situation in Vancouver is quite different with at least 35 nations represented in the city. (Local observers consider this to be a substantial under estimate of the diversity of the Aboriginal population in the city, even claiming that there are members of all of the almost 200 BC Native bands in the city.)

Retaining a focus on Vancouver, to illustrate the historical basis of that city's complexity, we could take account of the pre-existing settlement of differing and overlapping parts of the territory now covered by Greater Vancouver by the Squamish, Tsleil Waututh, and Musqueam nations. There is no part of the city with an almost exclusively First Nations population, although Vancouver East contains an estimated 50 to 70 percent of the

Aboriginal population (Todd, 2000). In Vancouver, therefore, models of self-government based neither upon Aboriginal nation nor upon territoriality can be readily expected to gain majority support from the urban Aboriginal population.

In its concluding comments, the NAFC and LCC (1999: 67) suggested "a new focus on the notion of community in grappling with urban governance," with a stress upon practices that incorporate dialogue and consensus. In general terms, this approach is consistent with conceptions of social sovereignty (Latham, 2000). It is broadly compatible with the notion of social citizenship, where governance may be organized around social organization other than the state, and is not necessarily constrained by territorial boundaries.

Projects to Programs: Organizations to Alliances

The growing history of policies towards urban Aboriginal people shows the changing role of federal government (Satzewich and Wotherspoon, 1993; Peters, 2001), municipal government and responses to differential patterns of mobility over a series of decades (e.g., Dosman, 1972; Wannell and Caron, 1994). The recommendations of the Royal Commission on Aboriginal Peoples (1996) on urban governance covered funding, responsibilities, and priorities for federal, provincial, territorial, and municipal governments. While these differing levels of government have been involved in the establishment of urban governance for Aboriginal people, the major factor in the development of Aboriginal governance has been the energy and commitment of Aboriginal people, albeit working in a context that has been partly structured by funding initiatives.

Studies of specific urban Aboriginal self-government projects and programs show progress with education projects (Calliou, 1999; Taylor et al., 2001); health programs (Williams and Guilmette, 2001; Mercer, 2001); and policing and criminal justice (Todd, 2001). In each case there has been an underlying difficulty or systemic set of problems, and a pragmatic attempt to provide a service to ameliorate or resolve the problems. In most cases, there are clear aggregate statistical data on issues to be addressed. Examples are those that show health inequalities, differential mortality rates, low high school completion rates, and high rates of children "in care" (see, for example, statistics compiled by the Ministry of Children and Family Development, British Columbia, 2002). In other cases, Aboriginal health, community, youth, and welfare workers have gained awareness of emergent problems through their day-to-day work in towns and cities. These relatively isolated programs and schemes accumulate to show a growing and increasingly extensive profile of urban activity. At the same time, the year-on-year experiences of seeking to resolve problems without being able to address the underlying causes, and of needing to integrate and liaise with a range of agencies, point toward urban solutions for Aboriginal governance that are broadly community based, rather than only specifically oriented toward particular projects.

Progress with establishing new integrative organizations in Vancouver can be taken as an example of recent developments in self-government for urban Aboriginal people that are not limited by nation, or band membership but which are more extensively based upon community membership. Following the demise of a council for Aboriginal people in the city in 1997, the BC Association of Friendship Centres and the United Native Nations established a body with the title Aboriginal People's Council, in November 1998. The range of issues covered by the Council is considerable, including child and family services, economic development, education, health, housing, economic development, employment, land issues, social services, and justice (Todd, 2000). This new initiative on self-government was grounded in an understanding of the difficulties of Aboriginal people in the city, was a reaction against what was judged to be the negative impacts of federal, provincial, and First Nations policies, and was impelled by concerns to ensure that the urban Aboriginal community was represented on all major issues.

The Aboriginal Council gained provincial support in late 1998 for a program of collaborative development with the Ministry for Children and Families for off-reserve Aboriginal communities. More recently, further dialogue about principles for Aboriginal self-government led to a provincial conference on Aboriginal child and family services governance (June 2002). Conference planning was principally organized by the United Native Nations, Lake Babine First Nation, Métis Provincial Council of British Columbia, the Union of BC Indian Chiefs, and Nil/Tu'o Child and Family Services. The Ministry's explicit willingness to consider a separate Aboriginal governance structure for child and family services was taken up by the Aboriginal participants, who developed a resolution (the Tsawwassen Accord) that "recommended the development of Regional Aboriginal Authorities as a necessary step towards asserting our inherent right to self-determination" (press release, June 2002). There was a call, within the Tsawwassen Accord for a commitment to implement the proposals. Subsequently (September 2002) the provincial government agreed, without committing new funding, to the call for Aboriginal control of their children.

This is a framework for governance that is still developing, and it is too soon perhaps even to consider how it is to be evaluated, let alone assess its possible outcomes. Nevertheless, the alliance of First Nations' representative bodies that spans the Aboriginal community, and the willingness of the province to accept Aboriginal governance in child welfare are signs of potential positive progress in addressing complex and difficult issues. Another significant aspect of this initiative is the objective of adopting a holistic approach to provision for Aboriginal children and youth.

Conditions for Effective Governance

There are two issues to be considered here: the requirements for successful governance in an urban context and the evidential base for schemes and programs of self-governance. Each of these issues is a focus of discussion among Aboriginal people involved in urban issues and in the growing literature on Aboriginal governance. First, what are the principles and practice of organizations that are conducive to good Aboriginal governance? Second, how do we know whether programs and policies are working?

There are overlapping and broadly consistent statements about the requirements of urban Aboriginal self-governance from First Nations representatives and organizations. There are also reflections on the problems of some projects and programs in urban Aboriginal governance that stem from policy analysis (e.g., Hylton, 1999). Phil Fontaine (1999: x), National Chief, Assembly of First Nations, stresses inclusiveness and transparency:

> First, we must accept our responsibility for all of our people wherever they reside. This involves empowering our people with electoral rights and with the right to share in resources. Second, we must have transparent and accountable governments that are a model for the world to see.

The NAFC and LCC have recommended a more extensive set of prerequisites. The focus on community, mentioned above, is combined with an emphasis on four common principles (NAFC and LCC, 1999). This requires balancing the tensions between an Aboriginal rights framework and that of liberal democracy, flexibility to take account of the diversity of the urban Aboriginal population, procedures that are fair, open, and inclusive, and sharing resources and skills between organizations and communities.

Inevitably, there have been difficulties and some unexpected (negative) consequences of self-governance programs. For example, in discussion of child welfare programs there have been reports of political interference by community leaders, lack of adequate funding, and an increase in the number of children entering care (Durst, 1999). Miller (2001: 201-2) following an analysis of Aboriginal justice in Coast Salish communities that reveals internal inequalities, and social exclusion, offers words of caution.

> The Coast Salish communities, with their own forms of internal differentiation in the period before contact, have been fractured in new ways, with new practices of internal domination. At the beginning of the twenty-first century, the problems of self-governance, particularly the management of justice systems that both promote and symbolize internal control, are exacerbated by these internal struggles and by the continuing pressures on indigenous communities imposed by the mainstream societies.

The resolution of difficulties, such as those mentioned above, will be dependent upon the development of infrastructures for urban governance that can accommodate internal evaluation and critique.

Finally, this is an era of evidence-based policy development. Aboriginal self-government, like any system of government, in order to be successful requires an appropriate evidential base. Policy and program evaluation in other fields of governance makes it clear that not everything works. Some projects and programs may be ineffective and some programs may do more harm than good. Some programs may introduce unintended outcomes that are positive or negative. There is a need for urban Aboriginal governance to establish answers to those general questions behind realistic evaluation (Pawson and Tilley, 1996). What works? For whom does it work? In what circumstances does it work?

The answers to these questions will depend upon appropriate measures, samples, and investigative designs to accompany the innovative programs that are growing out of urban Aboriginal self-government and to gauge program effectiveness. Two examples linked with Aboriginal youth can illustrate the methodological issues here. There are several reasons why the Royal Commission on Aboriginal People, the National Association of Friendship Centres, and Aboriginal self-government initiatives have focused upon young people. These include the high incidence of poverty, HIV infection rates, exposure to violence, abuse, and family breakdown.

La Prairie (1994) has documented the range of experiences and concerns of youth in inner cities, including reference to the diversity of experience. The NAFC and LCC (1999: 68) put the imperative this way:

> Added to their demographic weight within the Aboriginal population and their large relative size in contrast to non-Aboriginal youth, is the simple reality that today's youth are the main repository of hope for the renewal of Aboriginal societies and cultures, many of which are desperately fragmented.

A few years ago, the Vancouver Police and Native Liaison Society launched a project to educate young people, from schools in the city and from reserves in rural areas, about the realities of life in the city's Downtown Eastside. It was a reality-check program, using talks, videos, tours of the alleyways, and education about drug abuse, with a liaison worker, followed by token gifts of polished inscribed pebbles to act as a symbolic reminder of the visit. The direct and immediate feedback from young people who experienced the project suggested that they would be dissuaded from running away to the city and joining the homeless young Aboriginal people already living there. However, there were doubts voiced by some Aboriginal groups that the program might have unintended consequences. Might it serve, for some young people, as an attractant, as an introduction to the Downtown Eastside, rather than as a deterrent? The organizers of the program faced questions about its evaluation and queries about evidence derived from objective indicators. Their early positive appraisals have now been confirmed by long-term evidence, from the participants and from those who have responsibility for them. About 3,400 young people have now experienced the program. There are sound reasons to build careful evaluation, based upon rigorous methodology into each project or program: every initiative has its costs, every one has potential for further positive development, and every one runs the risk of unintended negative outcomes.

Similar methodological issues related to evaluation arise with relation to programs for young people at risk. Figures on children in care in British Columbia reveal that Aboriginal children constitute almost 40 percent of total children in care, with a steadily upward trend since 1997 (British Columbia, 2002). There are new programs involving Aboriginal organizations in provision of cultural support for families with Aboriginal children in care. Several evaluative questions then arise. What will be the effects of these interventions? If they work, how will they work? For whom will they work and not work? Figures on education, unemployment, and involvement in the criminal justice system of young people brought up in care suggest multiple, reinforcing patterns of disadvantage. This is a profoundly difficult situation to remedy: careful objective measurement and analysis are warranted to evaluate the input and effects of such programs and ensure their successful adaptation.

This is not just a call for more academic research. It is not to suggest that we only need further accumulation of statistics about Aboriginal people in cities. There is recognition here of the mutual respect between participants and researchers that is a condition for effective evaluation research. It is therefore to suggest dialogue and working partnerships with a commitment to evidence-based governance. From the design of programs of self-government and provision of services onwards, careful and appropriate evaluation – linked with the explanation of outcomes – and corresponding redesign of programs, can offer a contribution to the possibility of reversing the compounded difficulties of Aboriginal people in urban areas. A by-product of such dialogue and joint involvement in research might be a step toward reconciliation on the role and methods of research.

Conclusion

There have been rapid developments in Aboriginal governance as urban Aboriginal people have sought means of resolving some of the educational, health, and other difficulties that they have experienced. Alternative models for urban Aboriginal government – community, nation, or territorially based – have been a source of discussion and debate. Issues of group and individual rights and their inter-relationship have been considered in the context of political theory. At the same time, policy and practice in urban areas has led to the growth of projects and programs under Aboriginal control. The conditions for their successful development and implementation have included the need to form new organizational alliances and to address matters that go beyond the scope of limited projects. As experience with urban governance has accumulated, problems with organization and evaluation have been identified. These problems now form part of the agenda for further development. Their pragmatic resolution, partly through the process of group organization and partly through the process of evaluation, will contribute to an understanding of the underlying difficulties of urban Aboriginal people and may also contribute to discussion of governance in broader contexts.

References

British Columbia, Ministry of Children and Family Development (2002) *The Health and Well-Being of Aboriginal Children and Youth in British Columbia*, Victoria: Ministry of Children and Family Development, British Columbia.

Calliou, Sharilyn (1999) "Sunrise: Activism and Self-Determination in First Nations Education (1972 – 1998)," in *Aboriginal Self-Government in Canada*, John H. Hylton, (ed.), Saskatoon: Purich Publishing.

Dosman, E.J. (1972) *Indians: The Urban Dilemma*, Toronto, McClelland and Stewart.

Driedger, L. (1996) *Multiethnic Canada: Identities and Inequalities*, Toronto: Oxford University Press.

Durst , Douglas (1999) "The Wellness of Aboriginal Children: Seeking Solutions Through Self-Government," in *Aboriginal Self-Government in Canada*, John H. Hylton, (ed.), Saskatoon: Purich Publishing.

Fontaine, Phil (1999) "Foreword" in *Aboriginal Self-Government in Canada*, John H. Hylton, (ed.), Saskatoon: Purich Publishing.

Graham, Katherine A. (1999) "Urban Aboriginal Governance in Canada: Paradigms and Prospects," in *Aboriginal Self-Government in Canada*, John H. Hylton, (ed.), Saskatoon: Purich Publishing.

Hylton, John H., (ed.) (1999) *Aboriginal Self-Government in Canada*, Saskatoon: Purich Publishing.

La Prairie, Carol (1994) *Seen but Not Heard: Native People in the Inner City*, Ottawa: Department of Justice of Canada.

Latham, R. (2000) "Social Sovereignty," *Theory, Culture and Society*, 17(4) (August): 1-18.

Mercer, Geoffrey (2001) "Aboriginal Peoples: Health and Healing," in *Aboriginal People and Other Canadians: Shaping New Relationships*, M. Thornton and R. Todd (eds.), Ottawa: University of Ottawa Press.

Miller, Bruce G. (2000) *The Problem of Justice: Tradition and Law in the Coast Salish World*, Lincoln: University of Nebraska Press.

NAFC and LCC (National Association of Friendship Centres and Law Commission of Canada) (1999) *Urban Aboriginal Governance in Canada: Re-Fashioning the Dialogue*, Ottawa.

Pawson, Ray and Nick Tilley (1996) *Realistic Evaluation*, London: Sage.

Peters, Evelyn J. (1996) "Aboriginal People in Urban Areas," in *Visions of the Heart: Canadian Aboriginal Issues*, D.A. Long and O.P. Dickason, (eds.), Toronto: Harcourt Brace and Company.

—— (2001) "Developing Federal Policy for First Nations People in Urban Areas 1945-1975," *Canadian Journal of Native Studies*, XXI(1): 57-96.

RCAP (Royal Commission on Aboriginal Peoples) (1996) Volume 4: *Perspectives and Realities*, Ottawa: Minister of Supply and Services.

Satzewich, V. and T. Wotherspoon (1993) *First Nations: Race, Class and Gender Relations*, Scarborough: Nelson Canada.

Taylor, Donald M., Martha B. Crago, and Lynn McAlpine (2001) "Toward Full Empowerment in Native Education: Unanticipated Challenges," *Canadian Journal of Native Studies*, XXI(1): 45-56.

Todd, Roy (2000) "Between the Land and the City: Aboriginal Agency, Culture and Governance in Urban Areas," *London Journal of Canadian Studies*, 16: 48-66, <http://www.bbk.ac.uk/llc/LCCS/LJCS/Vol_16/index.html>.

—— (2001) "Aboriginal People in the City," in *Aboriginal People and Other Canadians: Shaping New Relationships*, M. Thornton and R. Todd, (eds.), Ottawa: University of Ottawa Press.

Wannell, T. and N. Caron (1994) "A Look at Employment-Equity Groups Among Recent Postsecondary Graduates: Visible Minorities, Aboriginal Peoples and the Activity Limited," Human Resources Development Canada, Labour Market Outlet and Statistics Canada, Sectoral Analysis Branch, Report no. 69.

Williams, Allison and Ann Marie Guilmette (2001) "A Place for Healing: Achieving Health for Aboriginal Women in an Urban Context," *Canadian Journal of Native Studies*, XXI(1): 1-27.

Urban American Indian Identity in a US City: The Case of Chicago from the 1950s Through the 1970s

James B. LaGrand
Department of History
Messiah College

Urban migration was one of the most striking trends in the lives of Native people in North America during the 20th century, and this trend seems likely to continue into the 21st century. The people known variously as Indians, Native Americans, and Aboriginal people transformed from having a very small proportion living in cities at the opening of the 20th century to a majority or near-majority at its close. Although powerful and widely felt economic factors drove Indian urbanization in both Canada and the United States, there were also differences between these two countries. First, urbanization occurred earlier and to a greater degree in the United States than in Canada. Where the most recent census in Canada found 49.5 percent of the Aboriginal population living in urban areas, the 1990 US Census found 63 percent of Indians living in cities, and 53 percent in 1980. These figures themselves rest on significant Indian urbanization that began in the 1940s and 1950s in the United States.[1]

Moreover, in the United States, Indian urbanization was accompanied by far more government encouragement than in Canada. During World War II when wartime needs shifted the population of the US and millions of rural Americans became urban dwellers, thousands of Indians were among those who moved to production centres in the west and midwest for wartime jobs. Taking note of this wartime migration, the federal government beginning in 1952 officially sponsored Indian urbanization through the relocation program. The Bureau of Indian Affairs (BIA) set up relocation field offices in Chicago, Los Angeles, Denver, and Salt Lake City, and encouraged Indians on reservations to participate by offering money to pay transportation costs and initial living expenses while Indians adjusted to their new urban homes. During the 1950s, the twin Indian policies of relocation and termination (the attempt to end tribes' sovereign government-to-government with Washington) together intended to assimilate Native Americans into the nation and into local communities.[2] On the eve of the relocation program's implementation, Indian commissioner Dillon Myer summarized the assimilations thrust of government Indian policy. "The job, in a word," Myer announced to a group of social service workers, "is one of furnishing these people with positive incentives for taking up a new life in ordinary American communities."[3]

This story – of mid-20th-century Indian policy that intended to assimilate Indian people – is quite well known due to the work of Donald Fixico, Larry Burt, and other historians. This article will move beyond this policy-centred examination to explore the ways in which the urban life partly spurred on by policy changed the way in which urban Indians thought of themselves. It will examine the way in which it resulted in the establishment of a new urban Indian identity characterized by its pan-Indian nature and an oppositional stance toward outsiders. Some recent social science research has studied urban Indians to determine whether they are distinguishable from other urban residents based on socio-economic measures.[4] This article examines a similar question, in this case whether urban Indians are distinguishable both from other urban residents and from other Indians based on notions of self-identity. It will conclude that indeed a separate urban Indian identity did develop, yet will acknowledge that it was not a simple, straight-forward, or consensual matter. It resulted from sometimes vigorous debates within Indian communities. Still, the majority of Indians who lived in US cities by the middle of the 1970s on the whole thought of themselves and their place in American society very differently than did their reservation-dwelling ancestors two generations previous.

Traditional notions of Indian identity inculcated in reservation communities proved relatively stable and secure over much of the 19th and 20th centuries. These notions would come under pressure, however, when significant numbers of Indians began moving to US cities in the 1940s and 1950s. Among the several elements of identity that often changed in Indians' migration from reservation to city were ideas concerning race, assimilation, and individualism. In contrast with urban life, which in many ways highlighted race and racial identity, on reservations the notion of race barely existed. It was simply not a salient category in the minds of American Indians. Identity instead revolved around membership in a particular family or band. The social, cultural, and economic pressures of assimilation which were evident in the city also were less apparent on most reservations. To be sure, government officials and missionaries tried to push Indian people in this direction, but the stakes were smaller and assimilation – at least total assimilation – remained an unattractive prospect for most

Indians. Even in the city, many shared this perspective, but at least here it seemed as if assimilation might bring with it greater material benefits individually and communally. Indians could conceivably connect it to a comfortable apartment, a white-collar office job, or a high-quality education for their children. In reservation communities, assimilation often could not offer even these modest material benefits. Finally, individualism was often discouraged in traditional reservation communities by means of complex social ceremonies and mores. This attitude, which some believed to be more necessary in the city, was seen as socially destructive on the reservation. In general, the older, traditional Indian identity that urban migrants carried with them was formed in much greater isolation; it had no need to respond to outside groups and influences. The experience of new types of Indians emerging in Chicago and other US cities would be quite different.

Pan-Indianism of the sort forged in cities such as Chicago had many political, social, and institutional causes. Politically, Indian people in all major U.S. cities through the 1970s played the role of "minority of minority groups." They were always outnumbered by African Americans, Latinos, and sometimes other ethnic groups, as well. The desire to be heard in the city in this environment made pan-Indianism seem necessary to many. Sticking together against stiff challenges was an understandable and reasonable adjustment strategy by Indian people moving to the city.

In thinking about the social causes of and aspects of pan-Indianism, it bears noting that in some ways the developing urban Indian identity resembled the ethnic identity that other immigrants have created in American cities, described by one group of scholars as "continuously being reinvented in response to changing realities both within the group and the host society." [5] Pan-Indianism, as it developed in Chicago and elsewhere, drew on both reservation and urban experiences. Although a pan-Indian spirit among Native Americans in Chicago was growing – especially by the 1960s and 1970s – the intensity varied by tribe, and sometimes in surprising ways. There have been significant numbers of Chippewas in Chicago since the 1950s and before, yet few of them were inclined to pour all their energies into pan-Indian activities and enterprises. Close to their reservations in Wisconsin, they tended more than other tribes to retain ties with home reservations and often did not fully commit to their new Chicago home. Navajos in Chicago were certainly far from home, but they too were usually reluctant to become fully involved in pan-Indian activities, in part because of the immense size of the tribe itself. In contrast to the Chippewas and Navajos, there were relatively few Winnebagos in Chicago, but they enjoyed influence beyond their numbers.

Finally, Indian identity in Chicago during the 1950s, 1960s, and 1970s was also greatly influenced by the institutions established during this time: the American Indian Center (AIC), American Indians-United (AI-U), Native American Committee (NAC), and Chicago Indian Village (CIV). Many members of Chicago's Indian community affiliated themselves with one or more of these organizations and worked through them to better conditions for themselves individually and for Indians as a group. Examining the history of these institutions, this article will suggest, helps track changes in urban Indian identity.

Chicago's The All-Tribes American Indian Center (as it was first called), opened in September 1953 as the first urban Indian center of its kind in the US or Canada, although others would soon follow. It occupied two floors of an office building in Chicago's Loop. Soon, Indians living in different parts of Chicago and from different tribal backgrounds were assembling here for powwows, club meetings, athletic contests and other games, dinners, and socializing. One of the most striking characteristics of the growing Indian communities in Chicago and elsewhere during this time was their tribal composition. Unlike reservation communities which usually contained members of only one tribe, in cities members of dozens of tribes mixed together. Nowhere was this more evident than at the Center's powwows. The Center began holding a large annual powwow starting in 1954, and smaller ones throughout the year. Even those who were knowledgeable about their own tribe's history and culture were often humbled upon encountering the dozens of tribes represented in Chicago. As the number of Indians in Chicago and of the tribes they represented increased during the 1950s, more cultural traditions were added. The Center's 1958 powwow, for example, had Yakima, Hopi, Pueblo, Winnebago, Omaha, Sioux, Mesquakie, and Kiowa dances, as well as the Friendship Dance, Kids Dance, Round Dance, and War Dance, which did not originate from any one tribe. The Center helped Indians in Chicago learn about one another in a variety of ways. The connections they formed in the city were unique, and differed considerably from those of reservation communities where the vast majority of people were from the same tribal background. Where reservation communities fostered tribalism, urban communities such as Chicago's were beginning to foster pan-tribalism as a means of Indian identity. [6]

The urbanization of Indians that took place in Chicago and other US cities in the 1950s and 1960s resulted in the establishment of a new national organization called American Indians-United that hoped to represent all urban Indians and urban Indian centres. The group emerged out of conversations over many years between urban Indian leaders and officials of the National Congress of American Indians (NCAI). Established in 1944, the NCAI was very much a reservation-centred Indian advocacy organization, and throughout the 1960s, the growing number of Indians living in US cities accused the group of ignoring them. The NCAI responded to charges from those claiming to be disenfranchised, and engaged in a debate concerning the role of urban Indians within the organization, including the possibility of giving them equal representation. The group's leaders eventually rejected this idea, though, deciding that NCAI could be most effective by continuing to focus on reservation-based programs, and support the creation of a new organization to serve as NCAI's urban counterpart, which became American Indians-United.[7]

From the perspective of those who would affiliate with the new urban group, the most significant part of this plan was the freedom it offered Indians in cities to tackle problems they saw as distinctly urban. Jess Sixkiller, a Cherokee man who was the first Indian detective hired by the Chicago Police Department, became American Indians-United's initial director after its establishment in 1968. Sixkiller consistently spoke of the unique aspects of urban Indians, noting at one meeting: "In the urban areas of the country today we're faced more and more with a different kind of crisis than our reservation brothers."

Yet unity among urban Indians – one of AI-U's main goals – was difficult to attain. Other organizations of urban Indians became jealous of AI-U after it won some grants, and charged that the group was insufficiently responsive to Indians and instead was controlled by foundations and government agencies which were helping it. There were also problems between the leadership of AI-U and other Indians in Chicago. Leaders at Chicago's American Indian Center seemed to have expected more money and resources to be funneled directly to Chicago, and became disappointed and disgruntled when this failed to happen.[8]

Even within Chicago itself, the Center would not long be alone in trying to mobilize and aid the city's American Indian population. In December 1969, a group of Indian young people established the Native American Committee (NAC), claiming that the Center no longer represented all Indians in Chicago, particularly the poor and young Indians. What most distinguished the Native American Committee from its counterparts at the Center was its willingness and, in some cases, eagerness to participate in direct action protests. Shortly after its emergence, the group occupied the BIA's local office to support the group of American Indians then occupying Alcatraz Island in the San Francisco Bay as an act of protest. A few months later, 23 members again staged a sit-in, this time in support of Indians in

Denver who were protesting that the BIA did not respond to their needs after "dumping" them in the city. The NAC protestors demanded more influence in decisions made by the BIA affecting Indians.[9]

The Native American Committee again saw the opportunity for a dramatic and media-friendly direct action protest when they learned that the National Conference of Social Welfare was planning to hold its annual convention at a Chicago hotel. For some young activist Indians, this organization represented the paternalistic welfare system that so frustrated them. When they learned that the BIA would also participate to report on its work among Indians, it seemed like the perfect protest opportunity.

Arriving at the hotel, NAC and other like-minded activist groups began by challenging the BIA exhibit at the convention which boasted of the good work the Bureau was doing on reservations. They replaced photos in the BIA exhibit with their own which they claimed were more realistic, and marked up the Bureau's pamphlets "to correct the lies." Then during a large plenary session, they co-ordinated efforts to interrupt the entire convention. AIM leader Russell Means seized the podium, while four others took control of the microphones on the floor. Having gained a captive audience, Means then spoke for all four groups, and demanded $250,000 from the National Conference of Social Welfare to start programs for Indians in Chicago, Milwaukee, Cleveland, and at Turtle Mountain. The social workers compliantly voted on the demand and approved it by a vote of 399 to 93, although the vote was not binding. Later, NAC members carried in cardboard boxes they had filled with old clothes, used pantyhose, and mismatched tennis shoes, and dumped them in front of the audience, which they claimed symbolized their contempt for a paternalistic welfare system.[10]

Protests like this episode in the ballroom of a Chicago hotel and the reactions of militant young Indians would be repeated many times in Chicago and elsewhere during the early 1970s. But the situation was fraught with a frustrating contradiction. On the one hand, these young people believed that white organizations, and perhaps whites in general, owed Indians special attention and resources. On the other hand, they became frustrated and angry when such exchanges or discussions of exchanges were quickly overlaid with paternalism. For young activist Indians, the apparent contradiction proved a difficult dilemma to solve.

Native American Committee's protests in 1969 and 1970 at the Chicago BIA office and the National Conference of Social Welfare clearly revealed the differences between the new organization and the American Indian Center. But the Center, while perhaps weaker, still held a prominent position through this time. This would change, however, in May 1971 with the death of long-time executive director Robert Rietz and with the turmoil that would plague the Center in the period following. In the subsequent years, the Center remained profoundly divided. Some thought tribal differences were the most powerful and harmful during this time. Others viewed religious differences as creating the factionalism. Leaders of an Indian evangelical church and non-church members sometimes competed for power and money in Chicago's Indian community. Throughout this time, the Center's financial problems persisted. By early 1973, the situation was so severe, it appeared as if the Center might have to close. Some donors who had helped the Center for many years had grown nervous at the constant turmoil there, and cut back their funding.[11]

Members of the Center and of the Native American Committee continued their war of words. On the one side, some at the Center argued that the very idea of "Indian power," as usually understood, was un-Indian and appropriated from non-Indian society. After various militant slogans were spray painted on the walls of the Center, presumably by Indian youths, a member wrote in the Center's newsletter decrying this "vandalism," and instructed Indian youth: "Those of you who profess to advocate 'Indian Power' are only borrowing these words from the non-Indian." Those affiliated with NAC, however, believed they truly represented the Indian community and filled their speeches and writings with references to the "community" and "the grass-roots," while suggesting the Center's programs were directed "from the outside" and thus not the product of true self-determination and not truly Indian.[12]

A last major split within Chicago's American Indian community during this era came in the summer of 1970 in the wake of a housing protest. It began when Carol Warrington, a Menominee woman separated from her husband and raising six children on her own, was evicted from her apartment for failure to pay rent. Warrington said that conditions in her building were very poor and that withholding her rent was the only way to get the landlord to improve conditions. After learning of her case, NAC members came to Warrington's aid by helping her get back her family's clothing and household items that had been removed from her apartment. Then they went to the Center to borrow the large ceremonial teepee used for powwows, and set it up in an empty lot across the street from the Warrington's apartment building, in view of Wrigley Field. A number of other Indians, who had learned of Warrington's situation and were sympathetic with her struggle to find housing, came to the lot and pitched smaller tents around the large teepee in a show of solidarity. Between 30 and 60 Indians gathered at the teepee, some staying only a few hours but some settling in. Two days after the tent village was set up, Steve Fastwolf led most of NAC's members in pulling out of the protest, believing that they had made their point and that NAC's efforts could be better used elsewhere. Others decided to stay, and called themselves the "Chicago Indian Village" (CIV). Thus, another faction was born, and a fateful division of the Chicago Indian community first surfaced.[13]

Among those who split with NAC and stayed with CIV was Mike Chosa, a Chippewa man who would become the new group's leading spokesman and strategist. Initially, Chosa focused CIV's protest on the poor housing conditions of many Indians in Chicago, particularly those in the Uptown neighbourhood which was a centre of American Indian population and the home of the Center. Speaking for "the American Indians of Chicago," CIV issued a manifesto which declaring "war on the slum conditions in and near the Uptown area," and demanding that local political officials force delinquent landlords to repair properties within 60 days. If the slumlords failed to comply, CIV said the city should fine them and, if necessary, seize their property. Yet not all Indians in Chicago approved of the strategy pursued by CIV and the tone they used in their frequent communications with the press. In June 1970, two leading figures in the community presented a petition against CIV. They claimed the new radical organization presented a "distorted picture of Indian life and Indian needs in Chicago." The petition had over 270 signatures attached to it. The signers also stated that, contrary to the impression made by CIV, many Indians in Chicago had indeed managed to find "good jobs, decent homes, and lives of dignity and decency." Some also expressed concern about reports of drunkenness and drug use at CIV.[14]

Chicago's American Indian community was again under polarizing pressure – this time from Chosa's CIV. Some Indian people grew increasingly embarrassed about the camp and its environment, while others expressed indignation that any Indian person would feel ashamed of a fellow Native participating in the protest. A meeting between CIV and Center representatives arranged in hopes of clearing the air and healing some rifts only served to exacerbate the divide between CIV members and leaders at the Center. Chosa, who had earlier referred to the Center as the "American Apple Center," at the meeting characterized his followers as savvy "street Indians" and dismissed those at the Center as "educated Indians." A member of the Center's board of directors, in turn, angered some CIV residents when he characterized himself and others opposed to the protest as "working Indians," who he said should have more time to present their position.[15]

In June 1971, after a few months living in an abandoned building that had recently gone into receivership, the members of CIV were ready for a truly dramatic venture as they headed for the old Nike missile base on the shores of Lake Michigan. No longer an active military site, it was guarded overnight by an elderly unarmed private watchman. When CIV members approached him at 3:30 in the morning and told him they were "peacefully reclaiming land the white man has taken," and that he should leave, he complied. They proceeded to force the padlock on the gate and go in. Just three days after the last occupiers had been taken off Alcatraz Island in the San Francisco Bay, CIV had their own occupation on the shores of Lake Michigan and the beginnings of their own media event.[16]

The media attention focused on CIV's occupation was a mixed blessing. On the one hand, it brought donations. Food, clothing, blankets, cooking utensils, and furniture flowed in from white Chicagoans reading about the occupation every day in their newspaper. But it also tended to highlight the problems and tensions within CIV, particularly over the role drinking played within the group. Sometimes, Chosa and others in CIV who were not problem drinkers recognized that drunkenness had caused the entire group to suffer. For example, while camped in the abandoned building earlier, CIV members for a time had managed to repair it, but after a few parties and episodes of binge drinking, the building deteriorated to a hopeless point. Chosa, himself, held an ambivalent attitude toward alcohol and alcoholism, sometimes expressing sadness when drinking wreaked havoc on his group, but other times calling CIV "a bunch of drunks" with pride apparent in his voice. Sometimes it seemed that those at CIV thought that to be a "street Indian" – and so the opposite of the "educated Indians" at the Center – was to go through bouts of heavy drinking or at least not to shun those who did.[17]

After almost three weeks of being under the steady gaze of the media, CIV's negotiations with various federal officials at the Nike site proved unproductive. Chosa had been asking for 200 public housing units and an educational complex to be built for Indians by the federal government. Federal officials listened, but were unsure about whom to deal with even if a program was agreed upon. Frustrated with the slow pace of negotiations, officials gave their approval for Park District workers to take down the fence encircling the Nike site. CIV members were quickly awakened and rushed to the fence with buckets of water and iron bars to try to ward off the park workers, who said they had federal authorization to take down the fence. After the Indians began hitting workers' wire cutters – although not the workers themselves – with iron bars in order to stop their work, a large group from the Chicago Police Department stationed nearby in riot gear rushed to the scene to help the Park workers. During the melee, some CIV members drained the gas tanks of cars in the compound to make Molotov cocktails. The first six thrown over the fence failed to explode after shattering. Only one, thrown off-target toward a nearby marina, successfully exploded, burning an empty boat docked there. The two-hour battle between roughly 50 Indians and police and park workers ended with 12 Indians being arrested for mob action.[18]

From there, the members of CIV began a long, meandering, and increasingly ineffective trek throughout various suburban areas surrounding Chicago. By the end of 1971, CIV was still frequently on the move, but now having less success. The tone of newspaper accounts began to change, with more critical comments from Chosa's critics included. Columnists began to poke fun at Chosa's desire to remain in the spotlight and questioned why the housing offered his group was unsatisfactory. Splits emerged in the group, and by the summer of 1972, it had effectively dissolved.[19]

The troubles experienced by individual Indian organizations in Chicago from the 1950s to the 1970s should not obscure the larger point regarding Indian urbanization. Despite periodic debates about how an urban Indian identity should be configured and broadcast to the mainstream non-Indian society, what is striking about this account is how much all American Indians in Chicago during this time changed in how they thought of themselves. Members of different tribes who sometimes had previously considered each other foes began to focus on shared experiences and challenges, and so began to think of themselves as sharing a common Indian identity. An Oneida man in Chicago serves as one of many examples of this phenomenon. After recounting age-old tribal rivalries, he succinctly explained his experiences with members of other tribes: "When we get to the city we begin to think of ourselves more as Indians. Here, we all stick together."[20] This trend has continued since the 1970s as the American Indian Center of Chicago and new organizations established in recent years have worked to strengthen and draw resources from an ever-evolving urban Indian identity.

Chicago, though, is just one city among scores of cities in the US and Canada since the middle of the 20th century that have seen significant American Indian populations develop. Indeed, considering the majority status of urban Indians in the US since the late 1970s, it is surprising that relatively little historical work has yet been conducted on Indian communities in individual cities.[21] Yet even from the few accounts available, it appears that there are indeed some similarities between Chicago and other urban Indian centres.

There are many areas that might be productively examined in a comparative fashion. For example, some form of pan-Indianism began emerging in the 1950s in several US cities. Also, cities besides Chicago witnessed examples of Indian activism and militancy during the late 1960s and 1970s.[22] Yet the degree of urban Indian unity and the level of frustration seems to have been dependent on factors that vary from city to city. The size and tribal composition of a city's Indian community certainly has had an impact on community development. Chicago's mixture of many different tribes contributed to pan-Indianism there. Western cities with overwhelming Navajo populations appear to have followed tribal identity patterns to a greater extent. The racial make-up of a particular city had much to do with how Indian people viewed themselves and projected an identity for others watching. In Chicago, the city's large African-American population was carefully noted by Indian people who often went to great lengths to distinguish their identity and their goals from those of African Americans. US cities in the southwest with large Indian populations, however, have seen a different race relations dynamic from the mid-20th century to the present. Here, the relationship between Indians and Latinos has been more important. In other ways, as well, regionalism has played an important role in shaping various urban Indian communities. Particular features of cities, especially housing and employment opportunities, have played a role in Indian activism. Where the promises of urban life appear to have been broken, a pattern of opposition and even militancy can be seen.

Lastly, government policies toward Indian people contributed greatly to patterns of identity formation and activism among Indian people in Chicago and other cities. The overwhelming focus on assimilation by the BIA from the 1950s through the late 1960s sparked a backlash by many Indians who were not interested in abandoning their Indian identity and receiving the same treatment as every other ethnic and racial group. In Canada, the national government has not been as aggressive in pursuing Indian assimilation over the past several decades. In Canadian cities, it appears that Indian communities have not developed with the same type of oppositional focus to mainstream society and social structures as seen in late-20th century Chicago. Expanding this type of important comparative analysis, however, requires further examination of individual cities in the US and Canada. With this type of work, our understanding of the urban Indian experience in all its complexities will begin to respond to the importance of urbanization for Indian people in both the US and Canada.

Notes

1 Among the places where census data can be found is Thornton, Russell (1981) "Patterns and Processes of American Indians in Cities and Towns: The National Scene," *Urban Indians: Proceedings of the Third Annual Conference on Problems and Issues Concerning American Indians Today*, Chicago: The Newberry Library, p. 26; Shoemaker, Nancy (1999) *American Indian Population Recovery in the Twentieth Century*, Albuquerque: University of New Mexico Press, p. 77; Hanselmann, Calvin (2001) *Urban Aboriginal People in Western Canada: Realities and Policies*, Calgary: Canada West Foundation, September.

2 Examinations of US Indian policy during the 1950s can be found in Burt, Larry W. (1982) *Tribalism in Crisis: Federal Indian Policy, 1953-1961*, Albuquerque: University of New Mexico Press; Fixico, Donald L. (1986) *Termination and Relocation: Federal Indian Policy, 1945-1960*, Albuquerque: University of New Mexico Press.

3 Myer, Dillon (1951) "The Needs of the American Indian," Address December 12, 1951, Welfare Council of Metropolitan Chicago Files, 146-1, Manuscript Collections, Chicago Historical Society.

4 See for example, Hanselmann *Urban Aboriginal People*.

5 Neils Conzen, Kathleen et. al. (1992) "The Invention of Ethnicity: A Perspective from the U.S.A.," *Journal of American Ethnic History*, 12 (Fall): 4-5.

6 Chicago Field Relocation Office report, September 1952, Box 1, Reports on Employment Assistance, 1951-1958, Chicago Field Employment Assistance Office, Record Group 75, National Archives-Great Lakes Region, Chicago; "History of the American Indian Center," undated unpublished ms., American Indian Center, #0400, Section 1, Urban Records Collection, Community Archives, NAES College; "Constitution of the All-Tribes American Indian Center," Welfare Council of Metropolitan Chicago Files, 246-13, Manuscript Collections, Chicago Historical Society.

7 Minutes of Chicago Indian Ministry Committee, October 8, 1968, Church Federation of Greater Chicago Files, 29-3, Manuscript Collections, Chicago Historical Society.

8 Report from American Indians-United 1969 national convention, Church Federation of Greater Chicago Files, 34-2, Manuscript Collections, Chicago Historical Society.

9 *Chicago Today* (1970) "The American Indian NOW," (July 12); Dumont, Robert V. (1973) "Notes From a Visit to the City," *Youth Magazine*, (November 24): 30-37; Mucha, Janusz (1983) "From Prairie to the City: Transformation of Chicago's American Indian Community," *Urban Anthropology*, 12 (Fall): 362; Minutes of Chicago Indian Ministry Committee, April 6, 1970, Church Federation of Greater Chicago Files, 29-5, Manuscript Collections, Chicago Historical Society; *Chicago Tribune* (March 24, 1970); *Chicago Magazine* (1970) "Indians vs. the City," (April); *Chicago Tribune* (1970) "Indians Renew Attacks on Agency's Programs," (June 11); *Chicago Sun-Times* (1970) "Indian activists freed in sit-in," (July 3).

10 *Milwaukee Journal* (1970) "Indians Disrupt Welfare Conference, Demand Funds," (June 3); *Chicago Sun-Times* (1970) "The Indian Movement Here," (June 8); Means, Russell and Marvin J. Wolf (1995) *Where White Men Fear to Tread: The Autobiography of Russell Means*, New York: St. Martin's, pp. 158-159.

11 *Chicago Daily News* (1972) "Indian Center Aides Charge Exploitation," (December 15); *Chicago Tribune* (1973) "Local Indians Divided," (March 3).

12 *The Warrior* (April 1972); *Uptown News* (1972) "Indian Dream Meets City Reality," (November 25).

13 Browning Leveen, Deborah (1978) "Hustlers and Heroes: Portrait and Analysis of the Chicago Indian Village," Ph.D. dissertation, University of Chicago, pp. 107-112; Wilson, Natalia (1998) "The Chicago Indian Village, 1970," in *Native Chicago*, Terry Straus and Grant P. Arndt, (eds.), Chicago, pp. 155-162; *Chicago Sun-Times* (1970) "The Indian Movement Here," (June 8).

14 "Housing," May 12, 1970, Church Federation of Greater Chicago Files, 29-6, Manuscript Collections, Chicago Historical Society; *Chicago Sun-Times* (1970) "Petition of Indian Women Protests N. Side Village," (June 11).

15 Browning Leveen, "Hustlers and Heroes," p. 86; *Chicago Sun-Times* (1970) "Indians Here Square Off on Wrigley Field Village," (June 19); *Chicago Daily News* (1970) "There's a tempest in a teepee," (June 19).

16 *Chicago Daily News* (1971) "Indians Take Old Nike Base," (June 14); *Chicago Sun-Times* (1971) "Indians Seize Nike Site," (June 15).

17 *Chicago Tribune* (1971) "Indians Occupy Missile Base," (June 15); *Chicago Today* (1971) "Nike Site Indians Kid on Square," (June 15); Browning Leveen, "Hustlers and Heroes," pp. 203-227; *Chicago Daily News*, (1971) "Indian Tent-In Now in Lap of Percy, Nixon," (June 21); *Chicago Sun-Times* (1971) "Chippewa Mike Chosa a Different Kind of Indian," (August 15).

18 *Chicago Today* (1971) "Indians Battle Cops," (July 1); *Chicago Daily News* (1971) "Indians Leave Base After Battling Cops," (July 1); Browning Leveen, "Hustlers and Heroes," p. 217.

19 *Chicago Tribune* (1971) "Methodists Act to Oust Band of Indians," (November 27); *Chicago Tribune* (1971) "Indians Vow Daily Sit-In at Lion House," (December 1); *Chicago Sun-Times* (1972) "Fire Leaves 20 Homeless After Split in Indian Ranks," (January 9); *Chicago Tribune* (1971) "Chosa's Band Is Routed Again," (December 12); *Chicago Sun-Times* (1972) "Chosa's Indians go to Wisconsin," (July 5); *Chicago Sun-Times* (1972) "Chosa Indians Begin Moving Back into City," (July 20).

20 Garbarino, Merwyn (1971) "Life in the City: Chicago," in *The American Indian in Urban Society*, Jack O. Waddell and Michael Watson, (eds.), Boston: Little, Brown, p. 174.

21 The two historical case studies of American Indian urbanization are LaGrand, James B. (2002) *Indian Metropolis: Native Americans in Chicago*, 1945-75, Urbana, Ill.: University of Illinois Press; Danziger, Edmund Jefferson (1991) *Survival and Regeneration: Detroit's American Indian Community*, Detroit: Wayne State University Press.

Weibel-Orlando, Joan (1991) *Indian Country, L.A.: Maintaining Ethnic Community in Complex Society*, Urbana, Ill.: University of Illinois Press; Davis Jackson, Deborah (2002) *Our Elders Lived It: American Indian Identity in the City*, DeKalb, Ill.: Northern Illinois University Press are useful and suggestive anthropological case studies.

No monograph-length historical accounts of Aboriginal urban communities in Canada exist. Among the anthropological and sociological case studies of Canadian cities are Nagler, Mark, (1970) *Indians in the City: A Study of the Urbanization of Indians in Toronto*, Ottawa: Canadian Research Centre for Anthropology, Saint Paul University; Dosman, Edgar J. (1972) *Indians: The Urban Dilemma*, Toronto: McClelland and Stewart Limited; Barron, F. Laurie and Joseph Garcea, (eds.) (1999) *Urban Indian Reserves: Forging New Relationships in Saskatchewan*, Saskatoon: Purich.

22 One of the best accounts of Indian activism in the 1960s and 1970s is Smith, Paul Chatt and Robert Allen Warrior (1996) *Like a Hurricane: The Indian Movement from Alcatraz to Wounded Knee*, New York: Free Press.

The Way Forward

David R. Newhouse
Department of Native Studies
Trent University

Evelyn J. Peters
Department of Geography
University of Saskatchewan

The papers in this volume describe the complexity of the public policy landscape with respect to urban Aboriginal peoples. Urban Aboriginal populations are as complex and diverse as the cities within which they live. They are now an integral part of the multi-cultural nature of Canadian cities albeit occupying a different legal and constitutional space than other cultural groups. There is a strong desire to maintain Aboriginal distinctiveness in its many dimensions.

Urban Aboriginal populations comprise individuals and institutions. Urban Aboriginal populations comprise a mix of legal identities: Status Indians, Métis, Bill C-31 reinstatees and differing cultural identities, Cree, Ojibway, Iroquoian, Blackfoot, Nisgaa, Dene, to name a few. Some have strong ties to reserve and rural communities and maintain these ties through movement back and forth; others have lived in cities for several generations and consider themselves "urban." Urban Aboriginal populations range in size and proportion of total urban populations. However, regardless of size urban Aboriginal peoples come to the attention of local public policy-makers most often as a result of the social and economic difficulties that many have experienced. Public funding has fostered the emergence of a large institutional infrastructure over the last decade to assist individuals and communities in dealing with these issues. In addition, there is a small emerging Aboriginal middle class with interests in culture, tradition, and the arts. Sadly, however, at this time, Aboriginal peoples who live in cities tend to occupy positions of marginality with respect to education and employment. The 1981 Report of the Ontario Task Force on Native People in the Urban Setting: *Native People in Urban Settings: Problems, Needs and Services* described the situation using words that are still appropriate:

> Our research talked directly to the people and confirmed that the inadequate quality of life suggested by such indicators as unemployment, low job status, low levels of education and inadequate housing, was actually experienced by the respondents as inadequate. If the quality of life can be defined in terms of access to what people regard as the good things in life (for them), then the Native respondents living in urban settings do not have that access. They have neither the jobs, the income, the skills nor the knowledge to pursue for themselves an acceptable life.

What can be done to make significant improvements in the quality of life for urban Aboriginal peoples over the next decade? As these papers show, defining who is urban is a huge challenge as is deciding who ought to be involved and how. The issues surrounding choice of action necessarily involve research and investigation as solution and problem are intertwined A fundamental question for public policy-makers is choosing a framework for policy and programs. Should the focus be on individuals and their needs, desires, and goals? Should the focus be on institutions: community? neighbourhoods? organizations? Should the focus be on problem? If so, which problem: poverty? marginalization? discrimination? housing? health? Which approach: institutional development? community development? economic development? social development? governance? Who should be involved: local municipal governments? First Nations governments? Aboriginal women's' associations? friendship centres? Métis organizations? cultural education centres? chambers of commerce? business development groups?

Perhaps we can learn from the mistakes of the past. Aboriginal peoples have consistently expressed opposition to unilateral government policy-making. The public policy experience of the Canadian government since 1835 ought to have demonstrated that Aboriginal peoples will not allow themselves to have things done to them. Public policy development approaches that ignore the active consistent informed participation of Aboriginal peoples have proven to be difficult and unworkable. In fact, substantial citizen involvement is now considered to be consistent with contemporary public policy development approaches. Aboriginal public policy development ought to be approached with a high degree of Aboriginal involvement and participation. When dealing with urban Aboriginal peoples, this means seeking out effective means of facilitating the participation of local Aboriginal community leadership.

There is also within many Aboriginal communities a very strong desire to base public policy upon indigenous knowledge, (i.e., to use Aboriginal ideas about social order, etc. as the key informing notions of public policy). This approach is seen as consistent with a desire to maintain cultural distinctiveness by extending it into the realm of thought and everyday individual and collective action. Public policy approaches that don't consider this aspect will most likely not be successful and will be seem as continuing a process of assimilation.

There is also a clear desire for some form of urban Aboriginal governments to emerge over the next decade. Whether these forms are self-determination efforts like friendship centres, child welfare agencies, community health care organizations, or whether they develop along the lines of the recommendations of the Royal Commission on Aboriginal Peoples' "community of interest" governments with formal relationships to other governments (federal, municipal, or Aboriginal), it is important to recognize the diversity of approaches and to avoid one size fits all. Public policy approaches that do not recognize and deal with this desire in a respectful and supportive way will most likely be difficult to implement.

Aboriginal peoples occupy a position within Canadian society that is different in many aspects from other Canadian citizens. Allan Cairn's description of it as "citizens plus" in the 1966 Hawthorne Report on Indian conditions is an apt description. John Ralston Saul, in Reflections of a Siamese Twin, describes Canada as having three pillars: English, French, and Aboriginal. It is important not to ignore the urban aspect of the third pillar.

We argue that the best way forward is through clearly defined policy development partnerships that involve Aboriginal institutions. The shaping of Aboriginal public policy ought to be done largely by Aboriginal peoples. This is not to say that governments do not have a leadership role in this area. The confusing maze of constitutionality, jurisprudence, and jurisdictions surrounding Aboriginal peoples has been created by governments and needs to be dealt with by governments. In this respect, the federal government has a lead role in bringing its resources and jurisdictions to the table for discussion, facilitating the involvement of other governments (provincial, municipal, and Aboriginal), and developing multilateral responses.

We also argue that the vexed issue of representation of urban Aboriginal people needs to be addressed carefully. The issue is critical for several reasons. First, there is an increasing urban Aboriginal population that is not affiliated with any of the major Aboriginal political groups. Many individuals in this population wish to participate in Aboriginal organizations and communities. Second, unexamined initiatives can result in shifts that destroy longstanding organizations and community networks. While Aboriginal organizations may need to take the initiative on this issue, governments have a role to play in addressing divisive administrative categories and their accompanying implications for funding.

Finally, we argue that there also ought to be a concerted research effort directed at understanding better the characteristics and dimensions of urban Aboriginal populations. It is important to include as part of this research effort municipalities and provinces as well as institutions of Aboriginal communities. This research ought to go further than population characteristic. Important research topics range from the nature and practices of urban Aboriginal individual and community identities, to aspects of the relationship between Aboriginal institutions and local municipal machineries of government. Another significant area in which to build greater understanding has to do with Aboriginal and non-Aboriginal relationships in urban areas. This aspect was neglected by the Royal Commission, but not because the Commissioners thought it was unimportant. It is not a straightforward issue, but growing urban Aboriginal populations make it essential to find and highlight strategies that include Aboriginal communities in urban economic and social life, while celebrating their cultural contributions and remembering their unique legal position.

Canada is now a nation of cities. Fully 80 percent of the Canadian population now lives in urban centres. Cities are important to the economic, social, and cultural health of the country. Aboriginal people represent an important constituency in the attempt to build vibrant and attractive cities, and cities are increasingly important to the economic, social, and cultural life of Aboriginal peoples. Finding ways to improve the quality of life of both is the challenge over the next decade.

About the Authors

Renée Brassard holds a master's degree in criminology from the University of Montréal's School of Criminology. She is currently working on a PhD thesis at the School on Quebec Aboriginal women and their treatment by society and the law.

Eric Guimond is a demographer with experience in research and development, and is presently employed by Indian and Northern Affairs Canada, Research and Analysis Directorate. His educational background includes demography, community health, physical education, and Aboriginal studies. He is an expert in the areas of projection models of population and Aboriginal groups. He is currently completing PhD studies (U of Montréal) on the topic of ethnic mobility of Aboriginal populations in Canada (i.e., changes in self-reporting of ethnicity)

Calvin Hanselmann is a senior policy analyst with the Canada West Foundation, a western-based independent, non-partisan, non-profit public policy research institute. Calvin has a BA (High Honours) in public administration, and an MA in political studies, both from the University of Saskatchewan. His research interests are Aboriginal issues, urban affairs, and economic analysis.

Mylène Jaccoud is an associate professor at the University of Montréal's School of Criminology. She is the author of *Justice blanche au Nunavik*, published in 1995 by Éditions Le Méridien of Montréal. She has also published articles on the role of the law in excluding Aboriginal peoples, sentencing and healing circles, and the transfer of power to Quebec's Aboriginal communities. With co-author Andrée Lajoie, she produced a special edition of the *Canadian Journal of Law and Society* concerning Aboriginality and normativity.

Carl Keane is an associate professor in the Department of Sociology at Queen's University in Kingston. His research interests fall generally in the areas of urban sociology, organizations, and criminology. He has published in a variety of venues including the *Canadian Review of Sociology and Anthropology, Canadian Journal of Urban Research, Environment and Behavior* and the *Journal of Research in Crime and Delinquency*.

James B. LaGrand is associate professor and chair in the Department of History at Messiah College in Grantham, Pennsylvania. His work in 20th-century Native American history includes *Indian Metropolis: Native Americans in Chicago, 1945-75* (University of Illinois Press, 2002) and articles in the *Western Historical Quarterly* and the *American Indian Culture and Research Journal*.

Carol La Prairie received her MA in criminology from the Centre of Criminology, University of Toronto, and her PhD in sociology from UBC. She has worked for the federal government for the past 21 years both in the Department of Justice and the Ministry of the Solicitor General. She has conducted research and published quite extensively in the area of Aboriginal criminal justice. During her years in government, she has been seconded by the James Bay Cree (Quebec), Yukon Justice, the Ministry of the Attorney General in Nova Scotia, and Saskatchewan Justice to work on Aboriginal criminal justice issues. She was also the principal investigator for a study of Aboriginal people in the inner city cores of Edmonton, Regina, Toronto, and Montréal. Since 1997, she has worked on the evaluation of the Sentencing Reform Legislation, the Toronto Drug Treatment Court, and on secondment to the National Crime Prevention Centre.

Carole Lévesque has devoted her entire career to indigenous issues. She has a PhD in social and cultural anthropology (Sorbonne, Paris), and has worked closely with Quebec's indigenous communities, organizations, and institutions for the past 30 years. An independent researcher for many years, she is currently an associate professor at INRS-Urbanisation, Culture et Société (Institut national de la recherche scientifique-Université du Québec, Montréal, Canada). She has a wide range of experience and has carried out a variety of studies in the areas of social ecology, sustainable development, environmental and social impact assessment, history, and modernity.

David Newhouse is Onondaga from the Six Nations of the Grand River community. He is chair and associate professor in the Department of Native Studies and the Administrative Studies Program at Trent University. He serves as editor of the *CANDO Journal of Aboriginal Economic Development* and has extensive experience working in Aboriginal organizations and the public service. His research focuses on the way in which Aboriginal traditional thought and western thought are coming together and creating modern Aboriginal societies.

Mary Jane Norris is a Senior Research Manager with the Research and Analysis Directorate of the Department of Indian and Northern Affairs Canada. Prior to her current position, she also concentrated in Aboriginal research in the Demography Division of Statistics Canada. She has specialized in Aboriginal demography over the past twenty years. Her areas of research and publication include migration, population projections and Aboriginal languages. She is of Aboriginal ancestry, with family roots in the Algonquins of Pikwákanagán (Golden Lake), in the Ottawa Valley.

Evelyn Peters grew up in a farming community in southern Alberta. She completed her BA (Honours) at the University of Winnipeg, and her master's and Ph.D. in Geography at Queen's University. Between 1990 and 1993, she held a post-doctoral Canada Research Fellowship. Upon completing her doctoral degree, she taught at Carleton University for one year, before taking up a tenure stream appointment at Queen's University in Kingston. In 1994-95, she worked as policy analyst on urban Aboriginal issues with the Royal Commission on Aboriginal Peoples. In 2001, she moved to the Department of Geography, University of Saskatchewan, to take up a Canada Research Chair position. An urban social geographer by trade, her research has focused on Aboriginal people.

John Richards grew up in Saskatchewan, where he served one term in the legislature in Allan Blakeney's first government. He currently teaches at Simon Fraser University in Vancouver, and is a scholar-in-residence at the C.D. Howe Institute in Toronto. He has written extensively on various aspects of Canadian federalism and on social policy, and has written and edited numerous articles on Aboriginal policy over the last decade. He co-authored (with Helmar Drost) the recently published monograph, "Income On- and Off-Reserve: How Aboriginals are Faring" (available at <www.cdhowe.org>).

Andrew J. Siggner is currently senior advisor on Aboriginal statistics in the Housing, Family and Social Statistics Division of Statistics Canada. He has been the lead analyst on the 2001 Census release of data on the Aboriginal peoples in Canada. He also manages an Aboriginal statistical training program for which he has developed and delivers statistical courses to Aboriginal organizations across Canada. He is the permanent co-chairperson of the 2001 Aboriginal Peoples Survey – Implementation Committee. From 1995-98 Andy was senior analyst in the Census Analysis Division conducting research on Aboriginal demography. Between 1992 and 1995, Andy was on a three-year assignment with the Royal Commission on Aboriginal Peoples where he served as senior advisor on research statistics for the Commission. Prior to joining the Royal Commission he managed the 1991 Aboriginal Peoples Survey, which was a post-censal survey conducted by Statistics Canada. In the previous 20 years, Andy has held a variety of jobs, almost all related to Aboriginal demographic and statistical matters. He holds a BA (1969) and MA (1971) in sociology from the University of Western Ontario.

Philip Stenning, formerly with the Centre of Criminology, University of Toronto, is now a professor in criminology at Victoria University of Wellington, New Zealand. His principal research interests include public and private policing, the prosecution process, police and criminal justice accountability, firearms abuse and gun control, and Aboriginal policing and justice, and he has published in these and other areas of interest. He can be contacted at: philip.stenning@vuw.ac.nz.

Roy Todd is head of sociology at Trinity and All Saints, a college of the University of Leeds (U.K.). He was director of the Centre for Canadian Studies at the University of Leeds from 1995-98 and is currently a member of the Executive Committee of the Centre. His previous Canadian research has included work on multiculturalism in education and police-community partnerships. His current research is focused upon urban Aboriginal communities and Aboriginal conceptions and use of the land. Publications include (as co-editor) *Aboriginal People and other Canadians: Shaping New Relationships*, University of Ottawa Press, 2001.

Shelley Trevethan is director of the Community Research Division of Correctional Service of Canada. She received her Bachelor of Arts (Honours) in criminology from Carleton University in 1985 and her MA in developmental psychology from the University of British Columbia in 1987. She began her public service career in 1989 as a psychologist in the Personnel Psychology Centre. Over the past 10 years, she has worked as a researcher at Justice Canada and as chief of the Correctional Services Program at the Canadian Centre for Justice Statistics. Currently, she is responsible for programs of research in the areas of community corrections and Aboriginal offenders. Research interests include Aboriginal offenders, women offenders, restorative justice, halfway houses, victimization, family violence, youth justice, and recidivism. She has authored articles and made presentations on a variety of research projects in these areas.

Aidan Vining is the CNABS professor of government and business relations, Faculty of Business Administration, Simon Fraser University. He has PhD from the Graduate School of Public Policy, University of California, Berkeley. He writes on a variety of public policy issues. Recent articles have appeared in *Canadian Public Policy*, the *Canadian Journal of Administrative Sciences*, and the *Journal of Policy Analysis and Management*. His co-authored textbooks include *Policy Analysis: Concepts and Practice*, and *Cost-Benefit Analysis: Concepts and Practice*, (both from Prentice Hall).

Jerry White is a professor and chair of the Department of Sociology at the University of Western Ontario. He is a co-director of the First Nations Cohesion Project at Western and the past vice-chairman of the Health Professions Regulatory Council of Ontario (1992-99). Dr. White has authored and co-authored six books and articles on a range of issues including Aboriginal conditions, health care delivery and labour relations. His latest book, co-authored with Paul Maxim and Dan Beavon is *Aboriginal Conditions: The Research Foundations of Public Policy* with University of British Columbia Press.

Fred Wien completed his BA (Honours) in political studies and Spanish at Queen's University, Kingston, Ontario, in 1966, and his MA and PhD. In development sociology, Latin American studies and government at Cornell University in Ithaca, New York, in 1971. His first faculty appointment was at the University of Western Ontario, 1970-73. His appointments at Dalhousie University began at the Institute of Public Affairs in 1973 and continued at the Maritime School of Social Work in 1981, where he currently holds the rank of professor. He served as the School's director between 1981 and 1986, and on an acting basis more recently. Dr. Wien was deputy director of research with the Royal Commission on Aboriginal Peoples in the period 1992-96 with particular responsibility for managing the Commission's research program in the area of employment and economic development.

Terry Wotherspoon is head and professor of sociology at the University of Saskatchewan. He has conducted extensive research and published widely on social inequality and social policy, with particular emphasis on education systems, Aboriginal people, and racial and ethnic minorities. His recent books include *The Legacy of School for Aboriginal People: Education, Oppression, and Emancipation* (with Bernard Schissel, Oxford University Press, 2003); *First Nations: Race, Class, and Gender Relations* (with Vic Satzewich, Canadian Plains Research Centre, 2000); and *The Sociology of Education: Critical Perspectives* (Oxford University Press, 1998). He is a recent recipient of a Canadian Education Association-Whitworth Award for Educational Research.